# Collins | English for Exams

## Cambridge English Qualifications

# B1 PRELIMINARY

# 8 practice tests

T0381991

Published by Collins
An imprint of HarperCollins Publishers
1 Robroyston Gate,
Glasgow
G33 1JN

HarperCollins Publishers
Macken House
39/40 Mayor Street Upper
Dublin 1
D01 C9W8
Ireland

Second edition 2020

10 9 8

ISBN 978-0-00-836748-0

collinselt.com

A catalogue record for this book is available from the
British Library.

Author: Peter Travis
Series editor: Celia Wigley
For the Publisher: Lisa Todd and Sheena Shanks
Editor: Alison Silver
Typesetter: Jouve, India
Illustrations: Jouve, India
Photographs and illustration on page 58: Shutterstock.com
Photograph page 109: Cavan / Alamy Stock Photo
Printer: Printed and bound by Ashford Colour Ltd
Audio recorded and produced by ID Audio, London
Cover designer: Gordon McGilp
Cover illustration: Maria Herbert-Liew
Sample Answer sheets (pages 226–8): Reproduced
with permission of Cambridge Assessment English ©
UCLES 2019

All exam-style questions and sample answers in this
title were written by the author.

**About the author**

**Peter Travis** has taught English in various European
countries including Greece, Portugal and the UK and
authored course books and workbooks for major ELT
publishers. Peter is co-founder of Flo-Joe, the award-
winning portal for Cambridge English exams and runs
other popular ELT websites. Peter is also the author of
Collins Practice Tests for Cambridge English: First (FCE),
Practice Tests for B1 Preliminary for Schools and the first
edition of this book.

# Contents

| | |
|---|---|
| How to use this book | 4 |
| About B1 Preliminary | 6 |
| How to prepare for the test | 10 |
| Test 1 | 21 |
| Test 2 | 41 |
| Test 3 | 61 |
| Test 4 | 81 |
| Test 5 | 101 |
| Test 6 | 121 |
| Test 7 | 141 |
| Test 8 | 161 |
| Mini-dictionary | 181 |
| Audio scripts | 184 |
| Sample answer sheets | 218 |
| Answer key for the Reading and Listening papers | 223 |
| Model answers for the Writing papers | 227 |
| Model answers for the Speaking papers | 233 |
| Speaking paper: Additional practice by topic | 251 |

# How to use this book

## Who is this book for?

This book will help you to prepare for the *Cambridge Assessment English B1 Preliminary* exam. The exam is also known as the *PET* exam (*Preliminary English Test*). The exam was updated for 2020 and this book has been written for the new exam. This book will be useful if you're preparing for the exam for the first time or taking it again. It has been designed so that you can use it to study on your own, however, you can also use it if you're preparing for the *B1 Preliminary* exam in a class.

The book contains:

- **Tips for success** – important advice to help you to do well in the exam
- **About *B1 Preliminary*** – a guide to the exam
- **How to prepare for the test** – advice to help you to succeed in each paper
- **Practice tests** – eight complete practice tests
- **Mini-dictionary** – definitions of the more difficult words from the practice tests
- **Audio scripts** – the texts of the audio for the Listening and Speaking papers
- **Sample answer sheets** – make sure you know what the answer sheets look like
- **Answer key** – the answers for the Reading and Listening papers
- **Model answers** – examples of good answers for the Writing and Speaking papers
- **Speaking paper: Additional practice by topic** – more sample questions to help you prepare for the Speaking paper
- **Audio** – all the recordings for the practice tests as well as model answers for the Speaking papers are available online at **collins.co.uk/eltresources**

## Tips for success

- **Register for the test early** – If you're studying on your own, use the Cambridge Assessment English website to find your local exam centre. Register as early as you can to give yourself lots of time to prepare.
- **Start studying early** – The more you practise, the better your English will become. Give yourself at least two months to revise and complete all the practice tests in this book. Spend at least one hour a day studying.
- **Time yourself** when you do the practice tests. This will help you to feel more confident when you do the real exam.
- **Do every part** of each practice test. Don't be afraid to make notes in the book. For example, writing down the meaning of words you don't know on the page itself will help you to remember them later on.

## Using the book for self-study

If you haven't studied for the *B1 Preliminary* exam before, it is a good idea to do all the tests in this book in order. If you have a teacher or friend who can help you with your speaking and writing, that would be very useful. It is also a good idea to meet up with other students who are preparing for the exam or who want to improve their English. Having a study partner will help you to stay motivated. You can also help each other with areas of English you might find difficult.

Begin preparing for the *B1 Preliminary* exam by getting to know the different parts of each paper, what each part tests and how many marks there are for each part. Use the information in the *About B1 Preliminary* section to find out all you can. You can also download the *B1 Preliminary Handbook* from the Cambridge Assessment English website for more details. You need to know how to prepare for each of the papers in the best way possible. The *How to prepare for the test* section in this book will be useful. Try to follow the advice as it will help you to develop the skills you need.

In the practice tests in this book, you will see certain words highlighted in grey. These are the more difficult words and you can find definitions of these in the *Mini-dictionary* at the back of the book. The definitions are from Collins COBUILD dictionaries. It's a good idea to download the *Cambridge B1*

*Preliminary Vocabulary List* from the Cambridge Assessment English website. This is a list of words that you should understand at B1 level. Look through the list and make a note of the words you don't know. Then look up their meaning in a dictionary. You could use the Collins online dictionary: www.collinsdictionary.com. Knowing these words will help you to do better in the exam. Search 'B1 Preliminary Vocabulary List 2020' online.

## Preparing for the Writing and Speaking papers

When you are ready to try the practice tests, make sure you do the tasks in the Writing papers as well as the Speaking papers. You can only improve your skills by practising a lot. Practise writing to a time limit. If you find this difficult at first, start by writing a very good answer of the correct length without worrying about time. Then try to complete the tasks faster until you can write a good answer within the time limit. Learn to estimate the number of words you have written without counting them. Study the model answers at the back of the book. This will give you a clear idea of the standard your answers need to be. Don't try to memorise emails, articles or stories for the Writing paper or answers to the questions in the Speaking paper. If you work your way through the book, you should develop the skills and language you need to give good answers in the real exam.

The Speaking paper in this book has accompanying audio so that you can practise answering the examiner's questions. You will be Candidate B, so if you hear the examiner ask Candidate B a question, this means you should answer by pausing the audio on your computer and answering the question. In Parts 3 and 4 of the Speaking paper, you are expected to have a conversation with Candidate A. Again, you will be Candidate B and will respond to Candidate A's statements or questions. This experience will not be 100% authentic as Candidate A cannot respond to your statements or questions, however this book and the audio have been designed to give you an excellent opportunity to practise answering questions through the eight practice tests. Once you have finished the Speaking paper, you can listen to the model answers for Candidate B that have been provided for you. Another option is that you record your answers and then compare these with the model answers.

Please note that there are two versions of the Speaking Test audio:

- The first version contains the pauses for you to practise answering the questions in the Speaking tests. This is when you have to answer the questions for Candidate B. The scripts for this audio can be found from page 186 onwards in your book. For example, you'll see on page 186 that Test 1 Speaking audio track is labelled 'Track 05'. Look for Track 05 when you search for the audio online.

- The second version of the audio contains the Model Answers for the Speaking tests. These are for you to listen to, to see how a good student might answer the questions in the Speaking test. The scripts for this audio can be found from page 233 onwards in your book. You'll see that these audio files are labelled with an 'a' at the end, for example Track 05a, etc. Look for Track 05a when you search for the audio online.

At the back of the book you'll find more sample questions for the Speaking paper. These provide another opportunity to practise answering questions that an examiner might ask you. There are 16 topics and all the questions have been recorded. Try answering these questions as fully as possible. Don't just give a 'yes/no' answer but try to give a reason or an example in your answer. Finally, read as much as possible in English; this is the best way to learn new vocabulary and improve your English.

# About B1 Preliminary

The *Cambridge B1 Preliminary* test is an intermediate-level English exam delivered by Cambridge Assessment English. It is for people who need to show that they can deal with everyday English at an intermediate level. In other words, you have to be able to:

- read simple textbooks and articles in English
- write emails and articles on everyday subjects
- understand factual information
- show awareness of opinions and mood in spoken and written English.

The exam is one of several offered by Cambridge Assessment English at different levels. The table below shows how *B1 Preliminary* fits into the Cambridge English Qualifications. The level of this exam is described as being at B1 on the Common European Framework of Reference (CEFR).

|  | CEFR | Cambridge English Scale | Cambridge qualification |
|---|---|---|---|
| Proficient user | C2 | 200–230 | C2 Proficiency (CPE) |
|  | C1 | 180–199 | C1 Advanced (CAE) |
| Independent user | B2 | 160–179 | B2 First (FCE) |
|  | B1 | 140–159 | B1 Preliminary (PET) |
| Basic user | A2 | 120–139 | A2 Key (KET) |
|  |  |  |  |

The *B1 Preliminary* qualification is for students studying general English or those students in higher education. Cambridge Assessment English also offers a *B1 Preliminary for Schools* qualification. These two qualifications follow exactly the same format, the level of the exams is the same and the candidates are tested in the same skills. However, the content of the exams is a bit different. The 'for Schools' version is specifically designed to suit the interests and experiences of school-age candidates. If you're a school-age learner, it would be better for you to take the *B1 Preliminary for Schools* qualification and use the *Collins Practice Tests for B1 Preliminary for Schools* to prepare for the exam.

There are four papers in **B1 Preliminary** (each is worth 25% of the total mark):

- Paper 1: Reading (45 minutes)
- Paper 2: Writing (45 minutes)
- Paper 3: Listening (approximately 30 minutes)
- Paper 4: Speaking (12–17 minutes)

## Timetabling

You usually take the Reading, Writing and Listening papers on the same day. You take the Speaking test on the same day or several days before or after the other papers. If you're studying on your own, you should contact your exam centre for dates. The exam is paper based. You can also take the exam on computer in some countries. For more information, see: https://www.cambridge-exams.ch/exams/CB_exams.php.

## Paper 1 Reading (45 minutes)

### What is it?

The Reading paper tests how well you can understand general English texts. It includes different types of texts about lots of different subjects.

### Skills needed

In order to do well in the Reading paper, you must be able to:

- read real-world texts such as emails, notices and articles and understand the main ideas; understand details about the writer's opinion and their reason for writing; scan texts of different lengths to find a particular piece of information.
- answer questions within the given time.

The Reading paper has six parts:

**Part 1** has five short real-world texts, for example, notices, messages, emails and signs, and five multiple-choice questions with three options, A, B or C. You have to read each text and choose the correct answer. (Total marks: 5)

**Part 2** has five short descriptions of people and eight short texts. You have to match each of the descriptions with the correct text. (Total marks: 5)

**Part 3** has a longer text and five multiple-choice questions with three options, A, B or C. You have to understand details about the text as well as the writer's attitude or opinion on a particular issue and their purpose for writing. (Total marks: 5)

**Part 4** has a longer text with five sentences removed. Following the text are eight sentences, which include the five that have been removed. You have to find the missing sentences. (Total marks: 5)

**Part 5** has a shorter text with six gaps followed by six multiple-choice questions. You have to fill the gaps by choosing the correct word from four options, A, B, C or D. (Total marks: 6)

**Part 6** has a short text with six gaps. You have to fill the gaps by deciding what the missing word is. (Total marks: 6)

## Paper 2 Writing (45 minutes)

### What is it?
The Writing paper tests how well you can write an answer to a question using a good range of vocabulary and grammatical structures.

### Skills needed
In order to do well in the Writing paper, you must be able to:
- understand the instructions and identify the key points that you have to include in your answer.
- use a good range of B1-level vocabulary and grammatical structures.
- write emails, articles and stories.
- write a well-organised text that is easy for the reader to follow.
- rephrase information given in the instructions.
- write your answers within the word limits given in the instructions.
- write your answers within the given time.

The Writing paper has two parts.

**Part 1** tests how well you can communicate information clearly. You will need to write a short email (100 words). The instructions ask you to include four important points in your message. (Total marks: 20)

**Part 2** tests how well you can communicate, organise your ideas and use a range of language. This part gives you a choice of two different tasks: an article or a short story. Your answer must be about 100 words. For the article, you read an announcement from a magazine or website. For the short story, you are given a sentence which you have to use at the beginning of your answer. (Total marks: 20)

In each part, marks are awarded in the following ways:
- five marks if you include all the necessary information
- five marks if you express your message clearly
- five marks if you organise your message so a reader can follow it easily
- five marks if you use a good range of grammar structures and vocabulary

## Paper 3 Listening (about 30 minutes)

### What is it?
The Listening paper tests how well you can understand conversations, talks and recorded messages.

## Skills needed

In order to do well in the Listening paper, you must be able to:

- understand main ideas and details.
- understand a speaker's opinion and attitude.
- answer questions within the given time.

The Listening paper has four parts.

**Part 1** has seven short extracts from monologues (= a speech by one person) or dialogues (= speech by two people) such as conversations, recorded messages or radio programmes, and seven questions. For each question, you have to listen and choose the correct answer from three options, A, B or C. The options are pictures. (Total marks: 7)

**Part 2** has six dialogues and six questions. You have to listen and choose the correct answer to a question from three options, A, B or C. (Total marks: 6)

**Part 3** has a longer monologue and six questions. You have to listen and complete six gaps in a text. (Total marks: 6)

**Part 4** has an interview and six questions. You have to listen and choose the correct answer from three options, A, B or C. (Total marks: 6)

## Paper 4 Speaking (12–17 minutes)

### What is it?

The Speaking paper tests your ability to use spoken English. You take the Speaking test with another candidate (your partner) or sometimes in a group of three. You can't take it alone. There are two examiners: one asks you and your partner(s) questions, the other (the assessor) has the marksheets. They both listen carefully and give you marks. If you are taking the exam in a pair, it lasts about 12 minutes; if you are taking it in a group of three it lasts about 17 minutes.

You can only take the exam in a group of three if there is an uneven number of candidates in the session; the group of three is always the last to be examined in the session. You can't choose to take the exam in a group of three and you can't take the exam on your own.

Depending where you take the exam, you may already know the person you take the exam with, or you may meet them for the first time when you go into the exam. It doesn't make any difference to how well you do in the exam. The examiners listen to each of you very carefully.

### Skills needed

In order to do well in the Speaking test, you must be able to:

- talk about everyday subjects and express your opinions.
- ask and answer questions during a conversation.
- speak clearly for about a minute.
- speak using a good range of B1-level vocabulary and grammatical structures.

The Speaking paper has four parts.

In **Part 1** the examiner asks you questions about your personal details, daily routine, past experiences, future plans, etc. (Time: 2 minutes)

In **Part 2** the examiner asks each candidate to talk in turn. They give you a photo and ask you to describe it. You have to talk for about a minute. The examiner then gives your partner a different photo. Your partner also has to talk for about a minute. (Time: 3 minutes)

In **Part 3** the examiner describes a situation and gives you and your partner instructions to talk about it. They also give you a picture showing you the situation and different things to discuss. You have to make suggestions to your partner and reply to their suggestions, talk about different possibilities and agree about the situation.
(Time: 4 minutes)

In **Part 4** the examiner asks you and your partner questions related to the theme in Part 3. You have to talk to the examiner and each other and discuss the questions. (Time: 3 minutes)

## Marks and results

After the exam, all candidates receive a Statement of Results. Candidates whose performance ranges between CEFR Levels A2 and B2 (Cambridge English Scale scores of 140–170) also receive a certificate.

The Statement of Results shows the candidate's:

- score on the Cambridge English Scale for their performance in each of the four language skills (reading, writing, listening and speaking).
- score on the Cambridge English Scale for their overall performance in the exam. This overall score is the average of their scores for the four skills.
- grade – this is based on the candidate's overall score.
- level on the CEFR – this is also based on the overall score.

The certificate shows the candidate's:

- score on the Cambridge English Scale for each of the four skills
- overall score on the Cambridge English Scale
- grade
- level on the CEFR
- level on the UK National Qualifications Framework (NQF).

For *B1 Preliminary*, the following scores will be used to report results:

| Cambridge English Scale Score | Grade | CEFR level |
|---|---|---|
| 160–170 | A | B2 |
| 153–159 | B | B1 |
| 140–152 | C | B1 |
| 120–139 | Level A2 | A2 |

Grade A: Cambridge English Scale scores of 160–170

Candidates sometimes show ability beyond Level B1. If a candidate achieves a Grade A in their exam, they will receive the *Preliminary English Test* certificate stating that they demonstrated ability at Level B2.

Grades B and C: Cambridge English Scale scores of 140–159

If a candidate achieves a Grade B or Grade C in their exam, they will receive the *Preliminary English Test* certificate at Level B1.

CEFR Level A2: Cambridge English Scale scores of 120–139

If a candidate's performance is below Level B1, but falls within Level A2, they will receive a *Cambridge English* certificate stating that they demonstrated ability at Level A2.

Scores between 102 and 119 are also reported on your Statement of Results, but you will not receive the *Preliminary English Test* certificate.

For more information on how the exam is marked, go to: http://www.cambridgeenglish.org

Working through the practice tests in this book will improve your exam skills, help you with timing for the exam, give you confidence and help you get a better result in the exam.

Good luck!

# How to prepare for the test

## Paper 1 Reading

» **READING CHALLENGE 1: 'I don't know a lot of the words that I see in the texts or in the questions.'**

**SOLUTION**: Build your vocabulary. Start by downloading the *Cambridge B1 Preliminary Vocabulary List* from the Cambridge Assessment English website. This is a list of words at B1 level that you should understand. Look through the list and make a note of the words you do not know. Then look up their meaning in a dictionary. Knowing these words will help you to do better in the exam. Search 'B1 Preliminary Vocabulary List from 2020' for the latest version.

**SOLUTION:** Use a learner's dictionary when you study. Dictionaries such as the *Collins COBUILD Illustrated Intermediate Dictionary of English* have clear definitions, example sentences, and information about grammar and illustrations to help you to build your vocabulary.

**SOLUTION:** Use 'key' words and phrases that appear before and after unknown words to help you guess their meaning. Read the sentence with the unknown word carefully. You may also need to read the whole paragraph in order to work out the meaning. In the table below there are some ideas for how key words and phrases might help you to understand a word. The unknown word is underlined.

| Guessing the meaning of unknown words | | |
|---|---|---|
| **Ideas** | **Key words and phrases** | **Examples** |
| Pay attention to examples near the unknown word. If you understand the examples, you can use them to guess the meaning of the unknown word. | *such as*<br>*including*<br>*this includes*<br>*like*<br>*for instance*<br>*for example* | *The students had different <u>excuses</u> for not doing their homework, **such as** 'My dog ate it' or 'My mum washed it in the washing machine'.* |
| Look for key words that show the writer is contrasting two ideas. The unknown word might have the opposite meaning to the idea expressed in the sentence before or after it. | *but*<br>*while*<br>*Unlike X,...*<br>*On the other hand, X ...*<br>*However....* | *There is going to be a heat <u>wave</u> all this week. **However**, the weather will be much colder next week.* |

**SOLUTION:** Look at parts of words such as prefixes and suffixes to guess the meaning of unknown words. A prefix is one or more letters, e.g. *un-, dis-, pre-, co-, under-*, that go at the beginning of a word, e.g. *unhappy, disorganised*. A suffix is one or more letters, e.g. *-ful, -less, -ation, -y, -ment, -hood*, that go at the end of a word, e.g. *enjoyment, neighbourhood*. If you learn the meanings of common English prefixes and suffixes, you will be able to guess the meaning of many unknown words. For example, the prefixes *un-* and *dis-* give a word a negative meaning.

» **READING CHALLENGE 2: 'I often don't have enough time to finish all the questions.'**

**SOLUTION:** Read the text quickly using skimming and scanning skills to find the answers to questions. Skimming is when you read a text quickly, paying attention only to the most important ideas. In this way, you can often quickly find the important sections that many questions are based on. This will save you a lot of time. To be good at skimming, make sure you know where to find the most important ideas in a text. In the table following there is some information on where to find important ideas.

| Part of the text | Skimming strategy |
|---|---|
| Titles and headings | Read the title of a text; this sometimes gives you an idea of what the text is about. In the same way, paragraph headings may help you to find the topic of each paragraph. |
| Introduction | Read the last two or three sentences of the introductory paragraph. They often include the main idea of the text. |
| Main paragraphs | Read the first and last sentences of a paragraph. They usually include the main idea of the paragraph. |
| Conclusion | Read the first two or three sentences of the conclusion. They often say in a few words what the text was about. |

Scanning is when you read a text quickly in order to find specific key words or ideas. After you have read a question and its answer options, you should make a note of any key words or ideas such as names or numbers. Then scan the text, looking specifically for those key words or ideas. The answers appear in the texts in the same order as the questions so if you have found the part of the text that answers a question, the part of the text that answers the next question must be below that part.

You do not need to understand every word when you skim or scan a text. The most important thing is to find the information you need in order to answer the questions quickly and correctly.

To practise skimming and scanning, find an article in a newspaper or magazine. First, skim the article and write down the most important ideas on a piece of paper. Then scan it for key words or ideas such as names or numbers. The more you practise skimming and scanning, the better you will become, so try to practise every day.

**SOLUTION:** Time yourself when you do practice tests. While you work on the questions, be sure to check the time occasionally. Do not spend too long on any one question; if you cannot answer it, carry on to the next question and go back to it later. This will help you to avoid getting stuck on a question and wasting your time.

» **READING CHALLENGE 3: 'None of the multiple-choice answer options "feel" right.'**

**SOLUTION:** Make sure you understand the question types in each part of the paper and the skills you need to answer them. The same question types appear in every Reading paper. If you know which skills each part tests, you will avoid surprises in the real exam and you will be able to answer the questions with more confidence.

**SOLUTION:** Decide which answer options are clearly incorrect. Usually, you can ignore an option that has:
• information that is the opposite of the facts in the text.
• information that does not answer the question.

**SOLUTION:** If you find that you are spending too much time on one question and you are not sure of the answer, move on to the next question or the next part. If you have time, you can return to it later. Some people find it easier to answer difficult questions once they have had time to think about them.

**SOLUTION:** Find evidence for your answer in the text. For example, if you think option A is correct, find the part of the text where the answer is and underline it. Make sure you are not just matching words in the question to words in the text and be careful that the answer is correct as a whole. This is important in Part 2, where you have to match people and information with descriptions; a description may have some of the information but not all of it.

» **READING CHALLENGE 4: 'I find it hard to decide what the missing word is in Part 6.'**

**SOLUTION:** Some gaps need a 'grammar' word. These are words such as determiners (e.g. *a*, *the*, *much*, *many*), prepositions (e.g. *on*, *at*, *in*) and conjunctions (e.g. *and*, *but*, *because*). Make a list of all the types of grammar words you find in practice tests and learn them so you understand how they are used.

**SOLUTION:** Work with a partner and make your own text with gaps. Find a short text and cross out grammar words.

**SOLUTION:** Some gaps need words that are part of a set expression. For example, a text might have the expressions *at least* and *spend time*, and *at* and *spend* are in the gaps. Focus on the words around a gap and decide if the missing word is part of a set expression. Make a list of vocabulary 'chunks' like these and not just individual words.

**SOLUTION:** Skip the gaps you do not know and come back to them later.

## Paper 2 Writing

» **WRITING CHALLENGE 1: 'I'm not sure how much time to spend on each question.'**

**SOLUTION:** Know how much time you have. On the day of the exam, wear a watch. While you work, keep an eye on the time. Use this guide while you write.

| Part 1: 25 minutes | |
| --- | --- |
| **Time** | **What you should do** |
| 3 minutes | Read the instructions carefully. Underline the key words in each of the four points. |
| 5 minutes | Make notes and plan your answer. |
| 15 minutes | Write your answer. Make sure you answer all four points. Think about how you can express the ideas in the points using different words and structures. |
| 2 minutes | Check your spelling and watch out for mistakes in your grammar. |
| Part 2: 20 minutes | |
| 2 minutes | Read the instructions carefully. Decide which question you are going to answer. If you choose the article, underline the key words in the instructions. |
| 2 minutes | Make notes and plan your answer. Think about a good beginning, middle and end. |
| 14 minutes | Write your answer. |
| 2 minutes | Check your spelling and watch out for mistakes in your grammar. |

**SOLUTION:** Practise writing within a time limit before the real exam. Start by giving yourself 15 minutes more than the time limit in the exam and slowly cut this down until you can finish writing a few minutes early. You will need this time to read through your work to check for mistakes.

» **WRITING CHALLENGE 2: 'I'm afraid that the examiner won't understand the ideas in my writing.'**

**SOLUTION:** Use linking words. Linking words connect two sentences or clauses together. They work like signs on a road and show the reader where you are going in your text; they make it easier to understand. In the table following there are some useful linking words and expressions. Add new words or expressions as you learn them.

| Use | Examples |
|---|---|
| To show the order of events | *First*<br>*At the beginning, ...*<br>*Then ...*<br>*After that, ...*<br>*Next, ...*<br>*Finally, ...*<br>*In the end, ...* |
| To contrast two points | *but although*<br>*However, ...* |
| To give examples | *for example*<br>*for instance*<br>*like*<br>*such as* |
| To give more information, to add | *and*<br>*also*<br>*In addition, ...* |

**SOLUTION:** Practise your spelling. A few misspelled words will not affect your score but a lot of spelling mistakes may stop the examiner from understanding your meaning. One way to improve your spelling is to read a lot; the more often you see words in English, the easier it will be to remember how they are spelled.

**SOLUTION:** What are your spelling problems? Do you sometimes forget to add -*s* to plural nouns? Do you forget that some adjectives change when they are in the comparative form (e.g. *heavy – heavier, hot – hotter*)? Do you have difficulty remembering the past forms of irregular verbs? Make a list of your spelling problems and always check your work for these.

**SOLUTION:** Make sure your handwriting is easy to read. It does not matter if you use capital letters all the time and you do not have to join the letters together within words. But you should be confident that other people can understand your handwriting. Ask a friend to read some of your work and then tell you if it is clear or if any letters or words are difficult to read. Remember to organise your work into paragraphs, as this will help the reader identify the beginning, middle and end of your answer.

» **WRITING CHALLENGE 3: 'I find it difficult to write emails.'**

**SOLUTION:** Many words and phrases are used as set expressions in emails. If you can remember these words and phrases, you will find it easier to start your piece of writing and bring it to an end. In the table below there are some examples. Add new ones as you learn them. Using expressions like these will help you to create a friendly, informal style.

| Section of email | Set expressions |
|---|---|
| Beginning | *How are you?*<br>*I hope you're well.*<br>*Thanks for your email.*<br>*It was great to hear from you.* |
| Commenting on information you have received | *I'm sorry to hear ...*<br>*I'm / I was so pleased to hear ...*<br>*It's / It was great to hear ...* |
| Ending | *Write back soon.*<br>*Best wishes,*<br>*See you soon.*<br>*Take care.* |

**SOLUTION:** Keep a record of examples of the informal language you can use in emails. In the table following there are some examples. Add new ones as you learn them.

|  | Informal | Formal |
|---|---|---|
| Contractions | *I'm / You're / It's got* | *I am / You are / It has got* |
| Vocabulary | *Hi / Hiya*<br>*Brilliant!* | *Dear ...*<br>*Very good.* |
| Grammar | Active, e.g.<br>• Peter Jackson **directed** *The Hobbit*.<br>• They **sold** the house last year. | Passive, e.g.<br>• *The Hobbit* **was directed** by Peter Jackson.<br>• The house **was sold** last year. |
| Punctuation | Exclamation marks when you want to show your emotions, such as surprise, excitement (!) | Exclamation marks only when absolutely necessary |

» **WRITING CHALLENGE 4: 'I'm not sure what to include in the email.'**

**SOLUTION:** There are four notes linked by lines pointing to text in the email question. These notes are the content points and they tell you what you need to write about in your email answer. You must make sure you answer each of these content points. Quite often the first content point will be to reply with a friendly opening sentence. The next three content points may tell you to agree, disagree, give an opinion, explain, suggest, recommend, describe or ask something. If you answer each of the content points successfully you will immediately receive five marks for content. In addition, doing this should also mean your email is the correct length, at approximately 100 words.

» **WRITING CHALLENGE 5: 'I'm not sure how to improve my vocabulary for the exam.'**

**SOLUTION:** The Part 1 task might ask you to thank someone, to suggest something or to apologise about something. Make sure you record useful words and phrases to do these things. In the table below there are some examples. Add new ones as you learn them.

| Function | Expressions |
|---|---|
| Thanking | *Many thanks for ...*<br>*Thanks very much for ...* |
| Suggesting | *Why don't you ...?*<br>*What about ...?*<br>*Try ...*<br>*It would be a good idea to ...* |
| Apologising | *I'm sorry but ...*<br>*Apologies but ...* |

**SOLUTION:** Practise paraphrasing (= saying the same things using different words). Find a reading text from the Reading section of this book. Then choose a paragraph and read it carefully. Close the book and try saying what you have read by paraphrasing. When you have finished, compare your paragraph with the one in the book. Did you change key words by using synonyms (= words with the same meaning)? Did you change structures (e.g. active to passive)? Practise paraphrasing one paragraph a day until you feel confident about your paraphrasing skills.

» **WRITING CHALLENGE 6: 'I don't know how to write an article for the Part 2 question.'**

**SOLUTION:** The article task usually contains two questions you need to include in your answer. The article will always ask you to write about something you have experience of, so spend a minute or two thinking about your answer. Think about the kind of vocabulary you might include in your answer. For example, if the question asks you to describe your favourite film, try to show your ability to use appropriate words or expressions such as *actor, actress, director, thriller, horror film*, etc. During your studies, keep a list of topic vocabulary like this.

» **WRITING CHALLENGE 7: 'I don't know how to write a good story for the Part 2 question.'**

**SOLUTION:** If you have trouble thinking of something to write about in a story, use question words to help you think of ideas. Ask yourself questions beginning with *where, when, who* and *why*. Imagine you have to write a story with the opening sentence: *'It was late and I was lost.'* Ask yourself questions: *Where were you? When was it? Who was with you? Why were you there?* If you answer these questions, you will set the scene for your story. Then ask yourself: *What happened?* If you give details of what happened, you will describe the events.

**SOLUTION:** Ideas for your story can come from your own life. Give yourself a minute to think whether the opening sentence describes something that has happened to you or a friend. It does not have to be very exciting. If you can't think of something that happened to you, use your imagination – the story doesn't have to be true!

**SOLUTION:** You have to be able to use past tenses well when writing a story, particularly the past simple and past continuous. Practise using these tenses by keeping a diary. Every evening, write what happened during the day. For example:

*I woke up this morning at about 7.00. I got out of bed and went into the bathroom. While I was having a shower, I heard the phone ring.*

Keep it simple. Focus on making sure the verb forms are correct and using the two tenses correctly.

**SOLUTION:** You will get extra marks if you show you can use adjectives and adverbs correctly. Remember: an adjective is used to describe a noun. An adverb gives information about a verb. For example:

*There was a loud knock at the door and I got up quickly to see who it was.*

Be careful: if you use too many adjectives and adverbs, your writing will seem unnatural.

## Paper 3 Listening

» **LISTENING CHALLENGE 1: 'I'm worried that I won't know what to do.'**

**SOLUTION:** The instructions for the Listening paper are always the same. When you do the practice tests in this book, make sure you know what you have to do in each of the four parts in the Listening paper. In the exam and in the practice tests you will hear each recording twice so if there is something you don't understand the first time, listen for it again the second time. Always make sure you read the questions carefully before the audio starts. They give you lots of clues about what you will hear.

» **LISTENING CHALLENGE 2: 'I'm worried that I won't understand enough to answer the questions.'**

**SOLUTION:** In Part 1, read the question first, then look at the pictures. These will give you an idea of what each question is about. It is very likely that you will hear each of the pictures mentioned, but only one of them will be the correct answer. For example, you may hear words like *but*, *however* or other key words that will help you decide which of the three pictures is correct.

**SOLUTION:** In Part 2, read the questions and options carefully. This will help you get an idea about what the people will be talking about and you can guess what the answers might be.

**SOLUTION:** For Part 3, read the sentences before the recording starts and try to guess what the missing words might be. For example, are there words before or after the gap that indicate the missing word might be a date or a number? Is it likely the missing word is a noun?

**SOLUTION:** In Part 4, read through all the questions and options. This will give you a good idea of what the interview is about and the kind of things that are discussed. As you listen the first time, put a question mark next to the option you think is possibly correct. Make sure you listen carefully the second time for evidence that your choice is correct.

» **LISTENING CHALLENGE 3: 'I don't always understand the speakers. Sometimes they talk too fast.'**

**SOLUTION:** Listen as much as possible to natural English. The more you listen to native English speech, the better you will understand the English used in the *Cambridge Assessment English B1 Preliminary* exam. Try the following:

- Watch TV programmes or films in English. The programmes don't have to be educational – comedies and dramas have good examples of natural spoken English. If you find this difficult, watch English-language films with subtitles. Listening can be easier when you can read to check understanding.

- Join an English-language club. Your local university, library or community centre might have one. By joining, you will be able to practise speaking English and have the chance to hear native speakers.
- Join an online language community. There may be native speakers of English who want to learn your language and will be happy to practise talking to you using online tools like Skype™.

**SOLUTION:** Download English-language podcasts or radio programmes. At first, practise listening for only a minute or two at a time. As your comprehension gets better, listen for a longer time. When you listen, try to focus on the speakers' pronunciation as well as the meaning of the words. Listen as many times as you need to until you understand the main ideas.

## Paper 4 Speaking

» **SPEAKING CHALLENGE 1: 'I'm not sure how much I have to say when I answer the examiner's questions in Part 1.'**

**SOLUTION:** This part is just a simple conversation between you and the examiner. It is a chance for them to get to know more about you. You don't have to give very long answers but you should also say more than 'Yes' or 'No'. The examiner will make it clear if they want you to say a bit more, or they will tell you when to stop if you are talking for too long. You don't need to worry about this.

**SOLUTION:** When you answer Part 1 questions, give a reason for your answer or an example. If the examiner asks *Do you enjoy studying English?* say why you do or don't enjoy it. For example:

*Yes, I do. I love listening to music and I'm starting to understand the words to some of the songs.*

If the examiner asks *What kind of food do you like to eat?* don't just reply *Indian food* or *pizza*. Think of a meal you have eaten and why you enjoyed it. For example:

*I enjoy Indian food. I often go to a restaurant near my house and I always order something spicy to eat.*

» **SPEAKING CHALLENGE 2: 'I'm not sure I'll have anything to say in Parts 1 and 4.'**

**SOLUTION:** The questions in Part 1 and the conversation in Part 4 are about you and your experiences. The examiner might ask you to talk about your hobbies and interests, where you live, your family, your studies, etc. and you already know a lot about these subjects! Look at the table below. Think about the kind of questions the examiner might ask you about the subjects and how you would answer them.

| Subject | Possible questions |
|---|---|
| Where you live | *Do many tourists visit your town?* |
| Your hobbies or interests | *Have you always had the same hobbies and interests?* |
| Your friends and family | *Who do you look like in your family?* |
| Your daily routine | *What time do you usually get up?* |
| Your studies | *What was/is your favourite subject at school?* |
| Your favourite TV programmes/ films/books/music | *Have you read a book lately that you really enjoyed?* |
| The food you like/don't like | *What kind of food do people in your country like to eat?* |

**SOLUTION:** Try not to repeat the same words and phrases all the time. For example, the following expressions all mean *I like* or *I don't like:*

- I'm (not) fond of ...
- I'm (not) keen on ...
- I enjoy ...
- I can't stand ...

In the same way, don't keep using *I think*. Sometimes use *In my opinion* or *I feel*.

**SOLUTION:** Remember that Part 4 is a conversation. You'll do better in the exam if you ask your partner questions and respond to the things your partner says. This means you have to listen carefully because it will help you to keep the conversation going.

**SOLUTION:** Practise asking questions and using 'reply questions'. These are useful in a conversation. Here are some examples:

A: *I used to play football for my school.* B: *Did you? Were you good?*

A: *I've never eaten Spanish food.* B: *Haven't you? It's really nice.*

» **SPEAKING CHALLENGE 3: 'In Part 2 I worry that I won't have enough time to talk about my photo or that I won't have enough to say.'**

**SOLUTION:** Time yourself when you practise for the Part 2 task so you get an idea what it feels like to talk for one minute. By timing yourself, you'll learn not to speak too fast or too slowly and you'll be able to give a complete answer within the time. In the exam, the examiner will encourage you to say more if you haven't said enough or will tell you to stop talking when you have said enough.

**SOLUTION:** When you practise talking about a photo, spend a few seconds looking at the photo before you start. Ask yourself questions, such as: *What does the photo show? Who is in the photo? Where are they? What are they doing? How do they feel? What are they going to do next?* Then you can answer the questions when you talk about the photo. Practising like this will give you confidence for the exam.

» **SPEAKING CHALLENGE 4: 'In Part 2 I'm worried that my description will be disorganised and I'll get into a mess.'**

**SOLUTION:** Practise using a structure for your description. Here is a suggestion:

- Begin by saying what the photo is about. For example: *This is a photo of a birthday party. It looks like a children's birthday party.*
- Talk about the people in the photo and what they are doing. For example: *There are lots of children and two adults. The children are sitting at a table and the adults are serving them food...* (You could continue by describing what some of them are wearing or what they seem to be eating or doing.)
- Say what you think of the scene. For example: *It's similar to the birthday parties I had when I was young.*

**SOLUTION:** There are many words and expressions that you can use to help you to organise your thoughts. There are some common examples in the table. Add new words and expressions as you learn them.

| Use | Words and expressions |
|---|---|
| Comparing | *although*<br>*but*<br>*compared to/with*<br>*However, ...*<br>*On the one hand, ...*<br>*On the other hand, ...* |
| Giving reasons | *because*<br>*because of*<br>*so*<br>*in order to* |
| Giving examples | *for example*<br>*for instance*<br>*To give you an example, ...* |
| Adding | *The first reason is ...*<br>*The second reason is ...*<br>*Also, ...*<br>*What's more, ...*<br>*Finally, ...* |
| Concluding | *So, all in all ...*<br>*To sum up, ...*<br>*In general, ...* |

» **SPEAKING CHALLENGE 5: 'I'm worried that the examiners won't understand me. My pronunciation is bad.'**

**SOLUTION:** The examiner does not expect you to speak with the accent of a native speaker. In fact, having an accent is not a problem. The important thing is to speak clearly so that people can understand you.

**SOLUTION:** Ask your friends to listen to a recording of you speaking English. They might be able to tell you about pronunciation problems you don't notice on your own. In particular, ask them if it is easy to understand what you are saying. What words do they have difficulty understanding? Practise saying the words you had the most trouble with.

**SOLUTION:** Listen to as much English as possible. You could listen to English-language radio programmes or podcasts while you travel to work or watch English-language television in your free time. Start copying the sounds you hear.

**SOLUTION:** Practise speaking English with native English speakers. To find native English speakers in your area, try going to tourist attractions in your city. You could also join an English-language club. Check at your local library to see if there is one or start one yourself!

**SOLUTION:** Some speakers have trouble with certain sounds. For example, Spanish speakers sometimes add *e* to English words beginning with *s*, e.g. 'eschool'. Other speakers pronounce the letter *w* as a *v*. Find out if speakers from your country have a particular problem with English pronunciation and practise saying words with those sounds.

**SOLUTION:** If you want people to understand you when you speak, you have to stress words correctly. If you stress the wrong syllable, people might not understand you. For example, in the following nouns, the underlined syllable is stressed:

- cele<u>bra</u>tion
- ad<u>ver</u>tisement
- pho<u>tog</u>raphy

However, in the verb form, a different syllable is stressed:

- <u>cel</u>ebrate
- <u>ad</u>vertise
- <u>pho</u>tograph

Knowing how to pronounce words with more than one syllable is important and you should use a good dictionary to check the stress of any new words.

» **SPEAKING CHALLENGE 6: 'I don't know what to do if I make a mistake and if I should correct myself.'**

**SOLUTION:** Correcting yourself when you make a mistake is a good way of showing the examiner that you do know the correct word or item of grammar. But remember: you must also show that you can speak for quite a long time and this will be difficult if you correct yourself all the time. It is probably best to correct some mistakes but try to relax and speak as fluently as possible.

**SOLUTION:** Practise speaking English as much as you can before the exam. One way to do this is to speak to yourself when you are alone. The advantage of being alone is that you will be relaxed and less worried about making mistakes. Talk about what has happened during the day, what your plans are for the rest of the week or your opinion of anything that is in the news.

» **SPEAKING CHALLENGE 7: 'I don't know what to do if I don't understand what the examiner says.'**

**SOLUTION:** Always ask the examiner if you don't understand. They will repeat the instruction and make sure you understand. You won't lose marks for this.

» **SPEAKING CHALLENGE 8: 'I'm worried I'm going to feel very nervous when I take the Speaking test.'**

**SOLUTION:** Remember that a lot of people feel nervous when they take an exam, and the examiners understand this. There are lots of techniques to help you relax. Candidates often find that the worst part is waiting outside the room before they go in, and once they start speaking they relax. The examiners are there to listen to you, they don't want to frighten you!

**SOLUTION:** Remember that if you do plenty of practice before the exam you will feel more confident. If you work through all eight practice tests in this book you will learn about each part of the exam and you will know exactly what to expect in the Speaking test.

**SOLUTION:** Listen to the audio for the Speaking papers in the practice tests and practise answering the questions. Then listen to the model answers. Remember there is also an extra section at the back of the book to help you with the Speaking test – keep practising with the audio. The more you practise, the more confident you will feel.

# Test 1

# Test 1 READING

## Part 1

### Questions 1–5

For each question, choose the correct answer.

---

1

Hi Mary,

I've cancelled my trip to Grandad's tomorrow as I'm not feeling very well. If he calls can you tell him I'll phone him tonight?

Love, Mum x

A  Mary should call Grandad.

B  Grandad has cancelled the visit.

C  Mum will call Grandad later.

2

**Music School**

Guitar lessons 50% off from now until 31 August.

Classes must be booked in advance.

A  Lessons can be paid for on arrival.

B  Guitar lessons are half price for a limited period.

C  The school offers advanced music lessons.

3

**CAR PARK**
Parking for customers only.
1 hour maximum stay.
Management are not responsible for loss or damage to property.

A  Parking is limited to one hour.

B  Any damage should be reported to management.

C  Any lost property should be handed in.

**4**

> **To:**sjenner@hotmail.com
> **From**: tom668@gmail.com
>
> I've booked your tickets for the flight. They were the cheapest I could get. You can check in online but can only take hand luggage or you have to pay extra.
>
> Tom

A  There are cheaper flights available.

B  You have to pay extra for hand luggage.

C  There's no need to check in at the airport.

**5**

> **Sofa for sale**
>
> Almost new sofa needs a new home as we're moving to a small apartment. Buyer must collect.

A  The sofa is perfect for a small apartment.

B  The buyer must arrange to transport the sofa.

C  The sofa is brand new.

## Part 2

### Questions 6–10

For each question, choose the correct answer.

---

The people below all want to rent somewhere to live.
On the opposite page there are descriptions of eight properties to rent.
Decide which property would be the most suitable for the people below.

**6**    Mary is a young, single author and is looking for a one-bedroom property in a quiet location. She loves to get out daily to walk her dog. She needs parking space.

**7**    Michael is from Sweden. He has booked a three-month English course and is looking for accommodation. He is keen to experience the English way of life and would prefer to share with others.

**8**    Franco will be working in the UK for 12 months for a finance company and wants to share with a suitable person. He would prefer bills to be included in the rent.

**9**    Tom and Sally want to rent a home somewhere quiet. They need at least two bedrooms as Sally's elderly mother, who loves gardening, will be living with them. Local shops would be useful.

**10**    Paula starts a course at university soon and is urgently looking for accommodation. She doesn't drive and needs somewhere close to good transport links. She wants to share with others but doesn't like living with pets.

# Properties to rent

**A  Rowan Avenue**

One room available in a family home. We welcome international students looking for accommodation. You will have your own room, but you should be prepared to live as part of the family. We have two young children and a dog so it can get a little noisy at times! All meals provided.

**E  Birch Hill**

This ground floor, one-bedroom flat is perfect for the older person. The lounge opens onto a garden area shared by other residents. Limited parking but good transport links. Local shops nearby. Pets are welcome.

**B  Brooklyn Road**

This first-floor flat is in a great location. Excellent road and rail links with the station just a short five-minute walk away. This is a luxury property with new carpets and furniture in all rooms and so is not suitable for pet owners.

**F  The Crescent**

An opportunity to share a beautiful city-centre apartment situated in the centre of the business area. Looking for a professional person to share this two-bedroom property. Rent includes all bills. One-year minimum stay. No pets.

**C  Ash Lane**

A modern three-bedroom family home with a large garden. The property has its own garage. Situated in the heart of the countryside, there are excellent public transport links and a grocers and post office in the nearby village.

**G  Baker Close**

A second floor, one-bedroom flat perfect for a professional person. Situated close to the train station and local shops, great nightlife with clubs and restaurants just a short walk away. The property has parking at the back of the building. No pets allowed.

**D  College Street**

No bills to pay! Three spare bedrooms in this shared six-bedroom all-girl house. A regular bus and train service into the city centre and a short walk to the university. Share a very modern kitchen and living room. Hurry as rooms are going quickly!

**H  Meadow View Road**

Cosy one-bedroom cottage in the countryside with garage attached. Ideal for someone who wants to get away from the busy city. A car is necessary as there are no transport links into the local town. The local area is very popular with walkers and those wanting to enjoy nature. Pets welcome.

## Part 3

### Questions 11–15

For each question, choose the correct answer.

---

# Steve Cummins talks about starting his own business

I'd worked for the company for almost ten years. They were good employers and the money wasn't that bad. They trusted in my ability and always left me to get on with my work. And I shared an office and met some lovely people, so I certainly wasn't unhappy there. But I just couldn't stop wondering how better my life would be if I had my own business and could make my own decisions. And so one year ago this week I left my job.

We don't have a spare room at home, so the kitchen table has been my office. It was difficult to begin with, but I soon got used to working in this way. I started by visiting small businesses in the area to see if I could interest them in my services. My proudest moment was making my first sale, a website for a local cake shop. Soon after, I started getting calls from other people asking for help with websites of their own and I found myself getting quite busy.

Of course, there have been challenges. I'm not earning quite as much as before but it's enough. I don't have to pay for transport to work anymore so that means I'm not spending quite so much. My biggest problem has been managing my time. There's no boss to tell me what to do and I'm sometimes a little lazy. I have this rule that work stops on a Friday afternoon so I can spend time with the family at weekends, so I need to pay more attention to this.

So, I wouldn't say it's been easy, but I don't regret my decision at all. I've enjoyed being my own boss and I'm quite hopeful about the future. During the next 12 months I plan to rent some office space as I'd like to be able to separate work from my home life. I'm going to need to earn more money to pay for it but I think it will help me to focus on my work.

---

**11** Why did Steve leave his job?

    **A** He didn't like attending meetings.

    **B** He wanted more control of his work.

    **C** He had a great idea for a product.

    **D** He wanted to earn more money.

**12** Steve's greatest pleasure so far has been

    **A** getting his first customer.

    **B** not having to drive to work.

    **C** having his own office.

    **D** not having to answer the telephone.

**13** What does Steve say is the most difficult about working for himself?

    **A** working hard enough

    **B** not having a regular salary

    **C** feeling lonely

    **D** working at the weekend

**14** In the next year, Steve thinks

    **A** he will get an office job.

    **B** he will earn less money.

    **C** he might not need to work in his kitchen.

    **D** there will be much more competition.

**15** What would be a good introduction to this article?

**A**
> In this article, Steve Cummins explains the problems of starting your own business and dealing with difficult customers.

**B**
> Thinking of starting your own business? Steve Cummins did just that and now wishes he had done it sooner.

**C**
> Steve Cummins made a big decision last year to leave his job. Read on to find out about the ups and downs of being your own boss.

**D**
> Steve Cummins explains below how he dealt with not enjoying his job by leaving his employer and starting his own business.

## Part 4

### Questions 16-20

Five sentences have been removed from the text below.
For each question, choose the correct answer.
There are three extra sentences which you do not need to use.

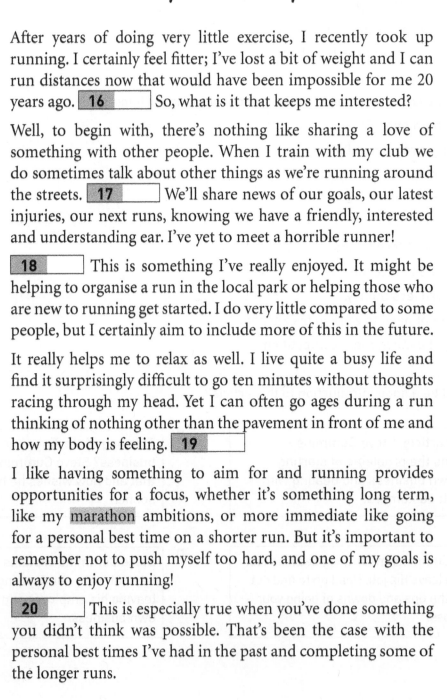

# My new hobby

After years of doing very little exercise, I recently took up running. I certainly feel fitter; I've lost a bit of weight and I can run distances now that would have been impossible for me 20 years ago. [ 16 ] So, what is it that keeps me interested?

Well, to begin with, there's nothing like sharing a love of something with other people. When I train with my club we do sometimes talk about other things as we're running around the streets. [ 17 ] We'll share news of our goals, our latest injuries, our next runs, knowing we have a friendly, interested and understanding ear. I've yet to meet a horrible runner!

[ 18 ] This is something I've really enjoyed. It might be helping to organise a run in the local park or helping those who are new to running get started. I do very little compared to some people, but I certainly aim to include more of this in the future.

It really helps me to relax as well. I live quite a busy life and find it surprisingly difficult to go ten minutes without thoughts racing through my head. Yet I can often go ages during a run thinking of nothing other than the pavement in front of me and how my body is feeling. [ 19 ]

I like having something to aim for and running provides opportunities for a focus, whether it's something long term, like my marathon ambitions, or more immediate like going for a personal best time on a shorter run. But it's important to remember not to push myself too hard, and one of my goals is always to enjoy running!

[ 20 ] This is especially true when you've done something you didn't think was possible. That's been the case with the personal best times I've had in the past and completing some of the longer runs.

**A**   And it's good for your health.

**B**   Then there's that sense of achievement.

**C**   But I don't think these are the reasons I go running.

**D**   Finding the time to run can be a problem.

**E**   I injured myself earlier in the year.

**F**   Running gives me a rest from anything that is on my mind.

**G**   Running also offers lots of opportunities to volunteer.

**H**   But mostly we talk about running.

## Part 5

### Questions 21–26

For each question, choose the correct answer.

---

# Drawing

Drawing is one of the earliest forms of communication and goes back much **(21)** ............... than the written word. However, despite its long history, it has not always been **(22)** ............. of as a form of art.

When paper became easily **(23)** .............. in the 14th century, the use of drawing in the arts increased. Some of the great artists of the Renaissance produced drawings of the highest **(24)** .............. and presented the human body in a more realistic way than ever before. However, it was often practised **(25)** .............. order to plan a larger painting and wasn't taken very seriously as a form of art.

Today, drawing is regarded as a **(26)** ............. skill and no less important than oil painting or other creative works.

---

| 21 | **A** wider | **B** further | **C** bigger | **D** greater |
|----|-------------|---------------|--------------|---------------|
| 22 | **A** taken | **B** seen | **C** thought | **D** made |
| 23 | **A** free | **B** open | **C** around | **D** available |
| 24 | **A** quality | **B** type | **C** kind | **D** sort |
| 25 | **A** for | **B** in | **C** on | **D** with |
| 26 | **A** valuable | **B** correct | **C** dear | **D** likely |

## Part 6

### Questions 27–32

For each question, write the correct answer.
Write **one** word for each gap.

---

### The Koala

We're leaving Australia soon and we've just met that well-known symbol of Australian wildlife, the koala. I've always called them koala bears, but they are a member **(27)** ............ the marsupial family.

They are only two centimetres long when **(28)** ............ first come into the world and spend the first six months living in their mother's pouch before moving on to her back for a further six months.

They live on eucalyptus leaves, which they eat huge amounts of, up to 1 kilogram **(29)** ............ day. One benefit of this diet is that they rarely need to drink water as they get **(30)** ............ from these leaves. They can live for up to 15 years in the wild and as long as 20 years when cared for in zoos or nature reserves.

Unfortunately, as more of these eucalyptus trees **(31)** ............ cut down, we are seeing a fall in **(32)** ............ number of koalas.

---

# Test 1 WRITING

## Part 1

You **must** answer this question.
Write your answer in about **100 words** on the answer sheet.

---

### Question 1

Read this email from your English-speaking friend Tania and the notes you have made.

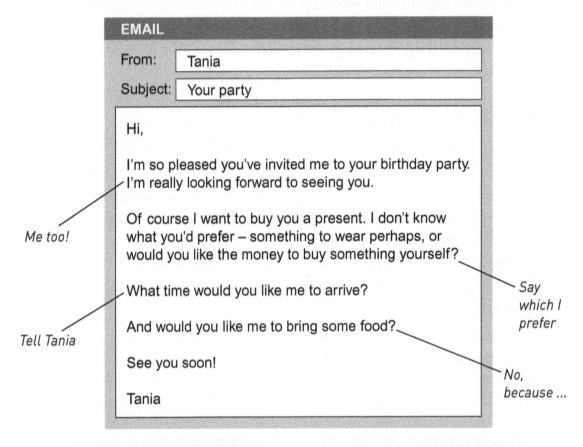

**EMAIL**

From: Tania

Subject: Your party

Hi,

I'm so pleased you've invited me to your birthday party. I'm really looking forward to seeing you.

*Me too!*

Of course I want to buy you a present. I don't know what you'd prefer – something to wear perhaps, or would you like the money to buy something yourself?

*Say which I prefer*

What time would you like me to arrive?

*Tell Tania*

And would you like me to bring some food?

*No, because ...*

See you soon!

Tania

Write your **email** to Tania using **all the notes**.

## Part 2

Choose **one** of these questions.
Write your answer in about **100 words** on the answer sheet.

---

## Question 2

You see this notice in an English-language magazine.

**Articles wanted!**

**WHAT KIND OF HOLIDAY DO YOU ENJOY?**

Have you got a favourite place you go to?

Are there things you like to do on holiday?

**Write an article answering these questions and we will put it in our magazine!**

Write your **article**.

## Question 3

Your English teacher has asked you to write a story.

Your story must begin with this sentence.

*When I opened the door, I couldn't believe my eyes.*

Write your **story**.

# Test 1 LISTENING

## Part 1

### Questions 1–7

For each question, choose the correct answer.

---

**1**   When does John offer to come?

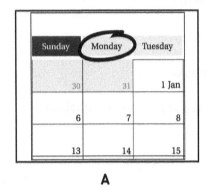

A                          B                          C

**2**   What did the woman enjoy doing at the party?

A                          B                          C

**3**   What will the weather be like in the morning?

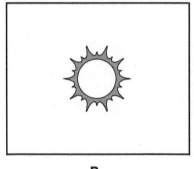
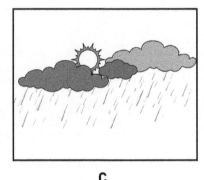

A                          B                          C

**4**  What time does the tour of the hospital start?

A

B

C

**5**  What isn't the daughter having for her birthday?

A

B

C

**6**  What size of shirt does the man want?

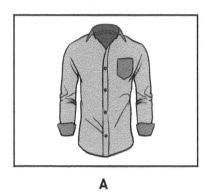

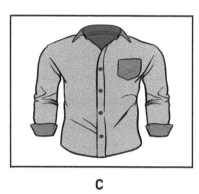

A

B

C

**7**  What are the police checking for next week?

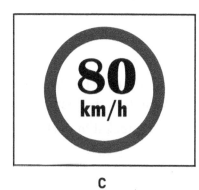

A

B

C

# Part 2

02

## Questions 8–13

For each question, choose the correct answer.

---

**8**  You will hear two friends talking about a film.
What does the woman say about it?

   **A**  It's only suitable for young people.

   **B**  The director doesn't usually make action films.

   **C**  It has already been on TV.


**9**  You will hear two friends talking about someone the woman lives with.
They think it would be a good idea

   **A**  to ask him to leave.

   **B**  to remind him to do the washing-up.

   **C**  to leave him a note of things to do.


**10**  You will hear a woman telling a friend about a holiday she is going on.
How does she feel about it?

   **A**  She is worried it might be expensive.

   **B**  She doesn't think she will be lonely.

   **C**  She doesn't like doing long walks.


**11**  You will hear two friends talking about meeting a relation at the airport.
To help the person find him, the man has decided

   **A**  to take a sign.

   **B**  to wear something colourful.

   **C**  to email her when she arrives.


**12**  You will hear two friends talking about getting to the train station.
The man thinks

   **A**  the bus will take a long time.

   **B**  a taxi is too expensive.

   **C**  the train will be late.


**13**  You will hear two friends talking about a new laptop.
What does the man say about the old one?

   **A**  He took it to work for a while.

   **B**  It was slow to start.

   **C**  It stopped working.

## Part 3

03

### Questions 14–19

For each question, write the correct answer in the gap. **Write one or two words or a number or a date or a time.**

---

You will hear a radio presenter called Erica talking about how we can help the environment.

## How to help the environment

Remember that when we're **(14)** ..................…..... we always have the choice to buy something somewhere else.

Take **(15)** ...................…... with you the next time you go shopping.

Recycle unwanted things by giving them to **(16)** ....................…....

See how you might be able to help with **(17)** ....................…... problems where you live.

Ask your friends to help you clear rubbish and litter from **(18)** ...................…..... and streets in your area.

Try car-sharing with your **(19)** ...................…..... if you work in the same area.

# Part 4

## Questions 20–25

For each question, choose the correct answer.

___

You will hear an interview with a woman called Sally Wainwright, who recently started singing classes.

**20** Sally explained that

    **A** people kept telling her to try something different.

    **B** she didn't enjoy art classes.

    **C** she had never been to a singing class.

**21** Sally wanted to sing because

    **A** her husband wanted her to.

    **B** her mother told her she would love it.

    **C** she didn't want to feel embarrassed about singing.

**22** What does Sally say she likes about the group?

    **A** The people are very kind.

    **B** You don't need to show you can sing well to join.

    **C** You only sing on your own if you want to.

**23** What does Sally say about the first session?

    **A** She had problems with her car.

    **B** She felt better after talking with the organiser.

    **C** She was asked to stand at the back.

**24** Since she has been singing with the group

    **A** Sally now sings with her children.

    **B** Sally has achieved all her goals.

    **C** Sally is more confident about singing on her own.

**25** What does Sally say about singing?

    **A** It can make you physically stronger.

    **B** She is sure it is good for her health.

    **C** She ends a session feeling cheerful.

# Test 1 SPEAKING

1A

1B

Audio scripts spend Model answers on pages 184–250.

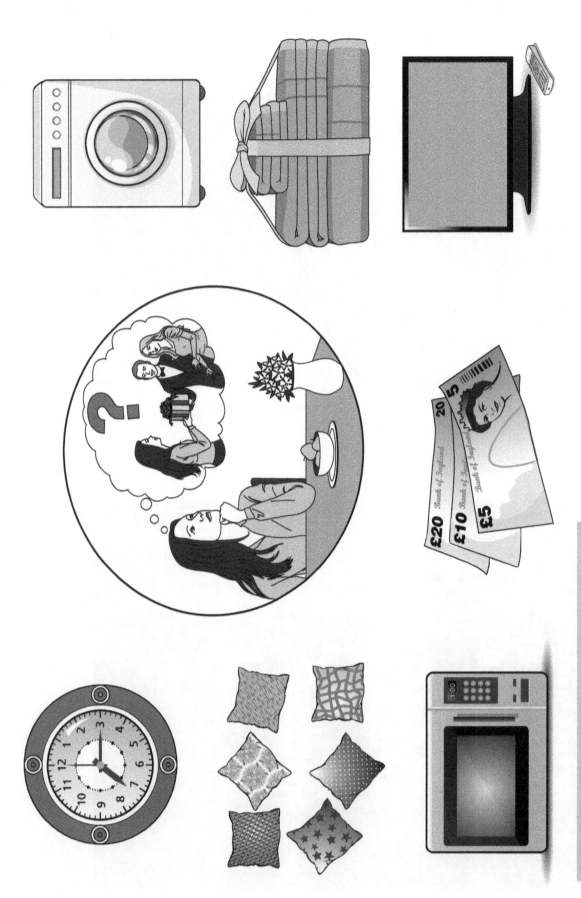

Ideas for a wedding present

Audio scripts and Model answers on pages 184–250.

# Test 2

# Test 2 READING

## Part 1

### Questions 1–5

For each question, choose the correct answer.

---

**1**

> Get £10 off
> when you spend over £50.
> Offer only available during our
> 2-week SALE!

A  Get £10 off all sales.

B  Offer lasts two weeks.

C  Spend up to £50 and save £10.

**2**

> Hi Paul
>
> Charles phoned to say he can't meet you until 9.00 as he's working late. Can you email him before he finishes work to say if this is OK?

A  Charles can't meet Paul at 9.00.

B  Charles will email Paul.

C  Paul should confirm that 9.00 is OK.

**3**

> **FOOD NOTICE**
> Please tell your waiter today if you have to avoid certain foods before you make your order.

A  The waiter will explain our special meals of the day.

B  Inform us of any issues with your diet.

C  Orders must be paid for before you eat.

4

| To: tracyhardy@yahoo.com |
| From: sheila@gmail.com |

Tracy, the boss has just called. Her train gets in at 1.00. If nobody from the office is around to pick her up could you call a taxi for her and let her know.

**A** Tracy needs to take a taxi to the station.

**B** The boss needs to be collected from the station.

**C** The boss doesn't know when the train arrives.

5

## Wanted!

Volunteer driver for local community centre. Would suit retired person as only 1 hour per day, Monday to Friday.

**A** Driver needed for five hours a week.

**B** Lifts available to community centre.

**C** Driver needed for retired people.

## Part 2

## Questions 6–10

For each question, choose the correct answer.

---

The people below are all looking for a job.
On the opposite page there are descriptions of eight jobs.
Decide which jobs would be the most suitable for the people below.

**6**  Sandra is doing a four-year degree in hair and beauty and wants to work as a volunteer for her third-year work experience. She likes to be part of a team and would enjoy dealing with customers.

**7**  Manuela is from Spain and is looking for work to support herself financially while she studies English at a local college. She can only work on Saturdays and Sundays and some evenings.

**8**  Stella is looking for work during the holidays. She's studying business at college and would love somewhere she can gain experience in a business environment and put her IT skills into practice.

**9**  John is looking for a job where he can work with customers. He recently completed a course in this area of work and is keen to find a job that would offer support in developing skills in managing staff.

**10**  Simon has a job but wants to work with teenagers during the weekend. He is planning a career change and is happy to work without pay in order to gain experience.

# Jobs Available

**A  ABC Computer Specialists**

Do you have customer service skills? ABC Computer Specialists are looking for sales advisers to join our growing customer service team. This is a full-time post, 37 hours a week, with great opportunities for the right person.

**E  Amega**

Would you like to work in a modern office environment, building relationships with customers, and working with our excellent team? If you've recently completed your studies at university and are looking for a career in the beauty industry, then please get in contact.

**B  Mansion House Hotel**

An exciting opportunity for students wanting work experience in the Mansion House Hotel on a part-time basis. You will be dealing with international customers and a second language would be an advantage. Hours of work can be agreed to suit your needs though you would be required to work some weekends.

**F  Peterfield Forum**

We are looking for keen volunteers to help run our summer school. You will have experience in working with young people and be prepared to accompany them on trips. The school is open from Monday to Friday and we need volunteers for at least two of these days.

**C  Susie's Hairdressing**

We are a new hairdresser's and we want a young, hard-working volunteer to manage our reception desk. You will take calls, make bookings and help build a relationship with our customers. Suitable candidates will be offered a one-year contract.

**G  Hall Green Community Centre**

This is a great opportunity to gain experience in youth work. We are looking for a volunteer with work experience to support our young people as they begin to enter employment. You would be expected to work on Saturdays from 9 a.m. to 5 p.m. with occasional Sunday sessions.

**D  The Daily News**

Our business is growing and we need an assistant for our customer service team. The successful person will assist in managing our sales staff and be responsible for reporting on sales. The successful person will receive training.

**H  Lucas Media**

Are you a student looking for work from Monday to Friday over the vacation period? We are offering a short-term contract to a keen young person to work with our sales team. You will get an idea of how a modern company operates, deal with customer enquiries and have the chance to help develop our website.

# Part 3

## Questions 11–15

For each question, choose the correct answer.

---

### Sarah Forbes talks about how she gets a good night's sleep

I can't remember when I started to have problems sleeping. As a student I seemed to spend half of my life sleeping. But after my graduation I found myself spending hours lying awake until the early hours of the morning. After a few weeks of this I decided to do something about it. I often went to bed at different times; perhaps there was a programme on TV I wanted to watch, or I'd be watching videos on my phone. So I tried going to bed at the same time each night. This took a while to get used to but slowly I found myself getting into a regular routine.

I also took the advice of a friend and made sure I did things to help me relax before I went to bed. I'd start by writing a list of things I needed to do the next day so I wouldn't end up thinking about them during the night. I got into the habit of having a nice warm bath before bedtime and then did some relaxation exercises like meditation. Reading also seemed to work, but not in the way I expected. I would sometimes just fall asleep in the middle of a chapter!

I also found some suggestions online about how to make your bedroom sleep-friendly. I used to have very thin curtains that let the light from outside shine through, so I changed these for thicker ones. I also removed all technology from the room like the TV and the laptop as these are not supposed to help you sleep, even if they are switched off. And of course I left the mobile phone downstairs!

And the result? I'm pleased to say it's worked. Of course, there are some nights where I find it difficult to go to sleep but mostly I'm getting a good seven hours' sleep a night. I started to make a note of my sleep patterns and this is also useful as it helps show things that were making me lie awake, like problems at work. So, I have to say it has been a very successful experiment.

---

**11** When did Sarah's sleeping problems begin?

    **A** when she was a student

    **B** after she finished at university

    **C** a few weeks ago

    **D** at different times during the week

**12** Writing a list of jobs to be done

    **A** helped Sarah read.

    **B** meant Sarah worked harder the next day.

    **C** was the first thing Sarah did at bedtime.

    **D** helped her think more clearly.

**13** What does Sarah say was the problem with her bedroom?

    **A** Her friends didn't like it.

    **B** It didn't have a TV.

    **C** She often left her laptop switched on.

    **D** It was too bright.

**14** Sarah says that now

    **A** she never finds it difficult sleeping.

    **B** she keeps a record of how well she sleeps.

    **C** she never thinks about work at night.

    **D** sleeping better is helping her at work.

**15** What would be a good introduction to this article?

**A**

| Our sleep expert Sarah Forbes explains how you can make sure you get a good night's sleep. |
|---|

**B**

| Sarah Forbes has not slept well for years. She told us how it affects her work. |
|---|

**C**

| Sarah Forbes suddenly found herself having trouble getting to sleep. But she took control of the situation. |
|---|

**D**

| Sarah Forbes knows what it's like not being able to sleep. Here she explains the dangers of lying awake at night. |
|---|

## Part 4

### Questions 16–20

Five sentences have been removed from the text below.
For each question, choose the correct answer.
There are three extra sentences which you do not need to use.

---

# Honey Bees

Honey bees are incredible insects and the worker bee perhaps the most interesting of all. You can be forgiven for not knowing about the lifestyle of these creatures while you enjoy your honey at breakfast. So here are some facts to consider the next time you buy a jar.

We all know that activity in the hive focuses on the queen. **16** But it's the workers, who have much shorter lives during the summer period and may only survive for up to six weeks, who do all the work.

Worker bees are female and during the first few weeks of their lives, when they are referred to as 'house bees', they will take on many different duties. **17** For example, they'll clean the cells where they were born and make sure bees that have died are removed. **18** Finally, they'll make sure the needs of the queen bee are met.

Towards the second half of their lives, the focus of their duties changes. They'll begin by acting as guard to the hive. **19** Then they'll move on to becoming 'field bees' when they'll leave the hive to collect nectar. However, this journey doesn't start until they have made sure they'll recognise the hive on their return.

They start by taking a short flight in front of the hive, flying backwards and forwards, up and down, getting a clear idea of where the hive is and what it looks like. **20** This careful approach is probably very wise as their search for nectar will take them a long way from home.

---

**A** They start by making sure the hive is kept clean and tidy.

**B** So most of the bees die during the summer.

**C** Then they'll act as nurse to newborn bees.

**D** They do this by controlling the temperature.

**E** Slowly they move further and further away from the hive.

**F** But you should always take care around worker bees.

**G** She can live for five years and lays eggs for future generations.

**H** They will make sure that only bees in the family enter.

# Part 5

## Questions 21–26

For each question, choose the correct answer.

---

### Fear of Flying

A fear of flying, also known as aerophobia, is said to affect almost 10% of the **(21)** ............, although some experts **(22)** ............ it is much higher than this. Those suffering from this will often avoid flying completely, which has a negative effect on their quality of life. Those who face their fears can end **(23)** ............ feeling seriously anxious before and during the flight.

There are generally two different causes. Some people worry about whether they will **(24)** ............ silly in front of other passengers. The thought of being sick or losing control can be quite frightening. Some people fear the flight itself. The most **(25)** ............ things people worry about are bad weather conditions, the possibility that the plane will develop a problem or even that the pilot will become ill. The most worrying time of all is often when **(26)** ............ off and landing, points in the flight when most people will experience a little fear.

---

| 21 | **A** population | **B** people | **C** crowd | **D** society |
| 22 | **A** choose | **B** make | **C** believe | **D** decide |
| 23 | **A** at | **B** in | **C** of | **D** up |
| 24 | **A** see | **B** work | **C** show | **D** look |
| 25 | **A** high | **B** common | **C** normal | **D** real |
| 26 | **A** taking | **B** going | **C** moving | **D** lifting |

## Part 6

### Questions 27–32

For each question, write the correct answer.
Write **one** word for each gap.

---

# Carnival

Rio de Janeiro's Carnival is the biggest festival on the planet and
I **(27)** ............. been enjoying it with millions of people from
around **(28)** ............ world. There are street parties all over
the city organised by local community groups called 'blocos'.
They write the songs, organise the dances **(29)** ............
provide the musicians.

The main event takes place in a special stadium called
the Sambadrome. The audience sees samba schools from
different parts of Rio present their samba, which is performed
**(30)** ............ musicians and dancers and includes beautifully
decorated floats. All these schools compete against other schools
**(31)** ............ see which school can be judged the best. Schools
prepare these performances for many months and the result is
wonderful.

If you're planning to visit Carnival you should think about it
well in advance as hotels and tickets **(32)** ............ sold out
very quickly.

---

# Test 2 WRITING

## Part 1

You **must** answer this question.
Write your answer in about **100 words** on the answer sheet.

---

### Question 1

Read this email from your English-speaking friend Martin and the notes you have made.

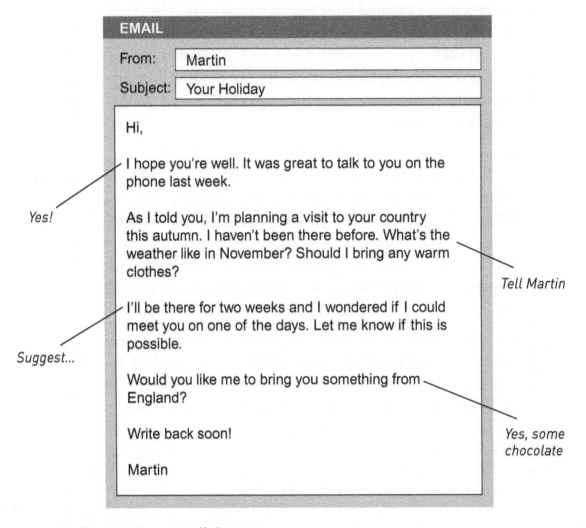

**EMAIL**

From: Martin

Subject: Your Holiday

Hi,

I hope you're well. It was great to talk to you on the phone last week.

*Yes!*

As I told you, I'm planning a visit to your country this autumn. I haven't been there before. What's the weather like in November? Should I bring any warm clothes?

*Tell Martin*

I'll be there for two weeks and I wondered if I could meet you on one of the days. Let me know if this is possible.

*Suggest...*

Would you like me to bring you something from England?

Write back soon!

Martin

*Yes, some chocolate*

Write your **email** to Martin using **all the notes**.

## Part 2

Choose **one** of these questions.
Write your answer in about **100 words** on the answer sheet.

---

## Question 2

You see this notice in an English-language magazine.

**Articles wanted!**

**HAVE YOU GOT A FAVOURITE MEAL?**

Is it something you eat at home?

Is there a restaurant where you like to order it?

**Write an article answering these questions and we will put it in our magazine!**

Write your **article**.

## Question 3

Your English teacher has asked you to write a story.

Your story must begin with this sentence.

*As the bus turned the corner, I saw my hotel at the end of the road.*

Write your **story**.

# Test 2 LISTENING

## Part 1

### Questions 1–7

For each question, choose the correct answer.

---

**1**   What does mum say Helen's brother can eat?

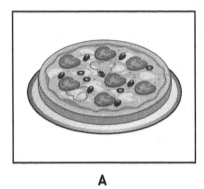

A

B

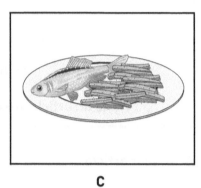

C

**2**   What does the man complain about?

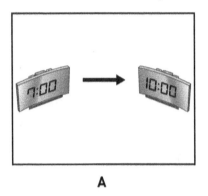

A

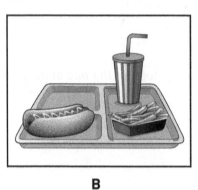

B

C

**3**   At what time might the road be OK to use?

A

B

C

**4** How much is a return flight to Paris at the moment?

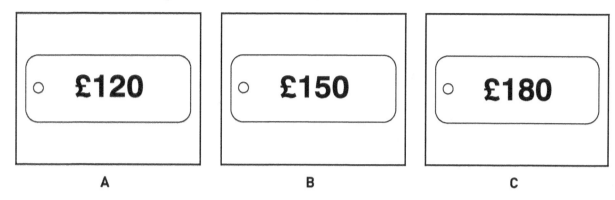

A       B       C

**5** Which programme has been cancelled?

A       B       C

**6** Which day has the most lectures?

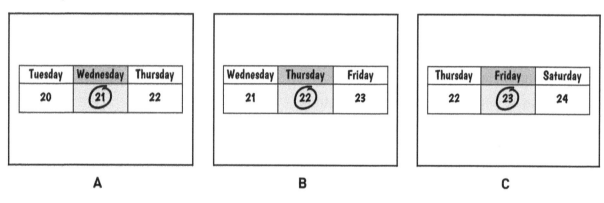

A       B       C

**7** Which item of food is not available?

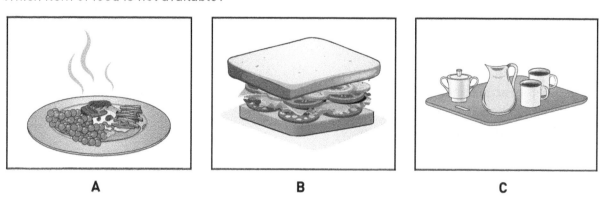

A       B       C

## Part 2

10

## Questions 8–13

For each question, choose the correct answer.

---

8   You will hear two friends talking about a new café in town.
    What does the woman say about it?

    **A**  It has just opened.

    **B**  The choice of food is too simple.

    **C**  She thinks it will be successful.

9   You will hear two friends talking about litter.
    They both agree

    **A**  there aren't enough street cleaners.

    **B**  people drop litter without thinking.

    **C**  people should tidy up litter in their street.

10  You will hear a woman telling a friend about a new car.
    What does she say about it?

    **A**  She has seen one she likes in town.

    **B**  A colleague has a similar car.

    **C**  She plans to drive to work.

11  You will hear two friends talking about a website they use.
    They both think

    **A**  it can be difficult to choose a date or time.

    **B**  it's cheaper if you book immediately.

    **C**  you get the tickets very quickly.

12  You will hear two friends talking about a photography competition.
    The man's brother

    **A**  gets permission before using a photo.

    **B**  has strangers asking him to take a photo of them.

    **C**  has never deleted a photo.

13  You will hear two friends talking about the man's birthday.
    What does he say about the morning?

    **A**  He usually has breakfast in bed.

    **B**  His son got up late.

    **C**  His son and daughter were laughing and joking.

## Part 3

11

### Questions 14–19

For each question, write the correct answer in the gap. **Write one or two words or a number or a date or a time.**

---

You will hear a radio presenter called Jonathan talking about the programmes on during the week.

### Radio Programmes

There are **(14)** ...................... to some of our programmes this week.

The wildlife documentary looks at **(15)** ....................... and how to identify them.

In Writers' World, discover how to get your work **(16)** .................... by using the web.

On Sports Night, there will be no discussions on last week's matches as they were **(17)** ....................

Join Sally at the new time of **(18)** ...................... to ask questions on Money Matters.

You'll find Sally at the entrance to the **(19)** .................... on Friday.

## Part 4

12

### Questions 20–25

For each question, choose the correct answer.

___

You will hear an interview with a man called Tom Walker, who is a personal trainer.

**20** Tom explains that

    **A** he is injured.

    **B** he used to compete against other cyclists.

    **C** he no longer cycles.

**21** Tom thinks that

    **A** people don't train properly.

    **B** he found it hard to push himself.

    **C** his injury was a useful experience.

**22** What does Tom say about his business?

    **A** It's difficult to get enough work.

    **B** He doesn't only train cyclists.

    **C** There are some people he chooses not to help.

**23** What does Tom say about using a gym for training?

    **A** He prefers to use the gym.

    **B** The gym can get too warm.

    **C** People work harder in a gym.

**24** Tom says that some customers

    **A** don't like being watched while they exercise.

    **B** dislike early morning sessions.

    **C** have training sessions before they go to work.

**25** What does Tom think about the summer period?

    **A** It is his busiest time.

    **B** He has to take a holiday.

    **C** It has advantages and disadvantages.

# Test 2 SPEAKING

1A

1B

Audio scripts and Model answers on pages 184–250.

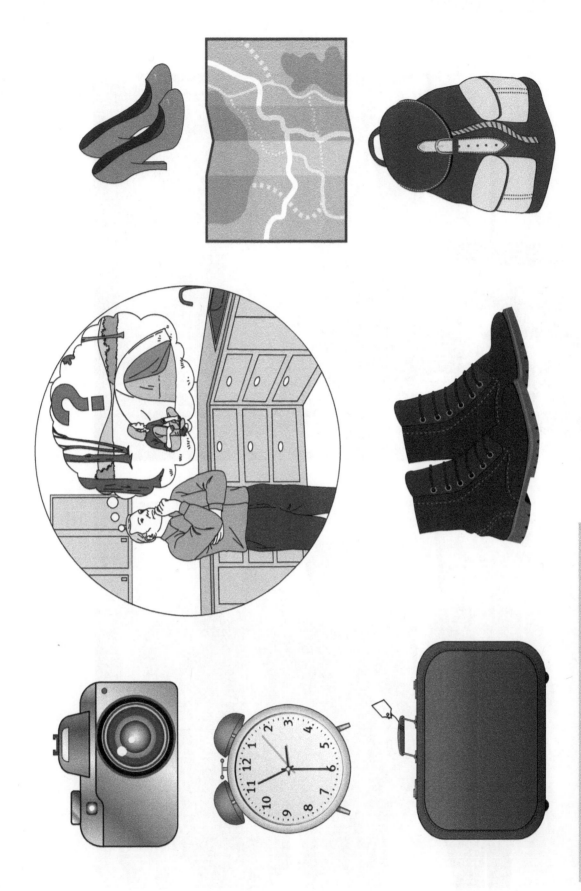

Things for a camping holiday

Audio scripts and Model answers on pages 184–250.

# Test 3

# Test 3 READING

## Part 1

### Questions 1–5

For each question, choose the correct answer.

---

**1**

> ### Man with a Van
> For help with pieces of furniture or smaller items and garden rubbish.
> Call 07785 65563

**A** Can only collect small pieces of furniture.

**B** Can transport large or small items.

**C** Large items should be broken into pieces.

**2**

> Hi Jenny
>
> Are you around this afternoon? I've got an important delivery coming and someone needs to sign for it. Can you let me know your plans so I can decide what to do?
>
> Gill

**A** Jenny should stay at home.

**B** Jenny has to sign for the delivery.

**C** Jenny has to contact Gill.

**3**

> **IN CASE OF FIRE**
> Operate nearest fire alarm and go to outside meeting point.

**A** Leave the building.

**B** Call an operator.

**C** The fire alarm is outside.

**4**

| To:megan@gmail.com |
| --- |
| **From**: kath123@gmail.com |

Hi Megan, I need to cancel my hair appointment tomorrow. I'm not sure what I'm doing next week but I'll email you soon to arrange another time.

Kath

A   Kath can't arrange an appointment yet.

B   Kath would like an appointment next week.

C   Kath will call next week.

**5**

**Spanish lessons**

Meet here in the coffee shop if you are local or online classes if not.

Call: 66700 533867

A   Do lessons online in the coffee shop.

B   Online classes not available.

C   Learn online if you do not live in the area.

# Part 2

## Questions 6–10

For each question, choose the correct answer.

---

The people below are all looking for something to do this weekend.
On the opposite page there are descriptions of eight events.
Decide which event would be the most suitable for the people below.

**6**  Ben has a teenage son who is taking exams at the end of the year. He would like an activity that his son can attend on Saturday to work on his art project.

**7**  Tina wants to get her children outside this weekend to enjoy the sunshine. She'd like to find something that will keep them active so they use up some energy.

**8**  Philip is looking after his ten-year-old nephew. He is looking for an activity on Sunday morning. He'd like something where he can sit down as he has a bad back.

**9**  Tania is looking for something to do on either Saturday or Sunday evening. She and her friend Susan are taking their children and would like somewhere they can listen to music and get something to eat.

**10**  Anna and her husband Tom are visiting the area this weekend and would like to take their 12-year-old son somewhere on Saturday evening. They would prefer something that's not too expensive.

# What's on this weekend?

**A  Open Air Entertainment**

From old black-and-white classics to the latest award-winning films. We open for the summer season this Saturday. Come along and enjoy your favourite film in the evening, outside under the stars – the weather looks good this weekend! Children under 13 enter for free.

**B  Find Robert the Rabbit**

Bring the children along to our annual 'Find Robert' event at Kings Shelley Park this Saturday morning. Each year Robert finds a different place to hide away, and this year we think the kids will find it hard to locate him. Lots of running around and fun for children of all ages!

**C  Open Gardens**

We're pleased to announce this popular summer event will be taking place this weekend. For anyone interested in gardens and gardening, now's your chance to have a look at some of the best in town as people open up their gardens to visitors any time between 9.00 and 5.00. Children are welcome.

**D  Tom and Larry's Garden Party**

This Sunday Tom and Larry will be performing your favourite tunes and a few new ones you may not have heard of. Entrance fee for the evening entertainment includes an evening of music, a buffet with a wide range of food and hot and cold drinks along with ice-cream for the kids.

**E  Mansfield Arts Market**

Come along this Sunday to check out some of the fantastic artistic talent the region has to offer. Have a look at some of the works and support our local artists by buying one to take home. We also have face-painting for the younger children and an art workshop for children who want to have a go themselves.

**F  Art Attack**

Come along to our art club for children this weekend. We offer a safe place where children from 6–16 can have time working alone or with others on a piece of art. And if your child needs help with their schoolwork there'll be someone available to offer help and advice.

**G  Wanted: Young Musicians**

For ages 14 and over, Middlechurch Musicians are holding a series of activities over the weekend for young people of any ability to learn or practise an instrument of their choice. Bring your child and their favourite instrument along, or if they haven't got to this stage let them try one of our own.

**H  Hassocks Green Festival**

In addition to our regular favourites, organisers this year have introduced a children's theme. Take a chair, then relax and enjoy action films and some of the funniest cartoons that will keep your kids entertained. The festival opens on Sunday at 10.00 and is free.

## Part 3

### Questions 11–15

For each question, choose the correct answer.

---

# Headteacher Mary Collins talks about healthy school days

Since I took up my role of Head at Franley Junior School I have been keen to educate our children on the importance of developing healthy habits. I started by working with our restaurant manager to come up with tasty new menus that contain lots of healthy ingredients. We change the menu Monday to Friday to encourage the children to try different things and keep unhealthy fried food to a minimum. The children have enjoyed the meals and eat a wide range of fruit and vegetables.

We've also rented an area of land near the school for a vegetable garden and made gardening a part of the school curriculum. Children now prepare the ground for planting, plant the seeds and watch as these turn into healthy fruit and vegetable plants. We're planning to create a child-friendly kitchen so our pupils can discover the pleasure of cooking. I believe all this gives the children an understanding of where our food comes from and very important skills that will stay with them for life.

To support this healthy-eating campaign, we have also made changes to the amount of physical exercise we get our children to do during the day. We start every morning before classes with a 'wake and shake' session in the playground when children get the chance to burn off energy with fun exercise routines. We also have different play times during the day so the playground isn't crowded, which means the children can run around safely. To support this we have also invested in sports equipment such as tennis, football and gym equipment to encourage the youngsters to take up sports.

But it's not just the children who are developing a healthy lifestyle. Several of our teachers have signed up for the Franley Fun Run this summer for the first time and have started a training programme in order to get fit. Many of our pupils have joined them and will be taking part in the run as well. I'm sure that seeing their teachers beside them will inspire them to finish. We have even had several parents show an interest in doing the event as well, so this is something we're all really looking forward to.

**11** Since Mary joined the school

    **A** fried food is no longer on the menu.

    **B** the school has employed a new restaurant manager.

    **C** the menu changes daily.

    **D** they serve food two days a week.

**12** What does Mary say about gardening?

    **A** It is part of a course of study.

    **B** The children are producing food for the school kitchen.

    **C** The children are learning to cook the food they grow.

    **D** It takes place inside the school.

**13** Play times

    **A** only take place at the start of the day.

    **B** result in the playground getting crowded.

    **C** are timed to prevent accidents.

    **D** have not cost the school any money.

**14** What does Mary say about the teachers?

    **A** They are all doing the fun run.

    **B** They are training with the children.

    **C** They have done the fun run before.

    **D** They are training with the parents.

**15** What would be a good introduction to this article?

**A**
Franley's new Head Mary Collins explains how she set about getting fit with the children.

**B**
Read how Mary Collins, the new school Head, reacted when she was ordered to improve the quality of food on the school menu.

**C**
Mary Collins explains how the first aim she set herself in her new job was to create a focus on healthy living.

**D**
Since taking on a new job at Franley Junior School, Mary Collins tells us how she has discovered the joy of healthy living.

## Part 4

### Questions 16–20

Five sentences have been removed from the text below.
For each question, choose the correct answer.
There are three extra sentences which you do not need to use.

---

# The Crime of the Century

When the Mona Lisa was stolen from the Louvre in Paris in 1911 it caused a sensation and left the art world and police puzzled as to how it had been taken and who had carried out the crime. It also helped make the work of art probably the most famous painting in the world.

At first, the police suspected artists who didn't like classical works of art of carrying out the crime. The poet Apollinaire was arrested and questioned for a few days. **16** _____

However, the true thief was an Italian man named Vincenzo Peruggia. He had a criminal record and had found work in the Louvre for a time. On the day the crime took place, he entered the museum along with other museum employees wearing the same white smock. **17** _____ He then took the painting off the wall and left the building with the work of art wrapped in his white smock.

Peruggia kept the painting for two years in his Paris apartment before eventually contacting an Italian art dealer, offering to return the painting to Florence for a reward. **18** _____ He argued he was returning the painting to its rightful home.

He was finally arrested after passing the painting to the dealer. However, many Italians saw his actions as those of a national hero. **19** _____ The painting was indeed shown off around Italy before it was eventually returned to Paris and the Louvre.

**20** _____ However, after being stolen and finally returned, it became more well known, its popularity grew and, as we know now, made the Mona Lisa smile famous around the world.

---

A   Previously, the painting had been admired by experts.

B   He waited until there was nobody in the gallery.

C   So the painting became popular in France.

D   Because of this, he only went to prison for a short while.

E   He said that he was doing his duty as a proud Italian.

F   But nobody knew it had disappeared.

G   Even the great Pablo Picasso was thought by some to be guilty.

H   It is now kept safely behind special glass.

## Part 5

### Questions 21–26

For each question, choose the correct answer.

---

## Surfing

Surfing grew throughout the 20th century to **(21)** .............. a popular sport all over the world, but surfers have been around for many years. The explorer James Cook saw surfing in action in 1778 during an **(22)** .............. to the Pacific. In fact, surfing took **(23)** .............. in the same areas then that have since become popular surfing resorts now, such as Hawaii and Tahiti. Surfing wasn't encouraged by local officials **(24)** .............. the 19th century but young Hawaiians took up the activity again in the early 1900s. Following the invention of lighter surfboards, surfing attracted people around the world. The 1960s saw a huge increase in the **(25)** .............. of surfers as the activity was promoted through the media and popular music. The hobby quickly became the professional sport it is now, and **(26)** .............. and national organisations were created that organised competitions and raised money to hold events.

---

| 21 | **A** create | **B** turn | **C** become | **D** play |
|----|----|----|----|----|
| 22 | **A** expedition | **B** travel | **C** drive | **D** move |
| 23 | **A** part | **B** place | **C** point | **D** position |
| 24 | **A** while | **B** along | **C** for | **D** during |
| 25 | **A** group | **B** total | **C** number | **D** sum |
| 26 | **A** near | **B** close | **C** next | **D** local |

## Part 6

### Questions 27–32

For each question, write the correct answer.
Write **one** word for each gap.

---

### Stonehenge

Stonehenge was one **(27)** .............. my favourite places on our tour of England last year. It's near the city of Salisbury. It's a ring of huge standing stones about 4 metres high. Experts think it **(28)** .............. built in three stages between 3,000 and 1,500 years ago.

Building something like that must **(29)** .............. been really important at the time but nobody knows for sure why they did it. Archaeologists have found evidence of human bone from **(30)** .............. far back as 3,000 years ago so it's possible it was a place where people were buried. Some people think that it could be a kind of calendar because of the location of the stones when **(31)** .............. sun rises. People have even suggested it was a landing site for visitors from outer space! **(32)** .............. the reason was for building it, I loved visiting it!

---

# Test 3 WRITING

## Part 1

You **must** answer this question.
Write your answer in about **100 words** on the answer sheet.

---

## Question 1

Read this email from your English-speaking friend Mark and the notes you have made.

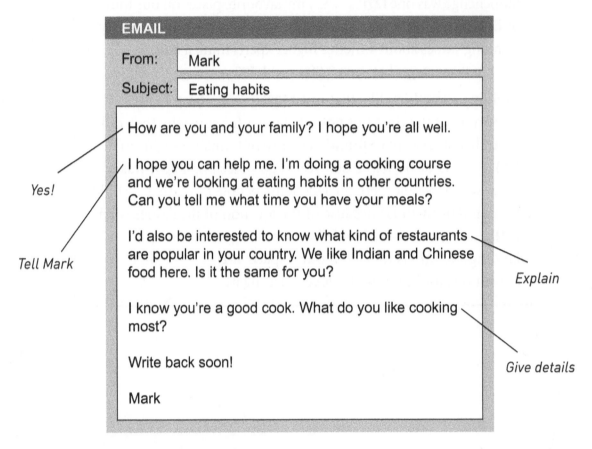

**EMAIL**

From: Mark

Subject: Eating habits

How are you and your family? I hope you're all well.

I hope you can help me. I'm doing a cooking course and we're looking at eating habits in other countries. Can you tell me what time you have your meals?

I'd also be interested to know what kind of restaurants are popular in your country. We like Indian and Chinese food here. Is it the same for you?

I know you're a good cook. What do you like cooking most?

Write back soon!

Mark

*Yes!*

*Tell Mark*

*Explain*

*Give details*

Write your **email** to Mark using **all the notes.**

## Part 2

Choose **one** of these questions.
Write your answer in about **100 words** on the answer sheet.

---

## Question 2

You see this notice in an English-language magazine.

| Articles wanted! |
| --- |
| **TELL US ABOUT YOUR HOBBY OR INTEREST**<br><br>Is it something you have done for a long time?<br><br>Why do you enjoy it?<br><br>**Write an article answering these questions and we will put it in our magazine.** |

Write your **article**.

## Question 3

Your English teacher has asked you to write a story.

Your story must begin with this sentence.

*The house was much bigger than I had expected.*

Write your **story**.

# Test 3 LISTENING

## Part 1

### Questions 1–7

For each question, choose the correct answer.

---

**1**   Which day is the carnival taking place this year?

A

B                                      C

**2**   Why has the woman decided to leave her job?

A

B

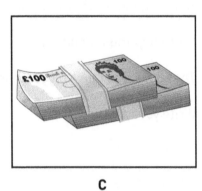

C

**3**   What should customers who have a problem with their telephone do?

A

B

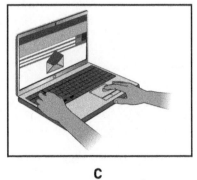

C

**4**   What does the man say he can't do?

A

B

C

**5**   What is today's special offer?

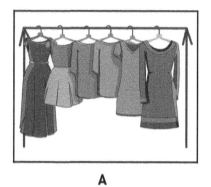

A

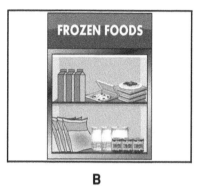

B

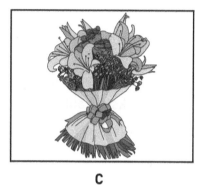

C

**6**   What time does Jamie suggest meeting?

A

B

C

**7**   What should passengers for the 10.15 train do?

A

B

C

# Part 2

18

## Questions 8–13

For each question, choose the correct answer.

___

**8** You will hear two friends talking about a dance performance.
What is the woman worried about?

   **A** They need more lessons.

   **B** They don't have anyone who can lead the group.

   **C** They don't have enough people in the group.

**9** You will hear two friends talking about a book they've read.
The man

   **A** finished reading it quickly.

   **B** thinks the author's other books are more complicated.

   **C** suggests trying a different author.

**10** You will hear a man telling a friend about a football match.
He thinks

   **A** there will be more people there than usual.

   **B** it was difficult to get tickets.

   **C** he might get a job selling tickets.

**11** You will hear two friends talking about a visit to the dentist.
What does the woman say about the appointment?

   **A** It was earlier than she wanted.

   **B** There wasn't a morning one available.

   **C** It's with a dentist she prefers.

**12** You will hear two friends talking about their evening meal.
What does the man say?

   **A** He'd like pasta.

   **B** They always eat takeaways.

   **C** He'd prefer a mild curry.

**13** You will hear two friends talking about a friend's birthday present.
What does the man say about Sandra?

   **A** She doesn't like reading books.

   **B** She isn't doing anything on Friday.

   **C** She doesn't like surprises.

## Part 3

19

### Questions 14–19

For each question, write the correct answer in the gap. **Write one or two words or a number or a date or a time.**

You will hear a manager called Sandra talking about a company training day.

---

### Company Training Day

Some of the training sessions may take place in a **(14)** .............. to the one in the programme.

Your training sessions will be confirmed by email on **(15)** ..............

Please complete the **(16)** .............. in the materials before you come to the training event.

Please give your completed questionnaire to the **(17)** .............. after the training day.

The **(18)** .............. will be closed on the training day.

Remember to check the noticeboard outside room **(19)** .............. for any last-minute changes.

---

# Part 4

20

## Questions 20–25

For each question, choose the correct answer.

---

You will hear an interview with a woman called Maggie Taylor, who is talking about garlic.

20  Maggie explains that

    **A**  she discovered garlic at university.

    **B**  you often find garlic in an English kitchen.

    **C**  people in the older generation don't like garlic.


21  Maggie says that because of learning about garlic

    **A**  she did a cookery course.

    **B**  she can now cook meals from other countries.

    **C**  she has travelled all over the world.


22  What does Maggie say about the health benefits of garlic?

    **A**  She thinks it can cure the common cold.

    **B**  It has been used as a medicine for many years.

    **C**  She has used it to help with a skin condition.


23  Maggie explains that

    **A**  garlic from the supermarket is OK to grow in an English garden.

    **B**  you can grow garlic in any climate.

    **C**  in the past it was harder to buy suitable garlic to grow in an English garden.


24  What does Maggie say about growing garlic?

    **A**  she wasn't successful the first time she tried.

    **B**  she has always had great results.

    **C**  you shouldn't dig it up while it's still green.


25  Maggie explains that

    **A**  her family like the soup she makes.

    **B**  her family dislike the smell of garlic.

    **C**  she doesn't worry what her family think.

# Test 3 SPEAKING

Audio scripts spend Model answers on pages 184–250.

**Activities to get fit**

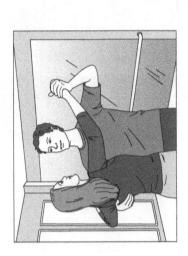

Audio scripts and Model answers on pages 184–250.

# Test 4

# Test 4 READING

## Part 1

### Questions 1–5

For each question, choose the correct answer.

---

1

**Instructions**

This product should be stored in a cool, dry place. Once opened, eat within 2 days.

**A** The product must be eaten by a certain time after it has been opened.

**B** The product will only last two days.

**C** This product is best eaten when it is cool.

2

Hi Fiona,

Will be home late. Just had an accident. No need to pick me up - the car can be driven home. Please text me the phone number of Steve the mechanic.

Jordan

**A** Fiona should go and get Jordan.

**B** Jordan needs Fiona to send him some information.

**C** Fiona should call the mechanic.

**3**

To: maggie@yahoo.com

From: Viviane@gmail.com

Excited about cooking for you tonight. Remember - catch the number 12 bus from the station. The number 1 takes the long route. You'll see the city but the food will get cold!

A  Viviane doesn't want the meal to be spoilt.

B  Viviane thinks it would be good if Maggie sees the city before she arrives.

C  There are two buses that Viviane recommends.

**4**

Clear dishes of food before putting them in the dishwasher.

Dishwasher must not be in operation after the office closes.

A  Empty the dishwasher before leaving the office.

B  Do not put food in the dishwasher.

C  See instructions for operating the dishwasher.

**5**

Phones are busy during office hours so check our 'Events' page for films this week. Other enquiries, call 08895 335832.

A  Call 08895 335832 if you have questions about films.

B  Check information on the website is correct by calling 08895 335832.

C  It is often difficult to speak to someone on the phone.

## Part 2

### Questions 6–10

For each question, choose the correct answer.

The people below are all looking for a restaurant.
On the opposite page there are reviews of eight restaurants.
Decide which restaurant would be the most suitable for the people below.

**6**
It's Jenny's 30th birthday and she would like to take a group of friends out for a meal. She'd like a party atmosphere with live music.

**7**
Kieran has an hour to wait before his train leaves. He would like somewhere that serves quality, fast food. He needs somewhere he can get to the station quickly.

**8**
Jon and his wife Debbie are celebrating their 20th wedding anniversary and would like to have a nice romantic meal somewhere not too busy. They love going on holiday to Italy.

**9**
Marie and her husband Harry want to take their young son for a meal. It would be good if there was something for him to do as he has a lot of energy!

**10**
Trevor is working late tonight at the office. He wants to order something over the phone to eat at his desk. He likes spicy food and is happy to pay for delivery.

# Restaurant reviews

**A  Southern Chicken Takeaway**

Ordered a takeaway chicken and chips from this place. Nice food but ordering was difficult. Someone in the kitchen was playing music really loudly and I could hardly hear what the man serving me was saying. I would have ordered over the phone but they don't deliver.

**B  The Noodle Bar**

This is what fast food should be like. From delicious Japanese soups to hot Thai main meals. Eat in or take away. They're very popular with locals and if you're eating at a table it can take a while to get served. They charge 10% delivery for takeaways.

**C  Spice World**

Phew! Just had one of the hottest curries I've ever eaten. I must say it was also one of the nicest meals I've had for a while. Unfortunately, it has only just opened, and they haven't organised a takeaway service yet but looking forward to ordering one when they do.

**D  Sandy's**

A fantastic restaurant just outside of town. Took our young daughter there last weekend and she loved choosing her own meals from the children's menu. If only they would provide something like a colouring book or an activity to keep children occupied as she soon started to get bored.

**E  Take a Tumble**

We had our grandchildren for the day and were lucky enough to find the new 'Take a Tumble' in town. Lots of activities for young children who can climb, slide or swim. They serve simple, cheap lunches that saved us the bother of finding somewhere else to eat.

**F  Macs**

I went to Macs, just opposite the entrance to the station last night. My friends had the fried chicken and I had pizza. We were all really happy with our meal. The food was at our table in ten minutes and it tasted great.

**G  Pasta della Piazza**

Whether it's a romantic meal for two or a memorable night with friends, Pasta della Piazza is the place to go. We enjoyed a fantastic night out with lovely Italian food and sang along and danced thanks to their regular pianist. You need to reserve to be sure of a table.

**H  Giovanni's**

This place is hidden away on the back streets of town. A tiny place with only five or six candlelit tables but with a wonderful atmosphere. Italian music plays softly in the background making you feel as if you've been transported to Florence or Rome.

## Part 3

### Questions 11–15

For each question, choose the correct answer.

---

# Robert Taylor talks about his new art show

Like all children, I was always getting myself and the kitchen table in a mess when I first took an interest in painting. Unlike many kids, who give up activities like art for other subjects when they go through school, I continued painting throughout my childhood. Now, after years of enjoyment, I've finally taken the scary decision to show off some of my favourite pieces of work by holding an exhibition at Glebe Street library. Inviting people to see my work is a new idea and one which I'm looking forward to.

I've never had any formal art training. When I was trying to decide what I should study at university, art as a subject never entered my head. I always thought my parents wanted me to follow a subject that would be useful when I was looking for a job, so I ended up taking a business course. Looking back, my parents would probably have supported me whatever my decision, but I decided to do what I thought was best for everyone.

And during my time at university, I rarely did much in the way of painting. It wouldn't have been easy to paint anyway as I lived in university accommodation and had very little space. I kept an interest in art though and visited local exhibitions whenever I could, but that was about it. It was later in my thirties while I was working that I discovered my love of the activity again. Since then I've made a point of spending at least one evening a week painting.

However, my works have only ever been seen by trusted friends and relatives. They've always given me plenty of support and encouraged me to continue with my art. But I've always wondered what people who I didn't know would think, people who could give me an honest opinion of my ability. The library have been very helpful and offered me a room for the show. They've asked me to supply questionnaires about the event and I've included a section for visitors' comments about the works. I'm very much looking forward to reading these opinions.

---

**11** What does Robert say about art?

    **A** Children usually continue doing it at school.

    **B** He had to give it up to do other subjects.

    **C** The thought of showing off his work is a little frightening.

    **D** He has often thought about letting people see his work.

**12** When deciding what to study at university

    **A** Robert didn't consider doing art.

    **B** his parents didn't want him to study art.

    **C** he thought he would need a job while he was studying.

    **D** Robert understood correctly what his parents wanted him to do.

**13** What happened while Robert was at university?

    **A** He didn't do any painting.

    **B** He discovered his love of painting again.

    **C** He was still keen on art.

    **D** He painted at least one evening a week.

**14** Robert is holding the exhibition because

    **A** his friends and relatives encouraged him to do this.

    **B** the library asked him to.

    **C** he is interested in getting opinions from friends and relatives.

    **D** he wants to know what strangers think of his work.

**15** What would be a good introduction to this article?

**A**
> Robert Taylor tells us how a love of art can lead to a change of career.

**B**
> If your child shows an interest in art, Robert Taylor will explain how to support this activity.

**C**
> After years in the shadows, Robert Taylor is about to face the public with his works.

**D**
> If you're keen on developing your artistic skills, Robert Taylor explains how to get support from friends and relatives.

## Part 4

### Questions 16–20

Five sentences have been removed from the text below.
For each question, choose the correct answer.
There are three extra sentences which you do not need to use.

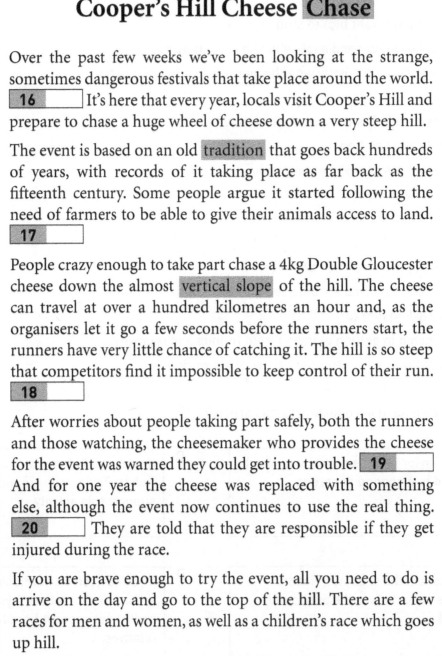

# Cooper's Hill Cheese Chase

Over the past few weeks we've been looking at the strange, sometimes dangerous festivals that take place around the world. **16** It's here that every year, locals visit Cooper's Hill and prepare to chase a huge wheel of cheese down a very steep hill.

The event is based on an old tradition that goes back hundreds of years, with records of it taking place as far back as the fifteenth century. Some people argue it started following the need of farmers to be able to give their animals access to land. **17**

People crazy enough to take part chase a 4kg Double Gloucester cheese down the almost vertical slope of the hill. The cheese can travel at over a hundred kilometres an hour and, as the organisers let it go a few seconds before the runners start, the runners have very little chance of catching it. The hill is so steep that competitors find it impossible to keep control of their run. **18**

After worries about people taking part safely, both the runners and those watching, the cheesemaker who provides the cheese for the event was warned they could get into trouble. **19** And for one year the cheese was replaced with something else, although the event now continues to use the real thing. **20** They are told that they are responsible if they get injured during the race.

If you are brave enough to try the event, all you need to do is arrive on the day and go to the top of the hill. There are a few races for men and women, as well as a children's race which goes up hill.

**A** The police told them they could be breaking the law if anybody was injured.

**B** So it is often shown on TV.

**C** Others believe it was a way of welcoming the beginning of spring.

**D** On the other hand, most people who enter are younger.

**E** Almost immediately they all start falling to the bottom.

**F** Because of issues like these, organisers make sure runners understand the dangers.

**G** This week we're visiting England, to a place called Gloucestershire.

**H** However, the cheese is made locally.

## Part 5

### Questions 21–26

For each question, choose the correct answer.

> # Light Pollution
>
> We are all familiar with air pollution, **(21)** ............ if we live in busy cities and suffer with pollution from factories and heavy traffic. But many of us don't take light pollution **(22)** ............ Compared to the skies of our grandparents, the night isn't **(23)** ............ as dark as it used to be because the use of artificial lighting has increased. As a result, this can create problems for migrating birds, which are not able to use the moon and stars to **(24)** ............ their journey. In addition, light from our neighbourhood, whether that is street lighting, **(25)** ............ lights or passing cars, can also **(26)** ............ our own sleep patterns. And of course, the night sky is harder for us to see unless we go to parts of the world free of artificial lighting.

| 21 | **A** really | **B** especially | **C** because | **D** when |
|---|---|---|---|---|
| 22 | **A** seriously | **B** real | **C** mainly | **D** important |
| 23 | **A** just | **B** quite | **C** equal | **D** same |
| 24 | **A** fly | **B** leave | **C** set | **D** complete |
| 25 | **A** danger | **B** security | **C** guard | **D** guarantee |
| 26 | **A** make | **B** create | **C** influence | **D** do |

## Part 6

### Questions 27–32

For each question, write the correct answer.
Write **one** word for each gap.

---

### What's in a smile?

Last week I went to an interesting lecture about smiling. We all love to see other people smile but it's supposed to be really good for us too. For example, **(27)** ............ you know smiling can make us appear better looking and even younger? It can also make us feel happier. **(28)** ............ is because various chemicals are delivered directly to the brain when we smile. They told us about some research that showed smiling just once can stimulate the brain by the same amount **(29)** ............ 2,000 bars of chocolate!

They explained that these results **(30)** ............ supported by our knowledge of how we avoid dangerous situations. Negative thinking, **(31)** ............ is often thought of as something we should avoid, helps us avoid dangers and defend ourselves. Smiling has **(32)** ............ opposite effect and can help our thoughts be more positive.

---

# Test 4 WRITING

## Part 1

You **must** answer this question.
Write your answer in about **100 words** on the answer sheet.

---

## Question 1

Read this email from your English-speaking friend Lisa and the notes you have made.

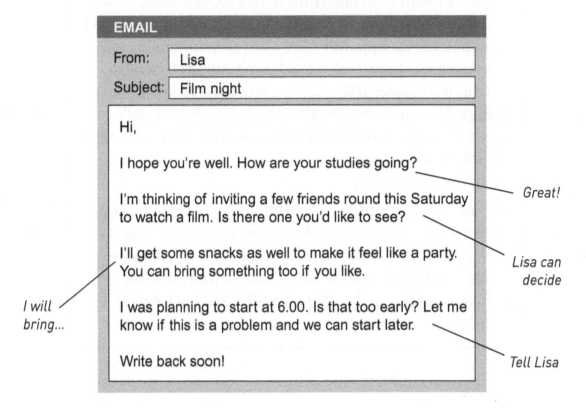

Write your **email** to Lisa using **all the notes**.

## Part 2

Choose **one** of these questions.
Write your answer in about **100 words** on the answer sheet.

---

## Question 2

You see this notice in an English-language magazine.

> **Articles wanted!**
>
> **WHY ARE YOU STUDYING ENGLISH?**
>
> Is it for a job, for studies or just for pleasure?
>
> How will it be useful in the future?
>
> **Write an article answering these questions and we will put it in our magazine!**

Write your **article**.

## Question 3

Your English teacher has asked you to write a story.

Your story must begin with this sentence.

*I left my car in the car park and went through the front door to the reception desk.*

Write your **story**.

# Test 4 LISTENING

## Part 1

### Questions 1–7

For each question, choose the correct answer.

---

**1**   Which activity wasn't available?

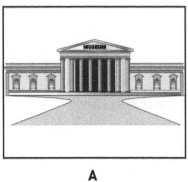

A

B

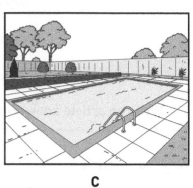

C

**2**   How does the man travel if there's a problem?

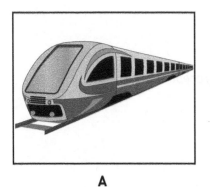

A

B

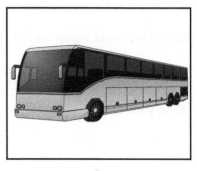

C

**3**   What is the building going to be used for?

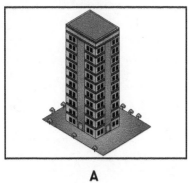

A

B

C

**4** Which membership allows a person to attend a presentation?

A        B        C

**5** When does the woman want to book a library computer?

A

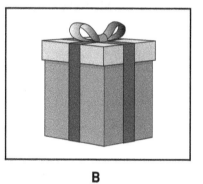

B

C

**6** What is the man doing on Saturday?

A

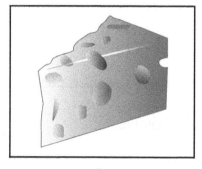

B

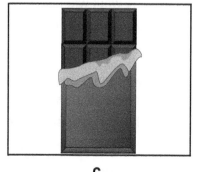

C

**7** Which item of food has the man's mother tried before?

A        B        C

# Part 2

26

## Questions 8–13

For each question, choose the correct answer.

---

8 You will hear two friends talking about a trip to the theatre.
What does the woman say about it?

   **A** The theatre offers cheaper entry to some students.

   **B** It's not always necessary to show student ID.

   **C** She is a part-time student.


9 You will hear two friends talking about the man's job.
The man

   **A** is looking for work as an accountant.

   **B** is prepared to earn less money.

   **C** knows what qualifications he needs.


10 You will hear a husband and wife talking about breakfast.
What does the wife say?

   **A** There isn't any cereal left.

   **B** They need to buy bread.

   **C** She would like to have the same drink as usual.


11 You will hear two friends talking about buying a bed.
The woman thinks the ones online

   **A** are better quality.

   **B** might be cheaper.

   **C** cost less in the furniture store.


12 You will hear two friends talking about going for a walk.
What do they both agree about?

   **A** The need to take an umbrella.

   **B** The walk will be a healthy thing to do.

   **C** They need to check the weather forecast.


13 You will hear two friends talking about a passport photograph.
What does the man say?

   **A** The shop assistants are really helpful.

   **B** The post office is open in the evening.

   **C** The nearest machine doesn't work.

## Part 3

27

### Questions 14–19

For each question, write the correct answer in the gap. **Write one or two words or a number or a date or a time.**

---

You will hear a man called Russell talking about a new club in the community centre.

---

**The Speakers' Club**

For business presentations to colleagues or to get ready for an
**(14)** ..................... Workshop leaders have a background in
business or **(15)** ..................... Sessions start at
**(16)** ..................... Members are invited to try one of our
**(17)** ..................... once a year. The first meeting is
**(18)** ..................... but remember to reserve a place.
Membership costs **(19)** ..................... per year or payment can
be made each month.

---

# Part 4

## Questions 20–25

For each question, choose the correct answer.

---

You will hear an interview with a student called Emily, who walks people's dogs.

**20** What does Emily say about walking dogs?

    **A** It's a good business idea.

    **B** It pays for some of her living expenses.

    **C** It helps people get out of their house.

**21** Emily says her first customer

    **A** was her neighbour.

    **B** was in hospital at the time.

    **C** made her accept some money.

**22** What does Emily say about becoming a dog walker?

    **A** She enjoyed what she was doing.

    **B** She had trouble arranging the walks around her studies.

    **C** She spoke to people in the local shops.

**23** Emily explains that

    **A** she didn't get any work straightaway.

    **B** she went to a customer's house.

    **C** she met her first customer at the weekend.

**24** Emily says that her customers

    **A** are very busy.

    **B** expect her to help them whenever they need it.

    **C** have well-behaved dogs.

**25** What does Emily say about payment?

    **A** She charges people per hour.

    **B** She discusses it with the customer.

    **C** She charges what her friends recommended.

# Test 4 SPEAKING

29–32

1A

1B

Audio scripts and Model answers on pages 184–250.

Things a person with a broken leg could do

Audio scripts and Model answers on pages 184–250.

# Test 5

# Test 5 READING

## Part 1

### Questions 1–5

For each question, choose the correct answer.

---

1

Hiya James

I've just phoned the cinema about the tickets. We only need to reserve seats if we want to sit next to each other. It seems like tickets are selling quickly

**A** They have to reserve seats.

**B** They should book tickets if they want to see the film.

**C** They should act quickly or they may have to sit apart from each other.

2

Employees only past this gate.

Please ring bell for help and someone will come to meet you.

**A** Ring the bell unless you work for the company.

**B** Employees should meet at the gate if the bell rings.

**C** Everyone must ring the bell for entry.

3

**REFUNDS**
Clothing must be in perfect condition and no refunds will be made for clothing that has been worn.

**A** Do not wear the item of clothing if you want your money back.

**B** Clothing that is not in good condition can still be returned.

**C** No refunds can be made for items of clothing.

**4**

| To: steven223@yahoo.com |
| From: chris112@gmail.com |

Sean says the laptop you
want is available on a
website he has seen.
He's going to email me the
link to the site. I'll send it to
you when I have it.

A  The laptop is on sale online.

B  The laptop can only be bought online.

C  Sean has offered to buy the laptop.

**5**

**NOTICE TO
PASSENGERS**
Is there a route you
prefer to take? Speak
to the taxi driver before
the journey starts.

A  Passengers must always tell the driver the route
they want to take.

B  The driver is willing to discuss the way to go.

C  Once the journey has started, do not speak to the
driver.

# Part 2

## Questions 6–10

For each question, choose the correct answer.

---

The people below all want to watch something on TV.
On the opposite page there are descriptions of eight TV programmes.
Decide which programmes would be the most suitable for the people below.

**6**  Lorraine is having a day off work with a cold. She wants to watch a quiz show during the afternoon especially one with cash prizes.

**7**  Gary can't sleep and wants to see if there is anything on TV. He'd like to watch a film and enjoys crime thrillers or anything with lots of action.

**8**  Isabelle is babysitting a seven-year-old girl. She's looking for a children's programme that has anything to do with drawing or cooking so they can do it together.

**9**  Raj and his wife Grace are spending the evening at home and are keen to watch a film together. They would like to watch something romantic and not anything that's too long.

**10**  Robert has some friends coming round for the evening. He would like a programme showing live football that has experts discussing the game afterwards.

# TV programmes

**A  Show Me How**

In today's programme Gemma and her best friend Louise will show you how to make a delicious banana bread. Mums or dads should remember to get the ingredients ready so you can follow the friends' instructions during the show.

**B  The Big Chase**

When the police start their investigation into a series of robberies, they expect to be making an early arrest. However, they are not prepared for the danger around every corner. A very exciting story that is sure to keep you on the edge of your seat. This week's late-night film starts at 12.30.

**C  Brain of Britain**

On this week's quiz show for the very clever we have a taxi driver, a lawyer, a journalist and a gardener answering questions. The winner will go through to the final next month with the chance of being crowned Brain of Britain. See how many questions you can answer!

**D  Front Row**

Join our team of experts as they discuss the draw for the next round of the FA Cup. Find out who will be playing who when they meet for the next round in two weeks' time. We'll have reporters out and about interviewing players on their opinions of the draw.

**E  5-2-1**

Join your host Sam Daniels as a team of friends from university try to answer questions on general knowledge and their favourite subjects. Can they win the top prize of £20,000? Join us just after the lunchtime news at 1.30.

**F  Molly and Me**

In this week's programme Molly reads another story from a well-known children's author. For five- to eight-year-olds – sit together with your child and enjoy some quiet time as you follow the story with Molly and her friends.

**G  Last Summer**

When Greg and Sandra meet on a coach journey to Athens, they quickly realise they have so much in common. They decide to spend the following two weeks together, fall in love and dream of a future together. However, life gets in the way. A short but very enjoyable 90-minute film.

**H  Midweek**

In tonight's game you can see two teams both playing at their very best. The programme begins at 7.00 and the game starts at 7.30. Stay around after the match for views from our team of professional players and managers as they discuss the result and choose their man of the match.

## Part 3

## Questions 11–15

For each question, choose the correct answer.

---

# Paul Harris talks about how he studied by distance learning before going to university

I didn't follow the normal route to university. Most of my teenage friends stayed on at school, passed their exams, chose their favourite university and continued their education. I couldn't wait to get to work and left without any qualifications, feeling that having a salary was more important. I spent a few years doing different jobs but always wondered what might have happened if I had followed my friends' example.

It was ten years later, in my late twenties, and after I discovered a love of history, that I finally decided I wanted to go to university. I thought about giving up my job and spending a year at college getting the exams I needed for university, but I couldn't afford to do this. So I decided to study on a distance-learning course and keep my job. This was long before the internet and online learning. My course consisted of a parcel brought by the postman with all the books I needed for the year, a study plan and the contact details of my tutors. No telephone number, just an address of a business where I had to post my work.

I would spend a week or two studying the next unit, write an essay and post it to the tutor. I would then wait, usually for at least two weeks, for the tutor's reply. It was always a very exciting moment when the postman arrived and I opened the envelope to see how well I had done. My tutor's comments were always very helpful, though I often wished I could phone him for the chance to discuss some of the things he had written.

I passed the exams and did indeed go to university. And the distance-learning course taught me the importance of hard work and the need to focus. It wasn't easy studying like this without the technology available today. I wasn't able to ask the questions I had and get the quick response that communication tools now make possible. But I also think it was much easier to concentrate then. There was no mobile phone to turn to every five minutes or social media to follow. I'm glad I did it my way.

**11** How did Paul feel about going to university when he left school?

    **A** He wanted to be like his friends.

    **B** He didn't think he could get the qualifications he needed.

    **C** He wanted to earn money.

    **D** He regretted not going.

**12** Paul chose a distance-learning course

    **A** because he loved his job.

    **B** so he could continue working.

    **C** because he couldn't find a history course at college.

    **D** because it was too late to go to college.

**13** What does Paul say about the course?

    **A** He would have liked more contact with his tutor.

    **B** He didn't understand his tutor's comments.

    **C** His tutor's handwriting was difficult to read.

    **D** The post service was very poor.

**14** Paul thinks that

    **A** he would have done even better if the internet had existed.

    **B** it was difficult to focus during his studies.

    **C** online learning is more effective.

    **D** the internet can make studying difficult.

**15** What would be a good introduction to this article?

**A** Paul Harris warns against choosing distance learning after his negative experiences.

**B** Forget college: distance learning is the best way to get that university place, says Paul Harris.

**C** Paul Harris describes his experiences of studying at a distance without the use of modern technology.

**D** Distance learning should be avoided if you are not serious about your goal, writes Paul Harris.

## Part 4

### Questions 16–20

Five sentences have been removed from the text below.
For each question, choose the correct answer.
There are three extra sentences which you do not need to use.

---

# Baking and Me

I've always been keen on cooking and you'd often find me in the kitchen preparing the evening meal. [ 16 ] It started because of my young children, who were always ready to bake and loved the chance to make cakes at the weekend. I never realised at the time how important it would become in my life. What started as a way of entertaining the kids became a passion for me and one that I love to pass on to others. [ 17 ]

To begin with there's the preparation. Unlike normal cooking, baking requires a great deal of care. [ 18 ] Cooking a spaghetti or a curry does not require the same degree of attention. I find this interesting as being careful like this is not something that I have ever been strong at. Baking gives me the opportunity to challenge myself to get things right.

Then there's baking itself. Whether it's a loaf of bread or some of my favourite cakes, for around 30 minutes my attention is on the oven. I love going back into the kitchen every so often to check to see if the cake or loaf is rising as it should do, and my eyes are always on the clock to make sure I don't leave it in too long. [ 19 ] This is why people selling a house or flat are often advised to have a loaf baking in the oven when buyers arrive!

And finally, there's the chance to eat what you've made. [ 20 ] But cutting a slice and discovering it's just right inside as well is always extremely pleasing. After testing to see if it's OK, I love calling the family out to the kitchen to invite them all to try a piece. So yes, it's a hobby I think will stay with me for life, despite the fact that it might mean I put on weight!

**A**    The smell of freshly baked bread makes a house feel like home.

**B**    On one occasion, my baking was not successful.

**C**    So, what is it that makes baking such an enjoyable experience?

**D**    The cake or loaf might look perfectly cooked from outside.

**E**    However, the children always agreed to clear up the mess in the kitchen.

**F**    But my love of baking only began a few years ago.

**G**    Most of these problems have been due to the oven.

**H**    Ingredients need to be measured out exactly.

## Part 5

### Questions 21–26

For each question, choose the correct answer.

---

# The Black Mamba

A bite from the Black Mamba is **(21)** ............... 'the kiss of death' in South Africa and it is **(22)** ............. a very dangerous snake.
The venom can kill a person within 30 minutes to a few hours **(23)** ............. medical help. It is one of the world's fastest snakes as well and can travel at up to 16 kilometres an hour, though it uses this speed to **(24)** ............. danger rather than to attack. In fact, the Black Mamba is a rather **(25)** ............... creature and will avoid people if possible. It can measure anywhere between two and four metres long and, **(26)** ............. on the area where it lives, can be a different colour, from brown to green to grey. It gets its name from the inside of its mouth, which is ink black.

---

| 21 | **A** said | **B** made | **C** called | **D** titled |
|---|---|---|---|---|
| 22 | **A** certainly | **B** exactly | **C** just | **D** fairly |
| 23 | **A** outside | **B** besides | **C** away | **D** without |
| 24 | **A** break | **B** escape | **C** lose | **D** run |
| 25 | **A** shy | **B** brave | **C** afraid | **D** soft |
| 26 | **A** relying | **B** choosing | **C** depending | **D** taking |

## Part 6

### Questions 27–32

For each question, write the correct answer.
Write **one** word for each gap.

---

# El Capitan

We're coming to the end of our holiday in America and have just **(27)** ............ to Yosemite National Park, California. I had to come here after I saw the documentary about Alex Honnold, **(28)** ............ did what experts thought was impossible and became **(29)** ............ first person to climb El Capitan without the help of ropes. This kind of climbing is known as free soloing. El Capitan is a vertical wall of granite 914 metres high and it took Honnold 3 hours and 56 minutes to complete the climb. Much of the time **(30)** ............ spent with him hanging on to the smallest pieces of rock with **(31)** ............ fingertips and the edges of his shoes. Alex spent over a year preparing for the challenge and everything, including the final climb, was filmed for a documentary. You really should try to see **(32)** ............ if you get the chance.

---

# Test 5 WRITING

## Part 1

You **must** answer this question.
Write your answer in about **100 words** on the answer sheet.

---

## Question 1

Read this email from your English-speaking friend Maura and the notes you have made.

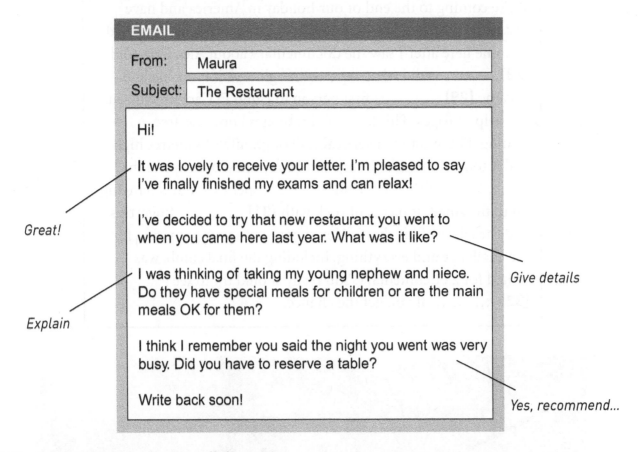

**EMAIL**

From: Maura

Subject: The Restaurant

Hi!

It was lovely to receive your letter. I'm pleased to say I've finally finished my exams and can relax!

*Great!*

I've decided to try that new restaurant you went to when you came here last year. What was it like?

*Give details*

I was thinking of taking my young nephew and niece. Do they have special meals for children or are the main meals OK for them?

*Explain*

I think I remember you said the night you went was very busy. Did you have to reserve a table?

*Yes, recommend...*

Write back soon!

Write your **email** to Maura using **all the notes**.

## Part 2

Choose **one** of these questions.
Write your answer in about **100 words** on the answer sheet.

---

## Question 2

You see this notice in an English-language magazine.

**Articles wanted!**

**HOW DO YOU LIKE TO SPEND YOUR WEEKEND?**

Is there something you do with friends?

Do you like to relax and do nothing?

**Write an article answering these questions and we will put it in our magazine!**

Write your **article**.

## Question 3

Your English teacher has asked you to write a story.

Your story must begin with this sentence.

*When I saw who it was, I ran across the road to meet her.*

Write your **story**.

# Test 5 LISTENING

## Part 1

### Questions 1–7

For each question, choose the correct answer.

---

**1** Which of the following needs attention?

A

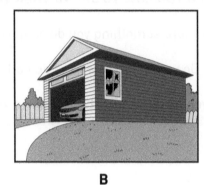

B

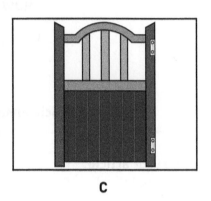

C

**2** Which item will be cheaper soon?

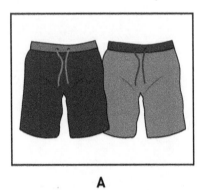

A

B

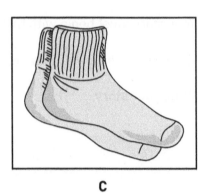

C

**3** When is the man starting his course?

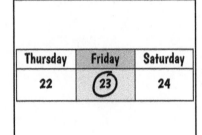

| Thursday | Friday | Saturday |
|----------|--------|----------|
| 22 | (23) | 24 |

A

| Friday | Saturday | Sunday |
|--------|----------|--------|
| 23 | (24) | 25 |

B

| Friday | Saturday | Sunday |
|--------|----------|--------|
| 23 | 24 | (25) |

C

**4**  What does the woman say they need for the party?

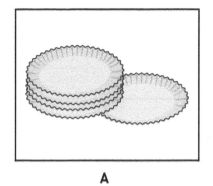

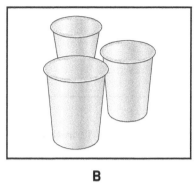

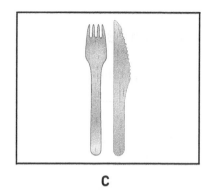

A                                       B                                       C

**5**  What did the man leave at work?

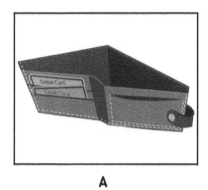

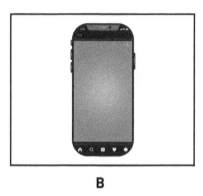

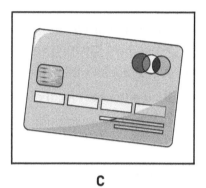

A                                       B                                       C

**6**  Where is the woman going on holiday?

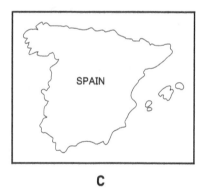

A                                       B                                       C

**7**  Which platform is the 9.30 train to London leaving from?

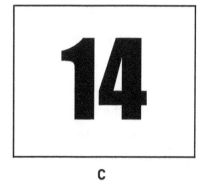

A                                       B                                       C

# Part 2

34

## Questions 8–13

For each question, choose the correct answer.

---

8  You will hear two friends discussing what to do in the afternoon.
   What do they agree to do?

   **A**  Go shopping.

   **B**  Decide after the next weather report.

   **C**  Buy something in town.


9  You will hear two friends talking about keeping fit.
   What does the man say about swimming?

   **A**  He doesn't think the woman should try it.

   **B**  It's the best form of exercise.

   **C**  The new swimming pool gets crowded.


10  You will hear a woman telling a friend about a handbag.
    What does she say?

    **A**  It is damaged.

    **B**  It costs a lot to return it.

    **C**  The one she has now is the wrong colour.


11  You will hear two friends talking about a new doctor.
    The woman thinks

    **A**  he's too young.

    **B**  he'll probably be busy.

    **C**  he doesn't listen to his patients.


12  You will hear two friends talking about a storm.
    The man says

    **A**  the storm was worse in the north.

    **B**  the next storm is going to be even worse.

    **C**  the storm will last until the end of the week.


13  You will hear a woman telling a friend about her noisy neighbours.
    What is the woman planning to do?

    **A**  Ask them to be quiet.

    **B**  Offer to have them for a meal.

    **C**  Get her husband to knock on their door.

# Part 3

35

## Questions 14–19

For each question, write the correct answer in the gap. **Write one or two words or a number or a date or a time.**

---

You will hear a radio presenter called William talking about a photography course he did.

---

### How to Take a Great Photo

The photography course lasted **(14)** ..................... and was for beginners.

Useful tips:

Make sure the camera is at the same **(15)** ................... as the person.

Stand the person in front of a **(16)** ................... background.

Taking photos in daylight can help make sure colours are **(17)** ...................

Take a photo of your subject when they are **(18)** ................... or looking out of the window.

Try to take at least **(19)** ................... of people every day.

---

# Part 4

36

## Questions 20-25

For each question, choose the correct answer.

___

You will hear an interview with a woman called Penelope Leigh, giving advice on how to revise.

20 What does Penelope say about understanding a subject?

   A  It's easy to do.

   B  Students don't like to do this.

   C  It helps you remember things.


21 Penelope thinks that

   A  explaining things to others can help you understand the subject.

   B  friends or relatives might be able to explain things to you.

   C  reading something more than once never works.


22 Why does Penelope say about managing revision?

   A  You should never revise just before an exam.

   B  Try to do it over a period of time.

   C  Only make notes occasionally.


23 What does Penelope say about some subjects?

   A  You should avoid studying boring subjects.

   B  They can be difficult if you don't find them interesting.

   C  Everyone has a subject they don't find interesting.


24 Penelope thinks listening to music while revising

   A  does not help.

   B  is OK if you listen to tunes you love.

   C  needs to be researched.


25 What is Penelope's final tip?

   A  Learning lists can help you remember.

   B  Imagine yourself being successful.

   C  Use creative ways to help you remember key points.

# Test 5 SPEAKING

37–40

1A

1B

Audio scripts and Model answers on pages 184–250.

A pet that would be suitable for a young boy

Audio scripts and Model answers on pages 184–250.

# Test 6

# Test 6 READING

## Part 1

### Questions 1–5

For each question, choose the correct answer.

---

1

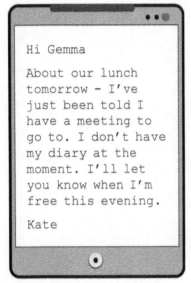

Hi Gemma

About our lunch tomorrow – I've just been told I have a meeting to go to. I don't have my diary at the moment. I'll let you know when I'm free this evening.

Kate

**A** Kate will contact Gemma later.

**B** Gemma has lost her diary.

**C** Gemma is going to be late for lunch.

2

**INSTRUCTIONS**

Please note that batteries are not included with this toy. These are available in our electrical department.

**A** The toy does not need batteries.

**B** There aren't any batteries in the toy.

**C** The toy is available in the electrical department.

3

**NOTICE**

Children under 13 must be accompanied by an adult at all times when using the swimming pool.

**A** Adults must stay with children under 13.

**B** Children under 13 are only allowed to use the pool at certain times.

**C** Children who can't swim must stay with an adult.

**4**

> ## NOTICE TO PASSENGERS
>
> Please have the exact fare ready when paying for your journey. The driver does not carry money on this bus.

A Please ask the driver for the cost of your journey.

B Passengers must have the right money for their journey.

C See our notice about fares on the bus.

**5**

> **To:** petra@hotmail.com
>
> **From:** isabelle@gmail.com
>
> Hi Petra
>
> I hope you're OK. Have you finished that book I lent you? I was talking about it to Stephanie and she wants to read it.
>
> Isabelle

A Isabelle would like to borrow the book.

B Stephanie recommended the book to Isabelle.

C Isabelle would like the book back.

# Part 2

## Questions 6–10

For each question, choose the correct answer.

___

The people below all want to do a local activity.
On the opposite page there are eight activities in the local area.
Decide which activity would be the most suitable for the people below.

**6**    Susie has a teenage son who is very keen to get into acting and learning how best to perform on stage. Because of other activities he cannot do Saturdays or Sundays.

**7**    Gareth is 21 and on summer vacation before going back to university. He is looking for voluntary work that will help him gain experience in working with customers.

**8**    Marcia would like to take her children to the park one day next week. She would like to show them the importance of doing something for local people.

**9**    Ella is a new mum with a three-month-old baby and is looking for exercise to help her relax. She is free on Monday and Tuesday and loves getting a bargain!

**10**    Jacob is looking for somewhere to take his son for something to eat at lunchtime any day this week. He would like to go somewhere that is outside to get some fresh air.

# Local activities

**A Friends of Hamley Park**

Come along to 'Friends of Hamley Park' for our monthly litter pick. Join our friendly team of adults and children every Sunday to help us keep our lovely local park tidy and something to be proud of. We provide all the tools and equipment you'll need. Just come along on the day and we'll find something for you to do.

**E Storytelling**

Storytelling has become popular lately, especially for those who want to tell their story on stage in front of a live audience. Join our one-day event on Wednesday – we'll be looking at how to feel confident and keep your audience interested.

**B Yoga sessions**

Yoga sessions with Petra aimed at your level. I know how important it can be for you mums to get out of the house and do some exercise. My fun weekly 'Mum and Child' yoga classes start on Monday 18 June. Buy five sessions and get one free.

**F Time to relax**

A new six-week yoga course for beginners. Help yourself become more focused, reduce your stress levels, sleep better and improve your mental health. I will be running these courses in the local community centre on Wednesday and Thursday mornings from 11.00 till 12.00. Childcare is available for babies and young children.

**C Broadchester Park**

You are invited to come along for our weekly picnic in Broadchester Park. Open to all, young and old, it's held every Tuesday throughout the summer at 12.00. Please note there will be a charge for food which will be supplied by the café.

**G The community café**

Our community café is looking for young volunteer waiters and waitresses to help us throughout the summer period. You'll learn skills that will be useful when you start your job search. We're looking for anyone who is at least 18 and would like you to be available for at least two days per week.

**D Poetry competition**

Come and see the winners of this poetry competition. The theme was the natural world and the poets will be performing their work in the beautiful surroundings of Kimberley Park. Entry costs £2. Children under 11 are free.

**H Creswell Youth Centre**

Are you interested in developing your acting skills? Creswell Youth Centre is offering young people aged from 7 to 19 the chance to join us for our next show. No experience is required as we can offer a role to all abilities. You will need to be available at weekends throughout the summer.

## Part 3

### Questions 11–15

For each question, choose the correct answer.

# Jon Leverson talks about working in comedy

At school I was always the one with the funny comment, the class clown who never took things too seriously. I enjoyed making my friends laugh, and to be honest, I seemed to be quite good at it. This was why, at university, I decided to join a comedy club, a small group of people who wanted to practise their joke-telling in front of a live audience. Once a week I would go on stage in front of a small group of people and tell my jokes. This was my introduction to becoming a comedian.

Over the past few years I've continued with my hobby. Instead of jokes I like to talk about things that I experience in life that I find amusing. I'm a dad to a young son and a lot of my act is about some of the funny things he does or about being a father. The events I perform at only attract small audiences, but you get a lot of support and people do at least try to laugh, even if they don't like your act.

I work in an office 9–5 and I perform at the weekend. But don't think for one minute that it's just a few hours' work. Thinking of ideas is difficult. And you need to test these ideas and see what makes people laugh and what doesn't. You then throw some things out completely or change them a bit and try again the next week. In addition to the content it's about finding your style –what makes you special – and that only comes with practice.

Some people say doing what I do must be quite scary. I'm not sure about scary, but it's certainly true that standing in front of an audience and trying to make them laugh is quite a challenge. But it's worth it when you're successful. It's great to make people feel happy and to know that all the time you've spent in preparation has worked. This will always be a hobby rather than a career for me, but one that will hopefully give me a great deal of pleasure for years to come.

**11** What does Jon say about his time at university?

   **A** It was where he discovered he could make people laugh.

   **B** He started a comedy club.

   **C** He performed in front of people.

   **D** He enjoyed watching other people tell jokes.

**12** At the events he performs at

   **A** the audience think he is funny.

   **B** people laugh even if they don't find him funny.

   **C** he gets support from other fathers.

   **D** he tells jokes.

**13** Jon explains that

   **A** his act doesn't last very long.

   **B** he often repeats his act but with changes.

   **C** the audience make him feel special.

   **D** he sometimes feels he has failed a test.

**14** What does Jon say about performing?

   **A** He finds it very scary.

   **B** He's not good enough to make a career out of comedy.

   **C** Making people laugh isn't easy.

   **D** It means he spends less time at work.

**15** What would be a good introduction to this article?

**A**
> In this article, Jon Leverson explains the difficulties of trying to make a career out of comedy.

**B**
> Do you think you're funny? Jon Leverson tells us the steps to take to become a comedian.

**C**
> In this week's personal story, Jon Leverson tells us about his unusual hobby – making people laugh.

**D**
> Life doesn't always go as planned, and Jon Leverson explains how he took a career change at university.

## Part 4

### Questions 16–20

Five sentences have been removed from the text below.
For each question, choose the correct answer.
There are three extra sentences which you do not need to use.

---

# Clothes Exchange

Are you like me and have clothes in your wardrobe that you have hardly ever worn? Perhaps you even have something with the label still attached. Before you put them in a bag and take them to your local charity shop or throw them away, consider another possibility. **16** _____

Clothes swaps are becoming very popular as they give people the chance to offer their clothing they don't want in exchange for something they'd like to have for themselves. These parties are great for the environment. **17** _____ They also allow you to update what's in your wardrobe and to do it without spending any money at all.

If you're thinking of organising one yourself, it's best to keep the event quite small, just inviting friends and relatives. **18** _____ In order to make sure there's something for everyone, and that everyone feels included, invite people who are of a similar size and age. Either that or make sure there'll be a wide range of sizes on offer. Finally, decide on the number of items that everyone should bring before the event.

On the day, each person is given a button for every item they bring. These are used instead of money. You might decide before you start that some high-quality items should be worth more buttons than a much cheaper item. **19** _____

Make sure items are presented nicely, not thrown on a table in a pile. The idea is to make the whole experience feel professional, almost as enjoyable as looking round your local clothes shop.

Allow 15 minutes at the beginning for people to look at what is on offer. **20** _____ Make sure nobody tries to take anything before the swap is supposed to start or it may result in an argument!

---

**A** For example, some people bring clothes that are damaged.

**B** Do this with another person so everyone knows it has been done fairly.

**C** Then when you're ready, the swap can begin.

**D** Why not organise a clothes exchange or clothes swap party?

**E** Firstly, people can recycle clothes that would otherwise end up as rubbish.

**F** That's why you'll have to find another location.

**G** With small numbers you can hold the event in your home.

**H** However, the idea became very popular with university students.

## Part 5

### Questions 21–26

For each question, choose the correct answer.

---

### The Penny Black

In 1840, The Penny Black became the **(21)** ............ sticky postage stamp in the world. Before this the **(22)** ............ of posting something in the UK was very expensive. This depended on distance and how many sheets of paper were being sent and was paid by the person receiving the post. The idea of paying in advance was **(23)** ............ to parliament and in 1839 this became law. A **(24)** ............ was held to find the best way of sending post. The first suggestion attempted was a special envelope or 'lettersheet' with a stamp attached, but this wasn't **(25)** ............ and in the end the stamp itself was used with a picture of Queen Victoria and the price – one penny. However, the colour was a problem as it was difficult to cancel the stamp after it had been **(26)** ............ This was eventually changed to red and black ink was used to cancel it.

---

21   **A** basic          **B** first          **C** beginning          **D** start

22   **A** money          **B** amount          **C** cost          **D** payment

23   **A** recommended          **B** said          **C** played          **D** ordered

24   **A** match          **B** prize          **C** competition          **D** race

25   **A** dear          **B** popular          **C** famous          **D** common

26   **A** near          **B** worn          **C** passed          **D** used

## Part 6

### Questions 27–32

For each question, write the correct answer.
Write **one** word for each gap.

---

### A Working Holiday

I'm just coming to the end of my working holiday. As you know,
I **(27)** ................ spent two weeks on a farm. I applied to take
part and received a list of small farms **(28)** ................ were
looking for help. Working outside in the fields all day can be
hard, but there was also **(29)** ................ chance to work with
the animals. The farm I'm working on has sheep and I've really
enjoyed working with them. In return for the hard work we've
been fed and given a comfortable bed for the night. I really
recommend it. **(30)** ................ you don't mind getting your
hands dirty and doing physical work, it's a great way to spend
your time. You don't need any skills, just the right attitude,
and you need to be reasonably fit. **(31)** ................ are about
ten people working on our farm of all ages, from teenagers up
**(32)** ................ a 75-year-old man.

---

# Test 6 WRITING

## Part 1

You **must** answer this question.

Write your answer in about **100 words** on the answer sheet.

## Question 1

Read this email from your English-speaking friend Kelly and the notes you have made.

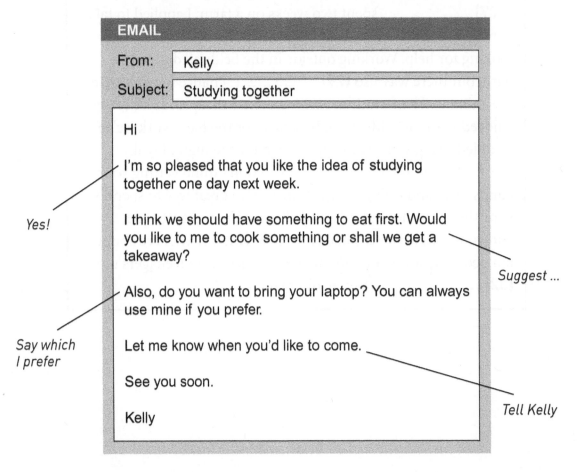

EMAIL

From: Kelly

Subject: Studying together

Hi

I'm so pleased that you like the idea of studying together one day next week.

*Yes!*

I think we should have something to eat first. Would you like to me to cook something or shall we get a takeaway?

*Suggest ...*

Also, do you want to bring your laptop? You can always use mine if you prefer.

*Say which I prefer*

Let me know when you'd like to come.

See you soon.

Kelly

*Tell Kelly*

Write your **email** to Kelly using **all the notes**.

## Part 2

Choose **one** of these questions.

Write your answer in about **100 words** on the answer sheet.

---

## Question 2

You see this notice in an English-language magazine.

**Articles wanted!**

**DO YOU SPEND MUCH TIME WATCHING TV?**

When do you watch TV?

Do you prefer watching things on your laptop?

**Write an article answering these questions and we will put it in our magazine!**

Write your **article**.

## Question 3

Your English teacher has asked you to write a story.

Your story must begin with this sentence.

*I was so pleased that the food tasted as nice as before.*

Write your **story**.

# Test 6 LISTENING

## Part 1

### Questions 1–7

For each question, choose the correct answer.

---

**1**  Where does the man think he last saw his keys?

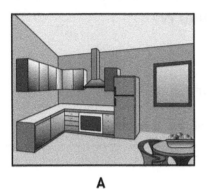  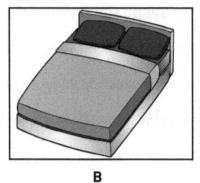  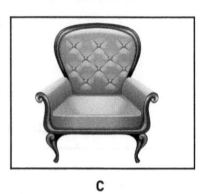

A                                  B                                  C

**2**  What does the man want to eat more of?

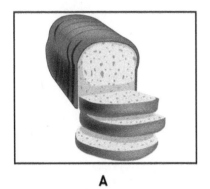  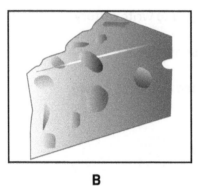  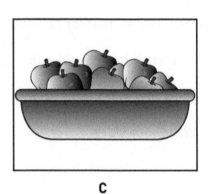

A                                  B                                  C

**3**  What is the woman going to do next Wednesday?

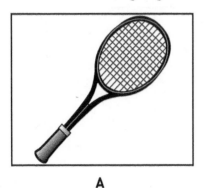    

A                                  B                                  C

**4**   What is the woman interested in buying?

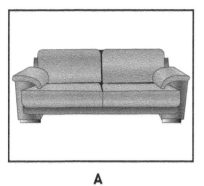   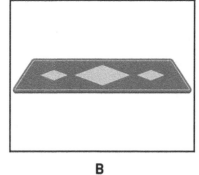   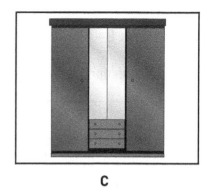

A                              B                              C

**5**   Why has the walk been cancelled?

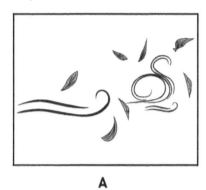   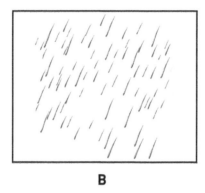   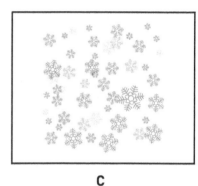

A                              B                              C

**6**   What did the woman enjoy most about her holiday?

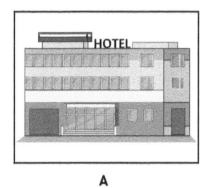   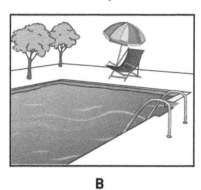   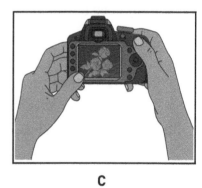

A                              B                              C

**7**   Which day does the man want to meet?

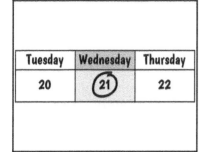

A                              B                              C

## Part 2

42

### Questions 8–13

For each question, choose the correct answer.

---

8   You will hear a wife and her husband talking about housework.
    The woman thinks

    **A**  the husband could be more organised.

    **B**  they should get the children to do more.

    **C**  they should employ a cleaner.

9   You will hear two friends talking about a university.
    What does the man think about the woman's choice?

    **A**  She has picked the best university for her subject.

    **B**  She already has friends at the university.

    **C**  Accommodation might not cost a lot.

10  You will hear two friends talking about the weather.
    The woman says

    **A**  she prefers it when it's cooler.

    **B**  the weather has been hotter than usual.

    **C**  they need it to rain.

11  You will hear two friends talking about a journey to work.
    What does the man say?

    **A**  The trains aren't reliable.

    **B**  He enjoys driving his car.

    **C**  He's thinking of using his bicycle.

12  You will hear two friends talking about the local swimming pool.
    The man doesn't use it because

    **A**  it gets too crowded.

    **B**  he doesn't have time.

    **C**  the changing rooms aren't safe.

13  You will hear two friends talking about visiting someone in hospital.
    What does the woman decide to do?

    **A**  Visit the following week.

    **B**  Take some grapes.

    **C**  Go by bus to the hospital.

## Part 3

43

### Questions 14–19

For each question, write the correct answer in the gap. **Write one or two words or a number or a date or a time.**

___

You will hear a radio presenter called Ellen talking about activities taking place over the summer.

---

## Summer Activities

For a full programme of events, text **(14)** .......................

The Activity Centre is running indoor **(15)** ......................
sessions for beginners.

There are also walks along the **(16)** ...................... to learn
about the local wildlife.

The Activity Centre is running an open day on
**(17)** ...................... June.

On the History Group walk you can learn about a famous
**(18)** ...................... who was born in the area.

If you're interested in writing **(19)** ...................... don't
forget to book a place with the Arts Centre.

---

## Part 4

44

### Questions 20–25

For each question, choose the correct answer.

---

You will hear an interview with a man called Matt Jennings, who helps people with online security.

**20** Matt says that
  **A**  people are taking better care about email safety.
  **B**  criminals notice when we don't do things correctly.
  **C**  we are inventing ways to beat the criminals.

**21** What does Matt say about some emails.
  **A**  He deletes them accidentally.
  **B**  He gets similar ones daily.
  **C**  They always come from the same company website.

**22** When you receive an email telling you to change your password, Matt says you should
  **A**  change your email password.
  **B**  keep a copy of the email.
  **C**  change your password on the company website if necessary.

**23** What does Matt say about an email he received?
  **A**  It came from an address he recognised.
  **B**  He thought it was OK.
  **C**  He replied to one the other day.

**24** After Matt received the email,
  **A**  he sent his friend an email.
  **B**  he phoned his friend.
  **C**  he received a second email.

**25** What does Matt say about passwords?
  **A**  People never remember them.
  **B**  Most passwords can be guessed easily.
  **C**  Try to use more than just letters and numbers.

# Test 6 SPEAKING

1A

1B

Audio scripts spend Model answers on pages 184–250.

**Things a woman could take on a business trip**

Audio scripts and Model answers on pages 184–250.

# Test 7

# Test 7 READING

## Part 1

### Questions 1–5

For each question, choose the correct answer.

---

1

**For Sale**

A microwave hardly ever used. Will sell for £50 or will accept a TV in good working condition.

A  A microwave and TV for sale.

B  The microwave was recently advertised on TV.

C  The microwave can be exchanged for a TV.

2

**To:** allstaff@luxuz.com

**From:** keith@luxuz.com

Hi

Lately office lights have been left on when the building is empty. Could you make sure that the last person to leave turns them off.

Thanks
Keith

A  Please leave lights on as some people are working late.

B  The last one to finish work should switch off lights.

C  Do not leave the office without leaving a light on.

3

Dear customer
Please do not eat food here you have bought somewhere else or you may be asked to leave.
Thanks.

A  Please do not leave food on the table.

B  You may be asked to leave if you don't order food.

C  Only food bought here should be eaten in our café.

4

Hi Mum

Thanks for the present. I love the shirt and the colour goes well with that skirt I bought. But do you have the receipt? I need to get a bigger size.

Bethany

A Bethany needs to change the shirt.

B Bethany wants to get a skirt the same colour.

C Bethany has lost the receipt.

5

**SHORT STORY COMPETITION**

Due to the summer holiday the last date for entry is now one week later on 31 August.

A You have one more week to enter the competition.

B You cannot enter the competition until 31 August.

C The competition is closed until the holiday period ends.

# Part 2

## Questions 6–10

For each question, choose the correct answer.

---

The people below all want to go shopping.
On the opposite page there are eight descriptions of shops.
Decide which gift would be the most suitable for the people below.

**6** Jim wants to buy some new shoes for work. He needs something reasonably cheap and, as he's working long hours, he needs a shop that is open late during the week.

**7** Hamid wants a shop where he can get measured for a new suit. He is happy to spend quite a lot but wants a place that has been recommended by other customers.

**8** Sheila wants to go shopping after she finishes work. She wants to buy an inexpensive dress or a skirt and would like to eat something made locally before her train leaves.

**9** Natalie is looking for a gift for her daughter who has passed her exams. She'd like to buy her something for university and wants to avoid the busy shopping centre.

**10** Manuela is on holiday in the UK and is looking for some chocolate for her friend. She would also like to buy something to read when she gets back to her hotel.

# Popular local shops

**A Wedges**

Take a break while you're shopping and try our delicious home-cooked hot meals. Popular with students, everything is reasonably priced. While you're here have a look at some of the second-hand clothes we have available.

**B New Street Corner Shop**

Get something to remind you of your visit here and look around at our wide range of souvenirs. We have lots of toys, sweets, locally made chocolates and attractive postcards and posters.
Looking for something to read?
Pick up a newspaper, a magazine or the latest novel for the journey home.

**C Stella's Boutique**

Late-night shopping in Stella's boutique. Many of our clothes are on special offer, with some items two for the price of one. Visitors can also enjoy locally made cakes and snacks in our café. Just a short two-minute walk from the train station.

**D Masons**

We're closing down next week and have a fantastic sale. Everything must go! We have the cheapest range of clothes in town and a great selection of men's wear, including suits, shirts and shoes. Open late this Saturday.

**E Henry's**

Henry's is known for its high-quality clothing, as our users' comments prove, whether that's dresses, skirts or stylish suits. Our highly experienced staff will measure you and make sure you get the perfect fit. A little more expensive than the high street shops but worth every penny.

**F Design Corner**

We're a new shop in the old part of town and away from the crowds. But there's nothing old about our goods. We sell dresses, skirts and blouses made by local designers, and beautiful posters, pens and pencils that will look great in the office or on a student's desk.

**G Walkers Department Store**

Visit one of the city's most popular shopping destinations. We sell the latest luxury designer clothes and everything for the home, and we have a restaurant with an international menu. You should reserve a table if you wish to eat as we can get quite busy!

**H Bartons**

If you're in town looking for a bargain don't forget to pay us a visit. Situated in the heart of the shopping mall, our popular sale has everything for the professional man, including suits, shirts and shoes. Don't forget our roof-top café! Late-night shopping Monday to Friday.

## Part 3

### Questions 11–15

For each question, choose the correct answer.

---

# Corinna Held talks about attending a music festival

I've always been mad about music, whether it's something I'm listening to on my headphones, dancing to at a club or enjoying at a concert. But my greatest love has always been going to music festivals. They are a great place to listen to your favourite musicians and to enjoy yourself with friends, and they are also an opportunity to meet new people. But the experience can be spoilt if you don't take care, so here are some things I've learnt along the way.

Let's start with what you should take. You can't be sure of the weather so I'd suggest preparing for anything. Take sun cream. If it's sunny you'll be out in the open all day. And don't forget something to keep you dry in a thunderstorm, even if it's only a large plastic rubbish bag. Your mobile phone and charger are essentials, of course, but apart from these don't take anything you wouldn't want to lose. Take comfortable shoes as you'll be on your feet all day, and if you're camping bring a tent that's easy to put up and weatherproof.

Once you're there, take a tour of the area so you know exactly where everything is. If you're with friends, agree on meeting points. Your tent is likely to be a long way from the action so you need places to find each other closer to the stages. This will help if you and your friends decide to see different bands, which is likely as your taste in music is probably not exactly the same. Be polite to people camping near you as they could become good friends. Drink lots of water and check the programme carefully so you don't miss your favourite acts.

And when it's all over? Here's my number one request: before you go home, please pick up all your litter in and around your tent. I can't believe the mess people create at festivals. Some people even leave their tent behind. And as you leave, enjoy the feeling that you've just felt, with a wonderful connection to all those around you. You've just had an amazing opportunity to see lots of different bands and make friends and generally had an experience you'll never forget.

**11** Corinna says that

    **A** music festivals are the best way to listen to music.

    **B** listening to music is her biggest love.

    **C** music festivals can be a great social event.

    **D** careless behaviour spoils music festivals for other people.

**12** What does Corinna advise people to do?

    **A** Be careful not to lose anything.

    **B** Be prepared for any weather.

    **C** Keep all your things in a plastic bag.

    **D** Leave your mobile phone at home.

**13** Corinna says you should agree on a meeting point

    **A** so you can find your way back to your tent.

    **B** in order to discuss which bands are on.

    **C** so you can talk about your taste in music.

    **D** because this is more convenient than going to your tent.

**14** What does Corinna say about litter?

    **A** People should request more litter bins.

    **B** You should clear the area where you've been camping.

    **C** People often leave litter in their tent.

    **D** Take it home with you.

**15** What would be a good introduction to this article?

**A**
> Going to a music festival? Corinna Held recommends some simple steps to make the experience a happy one.

**B**
> Music festivals can be a wonderful way to spend the weekend. Corinna Held tells us about her favourite events.

**C**
> With more and more of us attending music festivals, Corinna Held explains what it is about them people find so enjoyable.

**D**
> We all love listening to music. But do we get the best experience using our headphones? Corinna Held tells us why we should be going to music festivals.

## Part 4

### Questions 16–20

Five sentences have been removed from the text below.
For each question, choose the correct answer.
There are three extra sentences which you do not need to use.

# Why The Sea is Good For You

We all love spending time by the sea. The lucky ones might live on the coast and enjoy the benefits throughout the year. **16** Most of us would say we feel healthier by the ocean. In the past, doctors would actually recommend spending time by the sea to their patients. And research has shown that people who live on the coast are more likely to believe their health is good compared to those living in a city. So how do we benefit, exactly?

Well, to start with it's great for our mental health. **17** They have shown that watching, listening to or being in the ocean helps our brains slow down. The sound of the waves can help us relax and has a positive effect in reducing feelings of stress. This is why people who have trouble sleeping are often told to listen to recordings of the sound of waves hitting the shore to help them relax at bedtime.

**18** We go out a lot more when we're on holiday by the sea. We often become more active on holidays and people who live on the coast are usually more active too. And if you take your walks on the beach this is even better. **19** The sea air is also good for people with breathing problems. There is less pollution in the air near the ocean and in the autumn and winter the air is fresher. **20** It has even been found that the chemicals found in sea water are the same chemicals that help us have healthy skin.

No wonder then that we often feel so much better at the end of a seaside holiday and why we look forward so much to booking our next one!

**A**   Being by the sea is also good for our physical health.

**B**   This is healthier than the dry atmosphere in homes with central heating.

**C**   It's not just swimmers who know how to do this.

**D**   The rest of us have to wait for our next holiday.

**E**   However, in the end you'll notice the difference.

**F**   Walking on sand requires more effort than on the pavement.

**G**   Scientists have discovered that we have something called a 'blue mind'.

**H**   So scientists disagree about the reasons for doing this.

## Part 5

### Questions 21–26

For each question, choose the correct answer.

---

# The First Chess Champion of the World

Most chess historians agree that the first chess world championship
**(21)** ............ place in 1886 in the United States. On one side was an
Austrian chess champion Wilhelm Steinitz, who for many years
was **(22)** ............ to be one of the best in the world. Playing against
him was Johannes Zukertort from Poland, living in the UK, and
another player who many believed at the time was one of the world's
greats. According **(23)** ............ the contract, the match would be for
the championship of the world and would **(24)** ............ of 20 games
played in three different cities: New York, St Louis and New Orleans.
Steinitz won 10-5 and was world champion until 1894. Steinitz was
**(25)** ............ in how the game should be played and many of his ideas
had a big influence **(26)** ............ the modern game.

---

| 21 | **A** took | **B** went | **C** laid | **D** set |
|---|---|---|---|---|
| 22 | **A** held | **B** thought | **C** placed | **D** looked |
| 23 | **A** for | **B** in | **C** with | **D** to |
| 24 | **A** contain | **B** consist | **C** make | **D** include |
| 25 | **A** interested | **B** excited | **C** keen | **D** attracted |
| 26 | **A** to | **B** in | **C** on | **D** at |

## Part 6

### Questions 27–32

For each question, write the correct answer.
Write **one** word for each gap.

---

# The Marathon

Well, the time has finally arrived. I'm running in my first
marathon this weekend and I'm really looking forward
to it. Over the past 17 weeks I've **(27)** .....................
following a training plan. This has included four runs a week,
each **(28)** ................... different speeds to improve my
overall fitness. Sunday **(29)** ................. been the long
run day and I've slowly increased how far I go each week.
Some people argue you should try and get as close to the
full 40 kilometres **(30)** ...................... possible to increase
your confidence. However, the long runs have become
more and **(31)** .................... painful and I decided to
stop at 30 kilometres. I've also been in the gym twice a
week, working on strength-building exercises. I think I'm
ready for the challenge but of course I won't know for sure
**(32)** ................... I cross the finish line. I'll let you know
how I get on next week!

---

# Test 7 WRITING

## Part 1

You **must** answer this question.
Write your answer in about **100 words** on the answer sheet.

___

## Question 1

Read this email from your English-speaking friend Karen and the notes you have made.

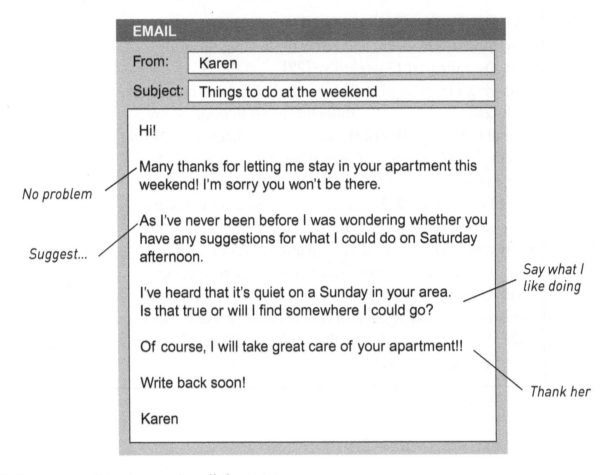

**EMAIL**

From: Karen

Subject: Things to do at the weekend

Hi!

Many thanks for letting me stay in your apartment this weekend! I'm sorry you won't be there. — *No problem*

As I've never been before I was wondering whether you have any suggestions for what I could do on Saturday afternoon. — *Suggest...*

I've heard that it's quiet on a Sunday in your area. Is that true or will I find somewhere I could go? — *Say what I like doing*

Of course, I will take great care of your apartment!! — *Thank her*

Write back soon!

Karen

Write your **email** to Karen using **all the notes**.

## Part 2

Choose **one** of these questions.
Write your answer in about **100 words** on the answer sheet.

___

## Question 2

You see this notice in an English-language magazine.

**Articles wanted!**

**WHAT'S YOUR FAVOURITE PLACE TO RELAX WHERE YOU LIVE?**

Do you enjoy a room where you can be with other people?

Do you prefer somewhere on your own?

**Write an article answering these questions and we will put it in our magazine!**

## Question 3

Your English teacher has asked you to write a story.

Your story must begin with this sentence.

*As my friend waved goodbye I wondered when we would see each other again.*

Write your **story**.

# Test 7 LISTENING

## Part 1

### Questions 1–7

For each question, choose the correct answer.

1   What time is the man's appointment?

A

B

C

2   Why is the woman going to be late for work?

A

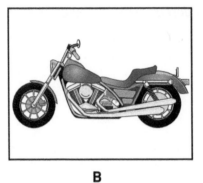

B

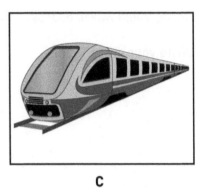

C

3   Which sport was the man unable watch on TV?

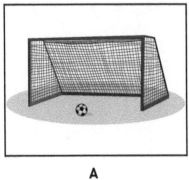

A

B

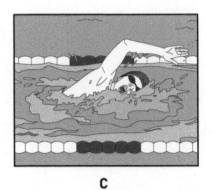

C

**4**     Where are floods expected to cause problems?

A                                    B                                    C

**5**     How many people are going to the party so far?

A                                    B                                    C

**6**     What does the woman finally buy to drink?

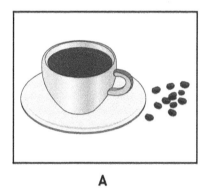

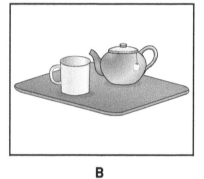

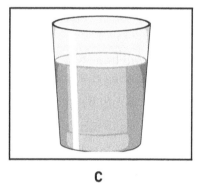

A                                    B                                    C

**7**     When does the caller want to move into the flat?

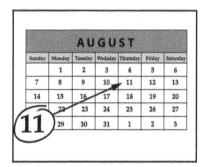

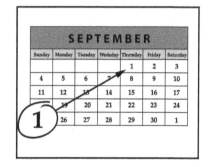

A                                    B                                    C

# Part 2

50

## Questions 8–13

For each question, choose the correct answer.

---

**8**  You will hear a man talking to his wife about a podcast.
The man thinks

    **A**  their daughter wouldn't enjoy it.

    **B**  it would be useful for their daughter's studies.

    **C**  it's free.

**9**  You will hear two friends talking about a new mobile phone.
The woman says

    **A**  it's not much better than her last one.

    **B**  it doesn't seem to be working properly.

    **C**  the screen is damaged.

**10**  You will hear a woman talking to her husband about washing clothes.
The man says the washing machine

    **A**  could be fixed quite cheaply.

    **B**  has never worked properly.

    **C**  doesn't need replacing.

**11**  You will hear two friends talking about living in the countryside.
What does the woman say?

    **A**  It would be good for her health.

    **B**  It's difficult to do your shopping.

    **C**  It can feel lonely.

**12**  You will hear two friends talking about travelling by plane.
The man thinks

    **A**  we should take more holidays at home.

    **B**  flights are too expensive.

    **C**  flying is faster than going by train.

**13**  You will hear two friends talking about a local businesswoman.
What does the man say about her?

    **A**  She is looking for a business partner.

    **B**  She supports local businesses.

    **C**  She is thinking of opening a new shop.

# Part 3

## Questions 14–19

For each question, write the correct answer in the gap. **Write one or two words or a number or a date or a time.**

You will hear an announcement in a supermarket.

---

### Milburn's Stores

At this Thursday's 'Special Buy' day you can get something for your **(14)** ……………..…..

There are jobs available for trainee managers and **(15)** …………….………...

Collect a **(16)** ……………..………… by the exit for information about how to apply.

On Friday the supermarket will open until **(17)** …………………..……..

This month Milburn's are supporting the local Arts Project and **(18)** ………..………….. …………….…….. Group.

You will be given a **(19)** …………………… when you pay to show your support.

---

# Part 4

52

## Questions 20–25

For each question, choose the correct answer.

___

You will hear an interview with a woman called Florence Adams, who helps people with job interviews.

**20** What does Florence say about starting preparation for a job interview?

   **A** Find out more about the company first.

   **B** Decide whether you would be happy to work in another country.

   **C** Ask people in the local area about the company.

**21** Florence feels it is very important that

   **A** the job is good for your career plans.

   **B** you focus on why you want to work for the company.

   **C** you only take the job if you really want it.

**22** If you don't have much experience in an area, Florence suggests

   **A** asking if the company can help.

   **B** not talking about these areas.

   **C** still arguing you are perfect for the job.

**23** What does Florence say about asking questions?

   **A** They should focus on what you will be responsible for doing in the job.

   **B** You should wait to be invited to ask questions.

   **C** They can tell employers more about you as a person.

**24** Florence suggests

   **A** reading some example interview questions available on the internet.

   **B** getting help from other people before the interview.

   **C** preparing answers for the interview.

**25** What does Florence say you should do when you walk into the room?

   **A** Find a chair to sit down.

   **B** Focus on the floor or ceiling to help you relax.

   **C** Act as if you are happy to be there.

# Test 7 SPEAKING

53–56

1A

1B

Audio scripts and Model answers on pages 184–250.

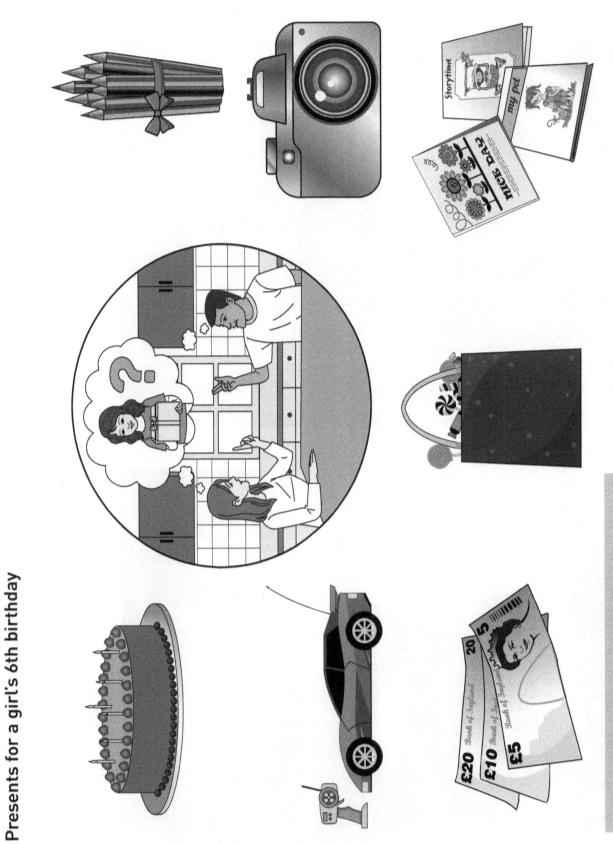

Presents for a girl's 6th birthday

Audio scripts and Model answers on pages 184–250.

# Test 8

# Test 8 READING

## Part 1

### Questions 1–5

For each question, choose the correct answer.

---

**1**

> **CUSTOMERS**
>
> Take no more than 2 items of clothing into the changing room unless you speak to an assistant first.

A   Speak to an assistant first before using the changing room.

B   Take at least two items of clothing into the changing room.

C   Ask for permission to take more than two items into the changing room.

**2**

> Jack
>
> We need more players for Saturday's game as a few others are ill. Call me if you fancy playing. Let me know as soon as possible so I can contact others if necessary.
>
> Michael

A   Michael is ill and can't play.

B   Jack should contact others to see if they are interested in playing.

C   Michael needs a quick reply.

**3**

> **LIBRARY**
>
> We will open at 9.30 on Wednesday 20 July because of staff training.
>
> Normal hours will continue next week.

A   Staff training starts at 9.30.

B   Opening hours are different on 20 July.

C   The library will open at a different time after 20 July.

**4**

To: Morris@hotmail.com
From: Chris@yahoo.com

Hi Morris

I can't make the concert tonight. If you want my ticket email me. I don't want any money for it! Have it as a gift!

A Morris can have the ticket for free.

B The ticket was a gift.

C Chris will email the ticket to Morris.

**5**

**LEFT LUGGAGE**
Our office will keep your luggage for up to 2 weeks. After this we will contact you at your email address

A Customers can leave luggage for no longer than two weeks.

B Customers must email the office if they cannot collect their luggage.

C Customers who have not collected luggage will be sent an email.

# Part 2

## Questions 6–10

For each question, choose the correct answer.

---

The people below all want to do something to keep fit.
On the opposite page there are eight descriptions of fitness activities.
Decide which activity would be the most suitable for the people below.

**6**

Theo is new to the area and wants to get fit for the first time in his life. He is more interested in team sports and would like to make friends as well.

**7**

Barbara loves running and would like to join a running club. She can't afford a membership fee to begin with but if she likes it, she'd be keen to sign up and volunteer as well.

**8**

Tracy has decided to join a gym. She wants to have someone who can help and encourage her to work hard. She'd also like to go swimming at the weekend.

**9**

Steve is looking for a personal trainer and is returning to exercise after hurting his ankle. He is busy at work and needs someone who is available any day.

**10**

Debbie is a keen athlete and wants to find somewhere she can train on a race-track and compete against other athletes. She likes to train early in the morning.

# Fitness activities

## A Stevie's Gym

Stevie's Gym is well known in the area for offering the best in everything to do with health and fitness. Relax in our luxury swimming pool or use the latest equipment in the gym. It's easy to lose interest if you don't have the right support, and our skilled team of trainers will get you started and help you stay focused.

## E Temple Health and Fitness

Whether you want to improve your fitness or lose weight, you can be sure to find the support you need to achieve your goals with our team of personal trainers. Visit our website to view their personal profiles and areas of expertise. Currently we are offering sessions at weekends only.

## B Blackwell Gym

The very best in personal service. Our members get a free health check when they join. We will then discuss your aims and design a personal programme to help you achieve your goals. Open six days a week, closed on Sundays.

## F Arena Leisure Centre

We know that some days are perfect for achieving goals in the gym, while others are best spent relaxing in the sauna. Whatever your needs, we can promise you a personal service. Please note the swimming pool is being used for competitions every Saturday and Sunday and is not open to the public on these days.

## C The Arcadian Harriers

We meet in the Arcadian Leisure Centre twice a week and set off on planned routes around the area. Join us on Tuesday for the 6k run and Thursday for the 10k. You don't have to become a member to run with us, but we'd love it if you did. We are also looking for people to help out with events.

## G Central Fitness and Leisure

We are one of the larger leisure centres in the area and can offer a huge range of activities at our 24-hour gym and 400-metre running track that is free to use for members. Sign up to our monthly league table and see how your times compare to other members.

## D JDC Gym

We offer personal, one-to-one training programmes for beginner and more advanced workouts. Our trainers are available seven days a week and can meet you at the gym or at a place that's more convenient to you. Build your strength and fitness and get help with any injuries you may have.

## H Sport Special

For those who want to focus on their own personal fitness, Sport Special provides members with a modern gym with the latest equipment. The leisure centre also organises group events such as five-a-side football or hockey. After the match, get to know your team mates in the café for tea, coffee and snacks.

## Part 3

### Questions 11–15

For each question, choose the correct answer.

---

# Georgina Johnson writes about the mobile phone

Looking back to when I was younger in the 1980s, I can remember dreaming of two inventions I thought would change my world but were probably not likely to happen in my lifetime. One was a tiny video camera that I could carry around in my pocket and film moments whenever I had the opportunity. The other was something I could use to see and speak to people miles away. I often saw them in science fiction films, and they didn't even need to be plugged in!

I find it incredible that during my adult life these two dreams have become a reality. And not even two separate inventions. Just one phone, small enough to keep in my pocket so that I hardly know it's there. I can video call or chat to friends and relatives, catch up with the latest news, watch videos of my favourite bands, check the weather forecast or send messages. Thanks to satnav I never have to worry if I get lost when I make a journey somewhere I have never been before. I can shop as much as I want and even take a course in any subject I want ... the list goes on.

Along with the internet, the mobile phone must be the biggest change in technology ever. So why do many of us feel slightly worried about how much time we spend on the phone in our lives? It's strange that the opportunities it has offered us for communication seem to have limited the time we actually spend talking to each other. We are all used to seeing friends and families who are always looking at their screens and taking very little notice of those around them.

The mobile phone is here to stay and we have to find a way of dealing with the problems it might create. I believe these are challenges we have to solve individually rather than expecting something or someone else to come to our rescue. It's up to us to be careful about the time we spend online and remember that it's good to talk with those sitting nearby. We can still feel amazed to have such a powerful piece of technology available when we need it.

**11** What does Georgina say about the 1980s?

    **A** She didn't have a TV.

    **B** Some inventions seemed a long way in the future.

    **C** People were always watching science fiction films.

    **D** She had friends who lived a long way away.

**12** Georgina says that a mobile phone

    **A** is easy to carry.

    **B** can be hard to know how to use.

    **C** is easy to lose.

    **D** is helping her with her studies.

**13** What changes does Georgina say the mobile phone has created?

    **A** We now depend on the internet.

    **B** It stops us seeing friends and relatives as often.

    **C** We communicate with people in a different way.

    **D** We spend more time communicating with people.

**14** Georgina thinks that people who use a mobile phone

    **A** don't realise how powerful it can be.

    **B** should speak to others for help.

    **C** are beginning to wish it hadn't been invented.

    **D** are responsible for using it sensibly.

**15** What would be a good introduction to this article?

**A**
> Georgina Johnson explains how her dreams have come true now the mobile phone has made her life so much easier.

**B**
> Are you spending too long on your mobile phone? Georgina Johnson warns of some of the dangers.

**C**
> One of the greatest inventions of all time or something we should be a little concerned about? Georgina Johnson gives her views on the mobile phone.

**D**
> Do you dream about what the future may be like and what technological inventions will occur? They are unlikely to come true says Georgina Johnson.

## Part 4

### Questions 16–20

Five sentences have been removed from the text below.
For each question, choose the correct answer.
There are three extra sentences which you do not need to use.

---

# The History of Fish and Chips

Fish and chips: the meal the UK is probably best known for around the world. It's unlikely you'll find many small towns or villages up and down the country that don't have a fish and chip shop on the corner.

However, neither fried fish nor chips were first eaten in the UK. It is believed that fried fish covered in flour was brought into the country by Jewish visitors from Spain and Portugal in the early 1800s. **16** It's difficult to say for sure which of these two countries started frying potatoes first, as to begin with this was street food sold as fast food snacks to poorer people. **17**

Experts are also not sure where fish and chips were first sold together in the UK. Some believe the prize should go to a man called Joseph Malin, who opened a shop in London around the 1860s. His family started by selling fried potatoes and then later added fish to the menu. **18** Records show that he was also selling fish and chips around the 1860s in a market in Lancashire in the north of England.

Until as recently as the 1980s the takeaway was served wrapped in old newspaper, a custom that some say started in order to save money. **19** Newspaper could only be used if the food was wrapped in more hygienic paper first.

The popularity of other takeaway meals such as pizza or burgers has certainly led to a decline in the number of fish and chip shops. There are now thought to be around 8,000 of them in the country. **20** But this is still a huge number when compared to some of the well-known fast food businesses.

---

**A**   Because of this, there is nothing to show where the practice actually began.

**B**   However, shops doing this were told to stop for reasons of people's health.

**C**   Then there's the difference of opinion about the size of chips.

**D**   Chips are also believed to have come from elsewhere, either France or Belgium.

**E**   There are no records to show which shop opened first.

**F**   However, others believe first prize should go to someone called John Lees.

**G**   This is compared to the 35,000 in the 1930s.

**H**   However, it is clearly not a healthy meal.

# Part 5

## Questions 21–26

For each question, choose the correct answer.

---

### The Great White Shark

The great white shark is thought of as a killer, but this is not really **(21)** .............. True, one look is enough to confirm how frightening these creatures are. They can be anywhere between four and five metres long and have around 300 teeth **(22)** ............ in rows. They can travel through the water at up to 24 kilometres an hour, speeding up when they attack. However, of the 100 or so shark attacks on humans that are **(23)** ............ each year, only around a half of these are made by the great white and most of these attacks do not lead to the person losing their life. Research has shown that the shark will often carry **(24)** ............ a test bite, and in many cases it has been shown they will release a human. Unfortunately, **(25)** ............ to the size of the creature's mouth this can still lead to the person being **(26)** ............ injured.

---

| 21 | **A** gained | **B** won | **C** fair | **D** corrected |
|----|----|----|----|----|
| 22 | **A** put | **B** done | **C** made | **D** arranged |
| 23 | **A** reported | **B** said | **C** told | **D** placed |
| 24 | **A** in | **B** up | **C** out | **D** on |
| 25 | **A** due | **B** since | **C** as | **D** for |
| 26 | **A** mainly | **B** importantly | **C** seriously | **D** strictly |

## Part 6

### Questions 27–32

For each question, write the correct answer.
Write **one** word for each gap.

---

## The Tower of London

I hope you like the photos of our holiday. My favourites are the ones **(27)** ............ the Tower of London. The big black birds you can see in one of the photos are called 'ravens'. The story goes that if ever these birds leave, the Tower will fall along with the country. **(28)** ............ are always supposed to be **(29)** ............ least six but the Tower keeps seven or more, just to be safe! The guide explained that it was King Charles II **(30)** ............ ordered this when he was warned of the dangers of killing the birds.

They don't want the ravens to fly away so one of their wings is 'clipped'. We were told that this doesn't hurt them at all but that it stops them flying away. All the birds are given names and I was surprised **(31)** ............ learn that the oldest one they've had was called Jim Crow, who lived **(32)** ............ he was 44 years old!

---

# Test 8 WRITING

## Part 1

You **must** answer this question.
Write your answer in about **100 words** on the answer sheet.

## Question 1

Read this email from your English-speaking friend Marcela and the notes you have made.

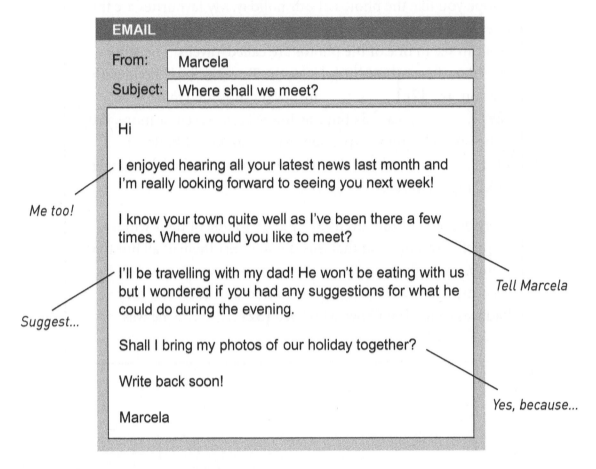

EMAIL

From: Marcela

Subject: Where shall we meet?

Hi

I enjoyed hearing all your latest news last month and I'm really looking forward to seeing you next week!

*Me too!*

I know your town quite well as I've been there a few times. Where would you like to meet?

*Tell Marcela*

I'll be travelling with my dad! He won't be eating with us but I wondered if you had any suggestions for what he could do during the evening.

*Suggest...*

Shall I bring my photos of our holiday together?

Write back soon!

Marcela

*Yes, because...*

Write your **email** to Marcela using **all the notes**.

## Part 2

Choose **one** of these questions.
Write your answer in about **100 words** on the answer sheet.

___

## Question 2

You see this notice in an English-language magazine.

| Articles wanted! |
| --- |
| **IS THERE A PERSON YOU LIKE TO SPEND TIME WITH?**<br><br>Have you known this person a long time?<br><br>What do you like to do together?<br><br>**Write an article answering these questions and we will put it in our magazine!** |

Write your **article**.

## Question 3

Your English teacher has asked you to write a story.

Your story must begin with this sentence.

*The van drove past and a box fell from the back of it.*

Write your **story**.

# Test 8 LISTENING

## Part 1

57

### Questions 1–7

For each question, choose the correct answer.

---

**1** What time does reception open?

A       B       C

**2** When is the best month to plant the seeds?

A       B       C

**3** Where did the man buy his shirt?

A       B       C

**4**   How much is one adult ticket to the football match?

A                                    B                                    C

**5**   What is it that needs replacing?

A                                    B                                    C

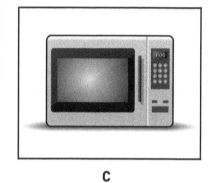

**6**   Where does the man want his wife to come?

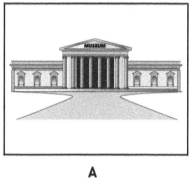   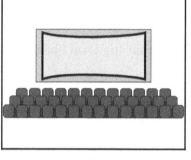   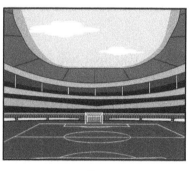

A                                    B                                    C

**7**   When is Janine's birthday?

A                                    B                                    C

# Part 2

58

## Questions 8–13

For each question, choose the correct answer.

_____

**8** You will hear two friends talking about a sales assistant.
The woman thinks

   **A** he knew when to ask for help.

   **B** he hasn't been working in the shop for long.

   **C** he is likely to become manager there.


**9** You will hear two friends talking about saving for when they retire.
The man thinks

   **A** people retire too soon.

   **B** younger people don't care.

   **C** people should start saving as early as possible.


**10** You will hear a husband and wife talking about a holiday.
The woman says

   **A** she would like to go somewhere they've visited before.

   **B** it's cheaper to book online.

   **C** she would like to go with friends.


**11** You will hear two friends talking about the local library.
The man says

   **A** families don't take their children to libraries.

   **B** people should have more books at home.

   **C** if a library closes it is unlikely to be replaced.


**12** You will hear two friends talking about doing a presentation.
What is the woman worried about?

   **A** The technology might not work.

   **B** She is worried about feeling too nervous.

   **C** She isn't sure of what to say.


**13** You will hear two friends talking about working from home.
The man says

   **A** it's difficult to concentrate.

   **B** he is more efficient.

   **C** he misses talking to people.

# Part 3

59

## Questions 14–19

For each question, write the correct answer in the gap. **Write one or two words or a number or a date or a time.**

You will hear a radio presenter telling new students about the first week at university.

---

### Your First Week at University

Make sure you bring information about your course and
**(14)** ………………..

Tell someone if you find anything that is **(15)** ……………..……....

The first place to meet new people is the **(16)** ………………..…

Clubs and societies are a great way to meet people who are
studying **(17)** ……………….…..

Avoid signing up for more than **(18)** ……………….….. groups.

Register with the **(19)** ……………….….. soon after you arrive.

---

# Part 4

60

## Questions 20–25

For each question, choose the correct answer.

---

You will hear an interview with a woman called Carrie Lewis, who is talking about her reasons for travelling.

**20** What does Carrie say about her reasons for having long holidays?

    **A** They have interrupted her career.

    **B** She might not be able to have them when she has a family.

    **C** If it were possible she would travel for longer.

**21** Carrie says she can afford a long holiday partly because

    **A** she finds work before she goes travelling.

    **B** she shares the cost with other people.

    **C** she avoids spending too much on accommodation.

**22** What does Carrie say about jobs?

    **A** It's not difficult to find work in a restaurant.

    **B** You have to start work early.

    **C** She once worked in a hotel.

**23** Carrie explained that this year

    **A** she had been offered a job.

    **B** she couldn't find a job in the French cities.

    **C** she wrote to a few restaurants while she was in France.

**24** What does Carrie say about the family restaurant?

    **A** nobody in the family spoke English.

    **B** one of the children employed her.

    **C** they had English-speaking customers.

**25** Why was the job perfect for Carrie?

    **A** The family had a boat she could use.

    **B** It gave her time to travel.

    **C** She could sometimes work on Sunday.

# Test 8 SPEAKING

61–64

1A

1B

Audio scripts and Model answers on pages 184–250.

Some things a teenager could eat on his way home before dinner

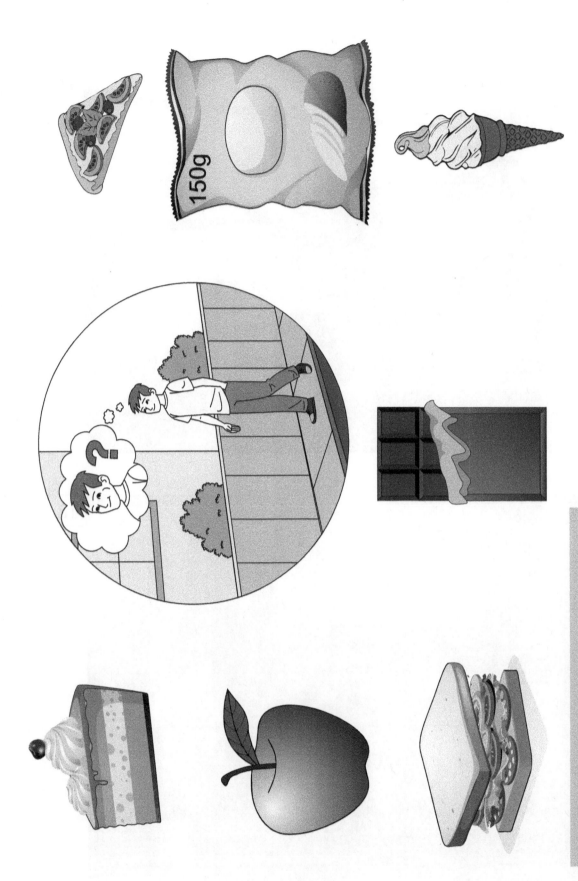

Audio scripts and Model answers on pages 184–250.

# Mini-dictionary

 Here are some of the more difficult words from the practice tests. Definitions and examples are from *Collins COBUILD Dictionaries.*

## TEST 1

**eucalyptus** /juːkəlɪptəs/ **(eucalyptuses)** NOUN an evergreen tree, originally from Australia • *The two greenhouses grow nothing but different species of eucalyptus.*

**marathon** /ˈmærəθən/ **(marathons)** NOUN a race in which people run a distance of 26 miles (= about 42 km) • *He is running in his first marathon next weekend.*

**marsupial** /mɑːˈsuːpiəl/ **(marsupials)** NOUN an animal such as a kangaroo or koala, that carries its babies in a pocket on its stomach. • *The furry little marsupials fit in the palm of one's hand.*

**nature reserve** /neɪtʃəʳ rɪzɜːʳv/ **(nature reserves)** NOUN A **nature reserve** is an area of land where the animals, birds, and plants are protected. • *It was created as a marine nature reserve to protect the dolphins.*

**pouch** /paʊtʃ/ **(pouches)** NOUN the pocket of skin on a kangaroo's stomach in which its baby grows • *The baby kangaroo's mother died while he was still in her pouch.*

**the Renaissance** /ðə rɪneɪsɒns/ NOUN **The Renaissance** was the period in Europe, between the 14th and 16th centuries, when there was a new interest in art, literature, science and learning. • *Science took a new turn in the Renaissance.*

## TEST 2

**cell** /sel/ **(cells)** NOUN the smallest area inside a beehive • *Honeycomb cells are built by the bees on frames.*

**hive** /haɪv/ **(hives)** NOUN a structure in which bees live • *Honeybees' ability to find their way back to the hive always amazes me.*

**meditation** /medɪteɪʃən/ NOUN **Meditation** means to remain in a silent and calm state for a period of time, often so that you are more able to deal with the problems of everyday life. • *Many busy executives have begun to do yoga and meditation.*

**nectar** /nektəʳ/ NOUN **Nectar** is a sweet liquid made from flowers, which bees and other insects collect. • *And, of course, bees drink nectar and make honey.*

**samba** /sæmbə/ **(sambas)** NOUN A **samba** is a lively Brazilian dance. • *Many Brazilians work nearby and dance the samba at local nightclubs.*

## TEST 3

**clove** /kloʊv/ **(cloves)** NOUN A **clove** of garlic is one of the sections of a garlic bulb. • *Fry a couple of cloves of whole, peeled garlic in olive oil.*

**dealer** /diːləʳ/ **(dealers)** NOUN A **dealer** is a person whose business involves buying and selling things. • *She used to be an antique dealer.*

**dietary requirements** /daɪətri rɪkwaɪəʳmənts/ PLURAL NOUN Someone's **dietary requirements** are things that they need to take into account about what they eat. • *Meals are served on request, allowing for special dietary requirements.*

**puzzle** /pʌzəl/ **(puzzles, puzzling, puzzled)** VERB to leave you feeling confused because you do not understand something • *My sister's behaviour puzzles me.*

**rightful** /raɪtfʊl/ ADJECTIVE If you say that someone or something has returned to its **rightful** place, they have returned to the place that you think they should have. • *This certainly helped Spain take its rightful place in Europe.*

**seed** /siːd/ **(seeds)** NOUN the small, hard part of a plant from which a new plant grows • *Plant the seeds in small plastic pots.*

**sensation** /senseɪʃən/ **(sensations)** NOUN If something is a **sensation**, it causes great excitement or interest. • *The film was an overnight sensation.*

**show off** /ʃoʊ ɒf/ (shows, showing, showed) PHRASAL VERB If something **shows** something else **off**, it emphasises its good features so that it looks especially attractive. • *The bus route shows off the beauty of the capital city.*

**smock** /smɒk/ (smocks) NOUN A **smock** is a loose piece of clothing that looks like a long shirt. • *Two little boys in white smocks came running down the road.*

**suspect** /səspekt/ (suspect, suspecting, suspected) VERB to believe that someone probably did something wrong • *The police did not suspect him of anything.*

**youngster** /jʌŋstəʳ/ (youngsters) NOUN a young person, especially a child • *The children's club will keep the youngsters busy.*

## TEST 4

**artificial** /ɑːˈtɪfɪʃəl/ ADJECTIVE made by people, instead of nature • *The city has many small lakes, natural and artificial.*

**chase** /tʃeɪs/ (chases) NOUN If there is a **chase**, someone goes after someone or something in order to catch them. • *The chase ended at around 10.30 p.m. on the motorway.*

**chemical** /kemɪkəl/ (chemicals) NOUN a substance that is used in a chemical process, or made by a chemical process • *The TV programme was about the use of chemicals in farming.*

**migrate** /maɪgreɪt/ (migrates, migrating, migrated) VERB to move from one part of the world to another at the same time every year • *Most birds have to fly long distances to migrate.*

**slide** /slaɪd/ (slides, sliding, slid) VERB When someone **slides**, they move smoothly across the ground. • *He watched the children sliding and laughing.*

**slope** /sloʊp/ (slopes) NOUN the side of a mountain, hill or valley • *A steep slope leads to the beach.*

**stimulate** /stɪmjʊleɪt/ (stimulates, stimulating, stimulated) VERB to make something more active • *America is trying to stimulate its economy.*

**tradition** /trədɪʃən/ (traditions) NOUN a type of behaviour or a belief that has lasted for a long time • *Afternoon tea is a British tradition.*

**transport** /trænspɔːʳt/ (transports, transported, transporting) VERB If you say that you **are transported** to another place, you mean that something makes you feel that you are living in that other place. • *Dr Drummond felt that he had been transported into another world.*

**vertical** /vɜːʳtɪkəl/ ADJECTIVE standing or pointing straight up • *The climber moved up a vertical wall of rock.*

## TEST 5

**chase** /tʃeɪs/ (chases) NOUN If there is a **chase**, someone goes after someone or something in order to catch them. • *The chase ended at around 10.30 p.m. on the motorway.*

**draw** /drɔː/ (draws) NOUN a choice at random of teams playing each other in a competition • *Today they are having the draw for the quarter-finals of the UEFA Cup.*

**flash** /flæʃ/ NOUN **Flash** is the use of special bulbs to give more light when taking a photograph. • *He was one of the first people to use high-speed flash in bird photography.*

**granite** /grænɪt/ NOUN **Granite** is a very hard rock used in building. • *They looked at the park's marble and granite monuments.*

**host** /hoʊst/ (hosts) NOUN the person at a party who has invited the guests • *I didn't know anyone at the party, except the host.*

**loaf** /loʊf/ (loaves) NOUN bread that has been shaped and baked in one piece • *He bought a loaf of bread and some cheese.*

**passion** /pæʃən/ (passions) NOUN a very strong interest in something that you like very much • *She has a passion for music.*

**pleasing** /pliːzɪŋ/ ADJECTIVE giving you pleasure and satisfaction • *The pleasing smell of fresh coffee came from the kitchen.*

**rope** /roʊp/ (ropes) NOUN a type of very thick string that is made by twisting together several strings or wires • *He tied the rope around his waist.*

**twenty** /twenti/ (twenties) NOUN if you are **in your twenties**, you are aged between 20 and 29. • *They're both in their twenties and both married with children of their own.*

**venom** /venəm/ **(venoms)** NOUN The **venom** of a creature such as a snake or spider is the poison that it puts into your body when it bites or stings you. • *Snake venom causes more than 100,000 deaths every year.*

**vertical** /vɜːˈtɪkəl/ ADJECTIVE standing or pointing straight up • *The climber moved up a vertical wall of rock.*

---

## TEST 6

**act** /ækt/ **(acts)** NOUN one of the main parts that a play or show is divided into • *Act two has a really funny scene.*

**comedian** /kəmiːdiən/ **(comedians)** NOUN a person whose job is to make people laugh • *Who is your favourite comedian?*

**offer** /ɒfəʳ/ **(offers)** NOUN If there is something **on offer**, it is available to be used or bought. • *Among the properties on offer is a ten-bedroom house.*

**swap** /swɒp/ **(swaps)** NOUN If you do a **swap** with someone, you give them something and receive a different thing in exchange. • *You may be able to arrange a swap with someone.*

---

## TEST 7

**charger** /tʃɑːˈdʒəʳ/ **(chargers)** NOUN A **charger** is a device used for charging or recharging batteries. • *He forgot the charger for his mobile phone.*

**chemical** /kemɪkəl/ **(chemicals)** NOUN a substance that is used in a chemical process or made by a chemical process • *The TV programme was about the use of chemicals in farming.*

**marathon** /ˈmærəθən/ **(marathons)** NOUN a race in which people run a distance of 26 miles (= about 42 km) • *He is running in his first marathon next weekend.*

**trainee** /treɪniː/ **(trainees)** NOUN A **trainee** is someone who is employed at a low level in a particular job in order to learn the skills needed for that job. • *He is a 24-year-old trainee reporter.*

**value** /væljuː/ **(values, valuing, valued)** VERB If you **value** something or someone, you think that they are important and you appreciate them. • *If you value your health then you'll start being a little kinder to yourself.*

**values** /væljuːz/ PLURAL NOUN The **values** of a person or group are the moral principles and beliefs that they think are important. • *The countries of South Asia also share many common values.*

---

## TEST 8

**household** /haʊshoʊld/ **(households)** NOUN Your **household** is your home and everything that is connected with looking after it. • *There is a never-ending list of household chores.*

**hygienic** /haɪdʒiːnɪk/ ADJECTIVE Something that is **hygienic** is clean and unlikely to cause illness. • *We went for a white kitchen that was easy to keep clean and hygienic.*

**race-track** /reɪstræk/ **(race-tracks)** NOUN A **race-track** is a piece of ground used for races, often by cars, motorbikes, and horses. • *Their first memories were also trips to the race-track to watch their dad race.*

**release** /rɪliːs/ **(releases, releasing, released)** VERB to stop holding someone or something [formal] • *He released her hand.*

**satnav** /sætnæv/ **(satnavs)** NOUN a piece of equipment in a car that tells you the best way of getting to a place • *We didn't have a satnav, so we had to use a map.*

# Audio scripts

These are the audio scripts for the Listening and Speaking papers of the tests. Listen to the audio online at: **www.collins.co.uk/eltresources**

## TEST 1    LISTENING

## Part 1

## Track 01

*Preliminary English Test, Listening.*
*There are four parts to the test. You will hear each part twice. We will now stop for a moment. Please ask any questions now, because you must not speak during the test. Now look at the instructions for Part 1. For each question, choose the correct answer.*

*Look at Question 1.*

**1**  *When does John offer to come?*

Man:    Hello, it's John the builder here. I've ordered the windows and they should arrive next Monday, so I can come and fit them on Tuesday. I did have a job with someone else on Thursday, but they've just called to say it's not convenient so I'm available any day next week, though perhaps we'd better forget Monday in case the windows arrive late in the day. Could you call me and let me know if this is OK?

*Now listen again.*

**2**  *What did the woman enjoy doing at the party?*

Man:    So what did you think of the party? I'm afraid I didn't really enjoy it that much.

Woman:    No. I'm glad we decided to leave early in the end. I didn't know anyone there and the food wasn't the best I've ever had. I tried talking with someone, but the music was so loud we couldn't hear each other. Still, I had a nice dance – that was fun but I was pleased to get home.

*Now listen again.*

**3**  *What will the weather be like in the morning?*

Woman:    Good evening. And now it's time for the weather forecast for tonight and tomorrow. The heavy rain and strong winds we have at the moment will continue through the night but should die out before early morning. It's looking like we'll be waking up to clear blue skies with lots of sunshine. We expect it to stay like this for rest of the day until the evening, when we might get a few showers.

*Now listen again.*

**4**  *What time does the tour of the hospital start?*

Man:    Are you interested in becoming a nurse? Then why not come along to our open day this Saturday at St John's Hospital? The activities will start with a presentation from our team of doctors at 1.00, followed by a tour with a nurse who will show you round the hospital at 1.30. And of course we will be available to answer any questions you may have. Join us at 12.30 for registration and a tea or coffee.

*Now listen again.*

**5**  *What isn't the daughter having for her birthday?*

Man:    Have you decided what you want for your birthday yet?

Girl:    Well, mum said you could buy me some driving lessons, but I don't think I'm ready yet.

Man:    OK, well, what if we give you the money instead or get you that nice dress you were looking at?

Girl:    Well, grandad's giving me money, so I think I'd prefer the dress.

*Now listen again.*

**6**  *What size shirt does the man want?*

Woman:    Hello sir. Can I help you?

Man:    Yes, I'd like to exchange this shirt, if that's possible.

Woman:    Yes, certainly. Is there something wrong with it?

Man:    No, it's fine but it doesn't fit me. I usually buy medium but this one seems a bit too small for me.

Woman:    Would you like to exchange it for a large?

Man:    I think I'll have a look round first and see if you've got something else in a medium, thanks.

*Now listen again.*

**7**  *What are the police checking for next week?*

Woman:    During the next week you'll see extra police on the roads in your area. Officers are looking out for drivers using their mobile phones when they're behind the wheel. Previously we focused on people not wearing seat belts or drivers going too fast and both were very successful. So, if you're thinking of checking social media or email on your way to work, think again. Our aim is to make the roads a safer place for everyone. Please drive carefully.

*Now listen again.*

*That is the end of Part 1.*

## Part 2

## Track 02

*Now look at Part 2. For each question, choose the correct answer.*

**8** *You will hear two friends talking about a film.*

Man: So, Storm Cloud. You saw the film last night, didn't you?

Woman: Yes, me and lots of teenagers all excited about seeing their action heroes. I enjoyed it! I think anyone would like it, whatever their age – lots of action, an exciting plot, a happy ending.

Man: It's quite a change for the director isn't it? An action film, I mean.

Woman: Yes. This is his first attempt at a film like this – he's mainly worked on TV programmes.

*Now listen again.*

**9** *You will hear two friends talking about someone the woman lives with.*

Man: I hear you're still having a problem with the new person in your flat?

Woman: Yes, his name's Steve. He doesn't do anything to keep the place tidy. He refuses to do any washing-up and never offers to cook. He says he just forgets to do things and that I should leave a note to remind him of jobs that need doing.

Man: I think you should ask him to find somewhere else to live.

Woman: Well, I didn't really want to do that, but I think you're right. He's never going to change.

*Now listen again.*

**10** *You will hear a woman telling a friend about a holiday she is going on.*

Man: So, are you looking forward to your holiday next week?

Woman: Yes, I really am. I'll be leaving next Friday. I booked it just in time before the price went up.

Man: You're very brave to go on your own, aren't you? Won't you feel a bit lonely?

Woman: Well, I'll be visiting friends once I'm there and they've promised to introduce me to their friends, so I don't think that will be a problem. I'm hoping to do some long walks in the countryside if the weather isn't too bad.

*Now listen again.*

**11** *You will hear two friends talking about meeting a relation at the airport.*

Man: Yes, so I'm meeting my cousin at the airport. Her plane arrives at about 9.00. I can't wait to see her for the first time and find out what she's like.

Woman: You've never seen each other before? How are you going to recognise each other?

Man: Well, I was going to take a sign so that she could find me in the crowds, but everybody carries them, don't they? So, I've decided I'm going to wear something

colourful instead. I haven't told her yet, so I need to send her an email.

*Now listen again.*

**12** *You will hear two friends talking about getting to the train station.*

Woman: What time shall we leave for the station in the morning?

Man: I was thinking about 9.00. That will give us time to catch the train.

Woman: Shall I come to your house or will you come to mine?

Man: Well, you're nearer to the station so I could get the bus to you. But they take ages at that time in the morning and I'm worried we'll be late and miss the train. It's more expensive, but a taxi might be quicker. I can order it and come to you.

Woman: OK. Let's do that.

*Now listen again.*

**13** *You will hear two friends talking about a new laptop.*

Man: I see you've bought a new laptop.

Woman: Yes, I've had the old one for years and I thought I'd get a newer model.

Man: What do you think of it?

Woman: It starts up really quickly, though to be fair the old one wasn't that slow. But it's so much lighter. I stopped taking the old one to work in the end as it was so heavy.

Man: Oh, the new one sounds much better, I'm sure you'll be pleased with it.

*Now listen again.*

*That is the end of Part 2.*

## Part 3

## Track 03

*Now look at Part 3.*
*For each question, write the correct answer in the gap.*
*Write one or two words or a number or a date or a time.*
*Look at Questions 14 to 19 now. You have 20 seconds.*
*You will hear a radio presenter called Erica talking about how we can help the environment.*

Erica: This morning we're continuing to look at environmental problems to see what we can do to help. And we can make a difference if we try. We often forget that as people who go shopping, we have a lot of power. If one company does something we don't like we can always shop somewhere else.

Then there's the amount of plastic that comes with the goods we buy. Try buying things that aren't wrapped in it. And if you're offered a bag and you don't need one, just say 'no thanks'. And any plastic bags you have at home, don't throw them away. Put them away somewhere until your next shopping trip and use them then.

On the subject of throwing stuff away, I try to keep things that other people might be able to use. There are always charity shops which are very happy to help you recycle your old clothes or things in the house. Knowing that someone else is getting pleasure from something you no longer need is a lovely feeling.

Pollution is of course a big problem, and we often feel that as individuals we have no power to make any difference. But that's not true. Find out what some of the local environmental problems are and see how you can help. Get together with friends and help to clear the rubbish from local rivers or collect litter from the streets around your home to keep the area looking tidy.

Finally, let's turn to energy. Cars are here to stay for the moment, and it would be difficult to ask people not to use them at all. But we should all try to avoid making unnecessary car journeys. Go by bike or public transport sometimes or, if you work in the same area as your neighbour, try car-sharing. Take it in turns to drive to work.

*Now listen again.*

*That is the end of Part 3.*

## Part 4

## Track 04

*Now look at Part 4.*
*For each question, choose the correct answer.*
*Look at Questions 20 to 25 now.*
*You have 45 seconds.*
*You will hear an interview with a woman called Sally Wainwright, who recently started singing classes.*

| | |
|---|---|
| Interviewer: | I'm speaking with Sally Wainwright, who recently started singing classes. What made you decide to do that, Sally? |
| Sally: | Well, I'd reached a time in my life when I wanted to do more, to meet new people, to try something different. I'd been to art classes, which were OK, and keep fit, which I hated. Singing classes were something I'd always wanted to try but never had the confidence to start. |
| Interviewer: | Why was that do you think? |
| Sally: | I always felt uncomfortable singing, even with my family. For example, going on holiday, my husband and children would sing along to the radio, but I never joined in. My mum had a great voice. I loved listening to her singing while she was cooking. I wanted to be able to do the same without feeling silly. |
| Interviewer: | Was it easy to find a class? |
| Sally: | Yes, a friend told me about one locally. I was worried I'd have to pass a test of some kind before they let me join but anybody was welcome, and you didn't need to prove how good your voice was. You just turned up for a practice session with other people. That was the best bit about it. We all sing together, not on our own. |
| Interviewer: | So how did you feel in that first session? |
| Sally: | Well, I was so worried before the session I nearly turned the car round and went home. People were already there waiting to start and, one of the organisers turned up. We talked about my reasons for coming along and, well, she gave me the confidence to give it a try. I found a space at the back of the group and just sang with everyone else. |
| Interviewer: | So, has it helped you become more confident? |
| Sally: | Absolutely, yes. Being in a group means you can sing without feeling silly. I've never been asked to sing on my own and I'm not sure how I'd feel if they did ask me, but now I join in with the kids when there's a good song on the radio. It's great to know I've achieved one of the goals I had when I started. |
| Interviewer: | So, would you recommend we all do something similar? |
| Sally: | Definitely. It's a great confidence builder, you'll make friends, and it's good for your health. There are supposed to be physical benefits from singing – something to do with increasing the oxygen levels, which makes us feel happier – I'm not sure about all that but I do know I always go home in a good mood. |

*Now listen again.*

*That is the end of Part 4.*

*You now have six minutes to write your answers on the answer sheet.*

*That is the end of the test.*

## TEST 1    SPEAKING

## Part 1

## Track 05

| | |
|---|---|
| Examiner: | Good morning. Can I have your mark sheets, please? I'm Fiona Evans and this is Michael Hale. What's your name, Candidate A? |
| Candidate A: | My name's Marta Gonzalez. |

Examiner: Where do you live?
Candidate A: I live in Madrid.
Examiner: And what's your name, Candidate B?

[PAUSE FOR YOU TO ANSWER]

Examiner: Where do you come from, Candidate B?

[PAUSE FOR YOU TO ANSWER]

Examiner: Candidate B, do you work or are you a student?

[PAUSE FOR YOU TO ANSWER]

Examiner: What do you do, Candidate B?

[PAUSE FOR YOU TO ANSWER]

Examiner: And Candidate A, do you work or are you a student?
Candidate A: I'm a student.
Examiner: What do you study?
Candidate A: I'm studying biological sciences. I'm going to finish my course next year.
Examiner: Thank you.
Examiner: Candidate A, do you enjoy studying English?
Candidate A: Yes, I do. I like being able to speak to other people in English and reading English books.
Examiner: Candidate B, what did you do last weekend?

[PAUSE FOR YOU TO ANSWER]

Examiner: Candidate A, what are you going to do next weekend?
Candidate A: I'm going to visit my grandparents. They live quite close to us and we're going there for dinner.
Examiner: Candidate B, what do you enjoy doing in your free time?

[PAUSE FOR YOU TO ANSWER]

Examiner: Thank you.

## Part 2

## Track 06

Examiner: Now I'd like each of you to talk on your own about something. I'm going to give each of you a photograph and I'd like you to talk about it.
Candidate A, here is your photograph. It shows two people on bicycles. Please tell us what you can see in the photograph.
Candidate B, you just listen.
Candidate A: OK, in this photograph I can see two people and they are riding bicycles. There's a young girl, she's on the left. She looks about ten years old. She's wearing a nice dress. Next to her, on the right is an older lady. I think it could be her grandmother. This lady is wearing jeans and a white shirt. They're in a park and there are trees in the background. Maybe it's summer because they're both wearing sunglasses. They're both

smiling and they look very happy. It's a nice family photograph.
Examiner: Thank you.
Candidate B, here is your photograph. It shows a group of children. Please tell us what you can see in the photograph.
Candidate A, you just listen.

[PAUSE FOR YOU TO ANSWER]

Examiner: Thank you.

## Part 3

## Track 07

Examiner: Now, in this part of the test you're going to talk about something together for about two minutes. I'm going to describe a situation to you. A woman has been invited to her friend's wedding. She is trying to decide what she could buy her friend for a wedding gift. Here are some things she could buy. Talk together about the different things she could buy and say which one would be best. All right? Now talk together.
Candidate A: OK, I think they're interesting presents but some are more expensive. Do you agree?

[PAUSE FOR YOU TO ANSWER]

Candidate A: Yes, I agree. I think if you need a washing machine you choose one yourself. The money would be a good idea. Her friend could buy something she needed.

[PAUSE FOR YOU TO ANSWER]

Candidate A: That's a good idea. I think the microwave and the television are too expensive. Shall we forget about them? There are also the towels and the cushions. What do you think about them?

[PAUSE FOR YOU TO ANSWER]

Candidate A: Yes, I agree with you.
Examiner: Thank you.

## Part 4

## Track 08

Examiner: Candidate A, do you enjoy going to parties?
Candidate A: Yes, I do. I enjoy talking and being with my friends. We always have a good time.
Examiner: And what about you, Candidate B?

[PAUSE FOR YOU TO ANSWER]

Examiner: Do you prefer to dance at parties or talk with people?

**187**

[PAUSE FOR YOU TO ANSWER]

| Examiner: | And how about you, Candidate A? |
| Candidate A: | I'm not very good at dancing so I usually sit with my friends and talk. When we know a song that's playing, we all sing as well. |
| Examiner: | What makes a good party, Candidate B? |

[PAUSE FOR YOU TO ANSWER]

| Examiner: | And what about you, Candidate A? |
| Candidate A: | Yes, I agree. The people are important. I also think it's good to have lots of food because people are always hungry. |
| Examiner: | Thank you. That is the end of the test. |

## TEST 2    LISTENING

## Part 1

# Track 09

*Preliminary English Test, Listening*
*There are four parts to the test. You will hear each part twice.*
*We will now stop for a moment.*
*Please ask any questions now, because you must not speak during the test.*
*Now look at the instructions for Part 1.*
*For each question, choose the correct answer.*
*Look at Question 1.*

**1**  *What does mum say Helen's brother can eat?*

| Woman: | Hiya Helen ... Hope you had a good day at college. We're so busy today and I won't be home from work until late this evening. There's a pizza in the freezer that should be enough for you, and your brother can have the pasta if he hasn't eaten already. Dad said he'll get himself fish and chips on the way home. |

*Now listen again.*

**2**  *What does the man complain about?*

| Woman: | I must say, I really enjoyed that film. What about you? |
| Man: | Yes, me too. I couldn't believe it was nearly three hours long. The time went so quickly, didn't it? It's the first time I've been to that cinema and I didn't know you can order food on your phone and have it delivered to where you're sitting. Next time I go I'll definitely get something. I just wish the people sitting in front hadn't spent the whole film talking. |

*Now listen again.*

**3**  *At what time might the road be OK to use?*

| Man: | And finally, let's turn to the traffic report for this Monday morning. I'm afraid it's not a good start to the week if you're driving in to work. There has been a serious accident on the Warwick Road, it happened around 6.00 this morning. Thankfully nobody was |

injured but there are long traffic jams. Drivers are being warned to stay away from the area until at least 10.00, when the road is expected to re-open. Keep listening and we'll update you at around 8.30 with our next traffic report.

*Now listen again.*

**4**  *How much is a return flight to Paris at the moment?*

| Woman: | I have a question about your cheap flights to Paris. |
| Man: | Yes, we have an offer this week. Is it just you flying, madam? |
| Woman: | It will be, yes, but I want to check the price first. It was advertised last week at £150, before the offer started, but I checked your website this morning and it's now listed at £180. |
| Man: | Sorry, that must be a mistake. Return flights are £120 this week, I'll get someone to update the information online. |

*Now listen again.*

**5**  *Which programme has been cancelled?*

| Woman: | Just a quick reminder to viewers of the change in tonight's TV schedule. With the whole nation excited about the Cup Final, football will be shown from 7.30 on Channel 1. Apologies to the gardeners out there as this means Gardeners' World will not be shown this week. For those of you who are not football fans, tune into Channel 2 this evening for the latest in our police drama 'Suspect', which follows the 7.00 news. |

*Now listen again.*

**6**  *Which day has the most lectures?*

| Woman: | Have you seen the lecture timetable? The university emailed it to me this morning. |
| Man: | Yes, it's not too bad, is it? |
| Woman: | No, there aren't any terrible days. Last week the secretary said Wednesday would be the busiest, but it looks like there's just one lecture in the morning. |
| Man: | Yes, Thursday has the most with one in the morning and another in the afternoon. I'm really not looking forward to Friday though. Only one in the morning, I know, but it's an 8.00 start. |

*Now listen again.*

**7**  *Which item of food or drink is not available?*

| Man: | Thank you for calling Yardley Over-50s Community Group. There is nobody available to take your call at the moment. If you are phoning about the menu this week, lunchtime sessions are still taking place as usual though building work means we've had to change the menu. We're unable to |

serve hot meals until Friday. There will be sandwiches available, however, and free tea or coffee as usual.

*Now listen again.*

*That is the end of Part 1.*

## Part 2

## Track 10

*Now look at Part 2. For each question, choose the correct answer.*

**8** *You will hear two friends talking about a new café in town.*

| | |
|---|---|
| Man: | I've just been into the shopping centre. There's a new café by the station. |
| Woman: | Yes, I know. I went there last week. I think it opened some time ago actually. |
| Man: | I only looked through the window. It looks really nice. |
| Woman: | Yes, it's nice and bright and the staff are really helpful. It's simple fast food. People might just want to grab something to eat before they catch a train, so it should do well. |
| Man: | OK, I'll go in and try it next time I'm in town. |

*Now listen again.*

**9** *You will hear two friends talking about litter.*

| | |
|---|---|
| Man: | Have you seen all that litter blowing around in the street outside? |
| Woman: | I know. It looks awful, doesn't it? |
| Man: | I don't know what we pay our taxes for. Why aren't the street cleaners out there tidying up? |
| Woman: | I know, but people don't seem to think about dropping litter. We shouldn't expect there to be a street cleaner running around behind everyone tidying up their rubbish. |
| Man: | Yes, I suppose you're right. But it does look so messy and someone needs to keep the streets clean. |

*Now listen again.*

**10** *You will hear a woman telling a friend about a new car.*

| | |
|---|---|
| Man: | Well done! I hear you've passed your driving test. Congratulations! |
| Woman: | Yes, I'm thinking about buying myself a nice little car now. |
| Man: | Really? What kind are you looking for? |
| Woman: | Nothing too expensive, that's for sure. A small one to drive around town. At first I wasn't sure I wanted to use it to go to the office, but I might car-share with a colleague to save on petrol. |
| Man: | That's a good idea. Just make sure you find someone you like to talk to in the morning! |

*Now listen again.*

**11** *You will hear two friends talking about a website they use.*

| | |
|---|---|
| Man: | You travel a lot by train, don't you? Do you book your tickets online? |
| Woman: | Yes, I use Train Track. It's my favourite site when I need to book anything. |
| Man: | Yes, me too. Some sites make it difficult to choose times and dates but that's never a problem on that site. |
| Woman: | I know. But have you noticed that sometimes the price of tickets goes up if you don't order straightaway? If you search the same journey later, it's more expensive. |
| Man: | Yes, I've noticed that too. |

*Now listen again.*

**12** *You will hear two friends talking about a photography competition.*

| | |
|---|---|
| Woman: | I heard about your brother winning that photography competition – that was very good. |
| Man: | I know. His photos are amazing. |
| Woman: | What kind of photos does he take? |
| Man: | The prize was for his photos of strangers in the street. |
| Woman: | Are people happy for him to take their photo? |
| Man: | He takes it first and then shows it to them on his camera. He always tells them what it's for and unless they ask him to delete it, he uses it. He says that people rarely complain. Some of them ask him to email them a copy. |

*Now listen again.*

**13** *You will hear two friends talking about the man's birthday.*

| | |
|---|---|
| Woman: | Happy birthday, Michael. Have you had a nice day? |
| Man: | Yes, it's been wonderful. Everyone has been so kind. |
| Woman: | Did the kids get you anything nice? |
| Man: | My daughter got up early and made me breakfast in bed. Toast and a cup of coffee. |
| Woman: | That must have been lovely. |
| Man: | It was. I'm certainly not used to that. My son was supposed to help but he forgot and woke up late. But he heard us laughing and joking and joined us when I was opening my presents. |

*Now listen again.*

*That is the end of Part 2.*

## Part 3

## Track 11

*Now look at Part 3.*
*For each question, write the correct answer in the gap.*
*Write one or two words or a number or a date or a time.*
*Look at Questions 14 to 19 now. You have 20 seconds.*

*You will hear a radio presenter called Jonathan talking about the programmes during the week.*

Jonathan: Before tonight's news let me tell you about some of the shows we have for you this week so you can make a note of them in your diary. There are a few changes to our regular programmes so listen carefully to make sure you don't miss any of your favourites.

Tonight at 8.30 John Seymour will present this week's wildlife documentary. John entertained us all previously with his trip to the safari park when he went along to meet the elephants. This time John will be telling us about how we can recognise the wildflowers in our gardens.

Then our first change of schedule. Apologies to listeners looking forward to Writers' World and our interview with Francis Selhurst, on how to get ideas for your next novel. We've had to rearrange this interview for next week as Francis is attending a conference. Instead, we'll be talking with an expert about how you can make use of the internet to get your next book published.

On Thursday at 8.00 we have Sports Night as usual, with a look at next weekend's football. Most of the games from last Saturday were cancelled due to the terrible weather, so there are no reports on those matches. But our experts will be looking forward to seeing some action this Saturday and will be trying to predict results as usual. Join our team at 8.00.

And finally, our reporter Sally Williams will be in town next Friday morning. She'll be interviewing people for our weekly programme Money Matters, starting from 10.00, not the usual 9.00. If you'd like the chance to speak to her and share your views of your experiences and any problems you may have, meet Sally at the main door of the library, not the normal meeting place at the Town Hall, which is closed due to building work.

*Now listen again.*

*That is the end of Part 3.*

## Part 4

## Track 12

*Now look at Part 4.*
*For each question, choose the correct answer.*
*Look at Questions 20 to 25 now.*
*You have 45 seconds.*
*You will hear an interview with a man called Tom Walker, who is a personal trainer.*

Interviewer: On today's programme I'm speaking to Tom Walker and finding out about being a personal trainer. Have you always done this Tom?

Tom: Hello, no actually, it's a long story but I was injured many years ago, which meant I had to stop a hobby that I loved: cycling. Stop is the wrong word really. I could cycle but I could no longer go in for competitions.

Interviewer: So how did this lead to you becoming a trainer?

Tom: Well, the reason for the injury was because I hadn't trained properly for events. I pushed myself too hard and finally injured my ankle very badly. It was a lesson in how not to do a sport and I decided I wanted a job where I could help other people train and compete safely.

Interviewer: Do you only train cyclists?

Tom: No, not at all. I see lots of people who are cyclists, but in order to get enough work I made the choice that I would try to support anyone. I help quite a lot of runners and people who just want to get fit. People of all ages too. My youngest customer is 16 and my oldest is 73.

Interviewer: Wow! Where do you hold your sessions?

Tom: It depends on the weather and what the person prefers. When it's dry and not too hot I simply meet them in the park and we do our exercises there. It's often cooler than using the gym and people are able to push themselves for longer and harder before they feel uncomfortable.

Interviewer: And of course, the park is free to use.

Tom: It certainly is. Sometimes it's not the right place to go though. Some customers feel a little shy or embarrassed about doing exercises in public. The sessions are sometimes early in the morning and you have people walking through the park going to work. So some customers prefer to meet in the gym.

Interviewer: It sounds like a lot of fun. Are you busy?

Tom: Definitely. I think people have become more concerned about their health and there's a growing interest in keeping fit. Some months are busier than others. During the summer people go away on holiday. But I get a lot of customers before their holiday who want to get into shape for the beach, so this period can also be a good time for business.

*Now listen again.*

*That is the end of Part 4. You now have six minutes to write your answers on the answer sheet.*

*That is the end of the test.*

## TEST 2     SPEAKING

### Part 1

## Track 13

| | |
|---|---|
| Examiner: | Good afternoon. Can I have your mark sheets please? I'm Steve Malpas and this is Sue Hudson. What's your name? |
| Candidate A: | My name's Stephan Eglin. |
| Examiner: | Where do you come from? |
| Candidate A: | I come from a small village in Switzerland. |
| Examiner: | And what's your name, Candidate B? |

[PAUSE FOR YOU TO ANSWER]

| | |
|---|---|
| Examiner: | Where do you live, Candidate B? |

[PAUSE FOR YOU TO ANSWER]

| | |
|---|---|
| Examiner: | Candidate B, do you work or are you a student? |

[PAUSE FOR YOU TO ANSWER]

| | |
|---|---|
| Examiner: | What do you study, Candidate B? |

[PAUSE FOR YOU TO ANSWER]

| | |
|---|---|
| Examiner: | And Candidate A, do you work or are you a student? |
| Candidate A: | I work. |
| Examiner: | What do you do? |
| Candidate A: | I'm a designer. I work in a design studio. |
| Examiner: | Thank you. |
| Examiner: | Do you like it where you live? |
| Candidate A: | Yes, I do. I enjoy living in a busy city. I live near the shopping centre and I like leaving my flat and being in crowds of people. |
| Examiner: | Candidate B, what about you? |

[PAUSE FOR YOU TO ANSWER]

| | |
|---|---|
| Examiner: | Candidate A, have you got any hobbies or interests? |
| Candidate A: | I play the guitar. I spend a lot of time practising on my own but I also play in a group with some friends. |
| Examiner: | Candidate B, what do you do to relax? |

[PAUSE FOR YOU TO ANSWER]

| | |
|---|---|
| Examiner: | Thank you. |

### Part 2

## Track 14

| | |
|---|---|
| Examiner: | Now I'd like each of you to talk on your own about something. I'm going to give each of you a photograph and I'd like you to talk about it. |

| | |
|---|---|
| | Candidate A, here is your photograph. It shows two people in a kitchen. Please tell us what you can see in the photograph. Candidate B, you just listen. |
| Candidate A: | This photo shows two people in a kitchen. It looks like a kitchen in someone's house, not one you see in a restaurant. There's a man and a woman preparing food. They look middle-aged and they might be a husband and wife. They are both wearing something to protect their clothes. I don't know the word for this, but everyone has one hanging in the kitchen and you put it on when you prepare food. It looks like the woman is getting the vegetables ready and the man is cutting something up, it looks like meat. I think they are making the evening meal and they both look very happy. |
| Examiner: | Thank you. |
| Examiner: | Candidate B. Here is your photograph. It shows people in a shopping centre. Please tell us what you can see in the photograph. Candidate A, you just listen. |

[PAUSE FOR YOU TO ANSWER]

| | |
|---|---|
| Examiner: | Thank you. |

### Part 3

## Track 15

| | |
|---|---|
| Examiner: | Now, in this part of the test you're going to talk about something together for about two minutes. I'm going to describe a situation to you. A man's daughter is going on a camping holiday. He wants to buy her something she can take with her. Here are some things he could get. Talk together about the different things he could get her and say which one would be best. All right? Now talk together. |
| Candidate A: | So, we need to choose something that's good for a camping holiday. I don't think the shoes are useful, do you? |

[PAUSE FOR YOU TO ANSWER]

| | |
|---|---|
| Candidate A: | I think the backpack is better than the suitcase. It's the kind of bag someone uses for camping, isn't it? |

[PAUSE FOR YOU TO ANSWER]

| | |
|---|---|
| Candidate A: | I agree, but the map is very cheap. I think her father would like to spend a bit more money on her present. I think your idea for him to buy walking boots is the best so far. What about the camera? |

[PAUSE FOR YOU TO ANSWER]

Candidate A:   Yes, let's say that.

Examiner:      Thank you.

## Part 4

## Track 16

Examiner:      Candidate A, have you ever been camping?

Candidate A:   Yes, but a long time ago. When I was younger I went with my family. I enjoyed cooking our food outside in a field.

Examiner:      And what about you, Candidate B?

[PAUSE FOR YOU TO ANSWER]

Examiner:      Candidate B, do you prefer a holiday in a town or the countryside?

[PAUSE FOR YOU TO ANSWER]

Examiner:      And how about you, Candidate A?

Candidate A:   I agree. That's the kind of place I prefer. When I go on holiday with my friends, we always look for places that have good shops but also a nice beach.

Examiner:      Candidate B, is it better to go on holiday on your own or with other people?

[PAUSE FOR YOU TO ANSWER]

Examiner:      And what about you, Candidate A?

Candidate A:   Yes, I agree. I think I would be lonely on my own. I like to have people to talk to on the journey and to have fun with on the holiday.

Examiner:      Thank you. That is the end of the test.

## TEST 3      LISTENING

## Part 1

## Track 17

*Preliminary English Test, Listening*
*There are four parts to the test. You will hear each part twice.*
*We will now stop for a moment.*
*Please ask any questions now, because you must not speak during the test.*
*Now look at the instructions for Part 1.*
*For each question, choose the correct answer.*
*Look at Question 1.*

**1**   *Which day is the carnival taking place this year?*

Man:        OK, we have activities for the carnival now but we need to decide on a date.

Woman:      We always hold it in July, don't we? On a Saturday. Last year the Saturday was the seventh of July. Shall we do that again this year?

Man:        I was thinking of moving it to the end of June around the thirtieth. But some of the acts can't make that date.

Woman:      Let's do it the same time as last year. This year that means Saturday the eighth of July.

*Now listen again.*

**2**   *Why has the woman decided to leave her job?*

Man:        Your mum was telling me you're starting a new job. Why's that?

Woman:      Yes, that's right. I've been with this company now for nearly three years.

Man:        So why are you leaving?

Woman:      They've always been great, never said 'no' if I was ill and needed time off or if I wanted to attend a training event. I just felt I needed a change. This other company offered me a higher salary so I decided it would be a good opportunity to move.

*Now listen again.*

**3**   *What should customers who have a problem with their telephone do?*

Woman:      Thank you for calling Intratek. All our operators are busy. If you are calling about a poor telephone connection, we are aware of a problem that is affecting customers in certain areas of the country. We are working with engineers to look into this matter. Please check our website for the latest updates. If you have a different enquiry, please email us at info@intratek.com for a quick reply.

*Now listen again.*

**4**   *What does the man say he can't do?*

Woman:      So can I book you to come round to tidy our garden?

Man:        Yes, that's fine this Friday at 11.00. Let's hope the weather is fine.

Woman:      Great. I'm looking forward to seeing the garden looking nice.

Man:        I'll cut the grass and I'll put all the things that can be recycled into green plastic bags. As I explained earlier, you'll have to find a way of getting these to a recycle centre yourself as I don't have my own transport.

*Now listen again.*

**5**   *What is today's special offer?*

Man:        Welcome to ABROSE Superstore this morning. Today we have an exciting selection of new clothing including a new range of women's dresses in the fashion section. And if you're wondering what to cook for tea tonight don't forget our frozen food section where you'll find some of your favourites at half price. And for our gentlemen visitors today, why not treat someone special to a nice bunch of flowers from our garden centre?

*Now listen again.*

**6**   *What time does Jamie suggest meeting?*

Man:        Emma, it's me, Jamie ... I was wondering what time you'll be free tomorrow afternoon. I should be able to leave college by 3.00 because my lecture has been cancelled. Is there any chance we can meet a little earlier than we planned? I can get the 3.15 train into town and get to you by 4.00 if that's OK. Call me back and let me know.

*Now listen again.*

**7** *What should passengers for the 10.15 train do?*

Woman: We regret to inform passengers that the 8.15 train to London has been cancelled. The next London train is at 10.15. Passengers can use their ticket for this train but should go to the ticket office for seat reservations. If you need an earlier arrival in London, a coach service has been arranged, leaving at 8.30. Passengers taking the coach should go to the coach stop now to check in any luggage. The next train to arrive at Platform 2 is the 8.00 to Watford Junction.

*Now listen again.*

*That is the end of Part 1.*

## Part 2

## Track 18

*Now look at Part 2. For each question, choose the correct answer.*

**8** *You will hear two friends talking about a dance performance.*

Man: Did you get the email? The date for the dance performance is 11 May.

Woman: Yes, I know. I'm sure we'll have enough time to prepare. We've got three lessons before the big day.

Man: Yes, I think we'll be OK. We've already learnt the basic steps, haven't we?

Woman: But the dance teacher's away on holiday for the next two weeks so we'll have to practise on our own. I'm not sure we have anyone in the group who's strong enough to take charge. You know how we argue so much.

*Now listen again.*

**9** *You will hear two friends talking about a book they've read.*

Woman: So, did you like that book?

Man: I loved it. I read it from cover to cover in one day!

Woman: Really? It took me a while to finish it. But I wasn't familiar with the author and I found it rather confusing.

Man: The plot is a bit complicated I agree, especially compared to his other books. But he really is a good author. Would you like to try one of his earlier ones?

Woman: OK, I'm happy to give him another chance.

*Now listen again.*

**10** *You will hear a man telling a friend about a football match.*

Man: Are you looking forward to going to the match this weekend?

Woman: I am, yes. Especially such a big game. It will be so exciting. I just hope we win.

Man: I can't wait! There should be a fantastic atmosphere in the ground and a bigger crowd than normal for such an important match.

Woman: I know. We were lucky to get two tickets, weren't we?

Man: It wasn't difficult at all. I know someone who has a job in the ticket office. He offered to save two for me.

*Now listen again.*

**11** *You will hear two friends talking about a visit to the dentist.*

Man: What time's your appointment at the dentist tomorrow?

Woman: It's the last one of the day at 5.30. I was hoping to get one earlier as my tooth is really hurting.

Man: Oh, poor you! Toothache is horrible.

Woman: I could have got one in the morning, but it would have been with a different dentist. I've heard he's not very good with nervous patients so I thought it would be better to see my usual one. She's gentle and explains everything to you clearly and calmly.

Man: Well, best of luck.

*Now listen again.*

**12** *You will hear two friends talking about their evening meal.*

Woman: OK, it's my turn to cook tonight. Is there anything you fancy?

Man: I love pasta although we've had it for the past three days so perhaps something else.

Woman Is there anything in the freezer? I don't really want to go shopping.

Man: I don't think so. We could always get a takeaway for a change. You could cook tomorrow instead.

Woman: OK. What about a curry?

Man: I'd rather have something that isn't too hot and spicy. There's a menu from the local restaurant in the kitchen. I'll go and get it.

*Now listen again.*

**13** *You will hear two friends talking about a friend's birthday present.*

Woman: It's Sandra's birthday this Saturday. Have you bought her a present yet?

Man: Not yet, no. I was thinking of getting her a book, but I have no idea what she likes.

| Woman: | There's an interesting play on at the theatre this weekend. Why don't we treat her to a night out? |
| Man: | That's a great idea. I know she's free on Friday so we could always book tickets and surprise her. She'd like that. |
| Woman: | OK, do you want to order the tickets? Hopefully we can get three seats together. |

*Now listen again.*

*That is the end of Part 2.*

## Part 3

## Track 19

*Now look at Part 3.*
*For each question, write the correct answer in the gap.*
*Write one or two words or a number or a date or a time.*
*Look at Questions 14 to 19 now. You have 20 seconds.*
*You will hear a manager called Sandra talking about a company training day.*

| Sandra: | Can I just say something about the training day next week. You should all receive your programme by email shortly. We've had to make changes to rooms and even now some of the training sessions may have to be held in a different building. But we'll let you know if this happens.
Some of you have asked about changing to a different session than the one you signed up for. We've tried to do this when it's been possible but as some training sessions are full it will sometimes not be possible. We will let you know by email on 13 September the full list of names of people going to each session. The trainers will email you the materials they'll be using during the sessions for you to have a look at before the training day. There are some tasks for you to complete in preparation for your session. Please make sure you print out these materials and complete the exercises before you attend.
At the end of the training day you will all be given a questionnaire for your comments on each of the sessions you attended. Could you please make sure you complete this and give it to the training manager. We are using a new company for this event and are keen to see how well the day goes.
Because staff in the company restaurant will also be attending training sessions, the restaurant will not be open. We are arranging cold food, teas and coffee for everyone. Could you email the restaurant manager before the end of |

this week and let him know if you have any special dietary requirements.
Finally, can I remind you to check the noticeboard outside room 134 for any last-minute changes. Yes, we'll email you all important information but several of you have complained that you haven't received our messages, so to be absolutely sure you're up to date, check the noticeboard.

*Now listen again.*

*That is the end of Part 3.*

## Part 4

## Track 20

*Now look at Part 4.*
*For each question, choose the correct answer.*
*Look at Questions 20 to 25 now.*
*You have 45 seconds.*
*You will hear an interview with a woman called Maggie Taylor, who is talking about garlic.*

| Interviewer: | On today's programme I'm speaking to Maggie Taylor and finding out about her love of garlic. Where did this all start Maggie? |
| Maggie: | I think it started when I went to university about 30 years ago. Garlic wasn't something you often found in many English kitchens at that time, not among the older generation anyway. My mum certainly never used it and when I went to university, I started seeing other students cooking with it for the first time. |
| Interviewer: | So how did it go from that to your current love of garlic? |
| Maggie: | I think my interest in it has just developed over the years. I studied cookbooks and of course discovered what a difference it can make to a meal. Actually, garlic turned me into a cook as I'd never really done much of that before. And because it's used all over the world, I've learnt to cook some interesting dishes. |
| Interviewer: | Garlic has health benefits too, doesn't it? |
| Maggie: | It certainly does. It has a very long history of being used as a medicine. Research shows that it can reduce heart disease. Some people believe that garlic can be used to fight off the common cold, though I'm not sure about that. I've even heard it can be used for some skin conditions. |
| Interviewer: | Have you tried to grow garlic yourself? |

| | |
|---|---|
| Maggie: | I have, yes. The first time I tried to grow it I used garlic from the supermarket, but I later discovered that this isn't really suitable for an English garden. You need to find garlic that has been selected for different climates. It used to be difficult to find the right type but these days it's quite easy to find the kind that grows well here. |
| Interviewer: | And were you successful? |
| Maggie: | Yes. I didn't do very well to start with, but I've been more successful recently. You must remember to plant it out in the autumn for best results, and it's usually ready to dig up around July when it's still green. Then you hang it somewhere warm and dry in the sunshine. Once you've picked it, garlic will last for up to a year. |
| Interviewer: | And finally, have you got a favourite recipe using garlic? |
| Maggie: | Well, there's a soup I cook that contains 25 cloves of garlic! I can't say my family like it. They're afraid it will make their breath smell. Personally, I think the smell of garlic is wonderful. But they're wrong to worry anyway, as when garlic is cooked slowly over a long period it becomes mild. |

*Now listen again.*

*That is the end of Part 4.*

*You now have six minutes to write your answers on the answer sheet.*

*That is the end of the test.*

## TEST 3    SPEAKING

### Part 1

### Track 21

| | |
|---|---|
| Examiner: | Good evening. Can I have your mark sheets, please? I'm Lorna MacDonald and this is Mark Farrington. What's your name? |
| Candidate A: | My name's Aleksandra Kaminski. |
| Examiner: | Where do you live? |
| Candidate A: | I live in Krakow in Poland. |
| Examiner: | And what's your name, Candidate B? |
| [PAUSE FOR YOU TO ANSWER] | |
| Examiner: | Where do you come from, Candidate B? |
| [PAUSE FOR YOU TO ANSWER] | |
| Examiner: | Candidate B, do you work or are you a student? |
| [PAUSE FOR YOU TO ANSWER] | |

| | |
|---|---|
| Examiner: | What do you do, Candidate B? |
| [PAUSE FOR YOU TO ANSWER] | |
| Examiner: | And Candidate A, do you work or are you a student? |
| Candidate A: | I'm a student. |
| Examiner: | What do you study? |
| Candidate A: | I'm studying Polish literature. |
| Examiner: | Thank you. |
| Examiner: | Candidate A, who do you live with? |
| Candidate A: | I live with my family. There's my mum, my dad and my two sisters. They're both younger than me. |
| Examiner: | And what about you, Candidate B? |
| [PAUSE FOR YOU TO ANSWER] | |
| Examiner: | Candidate A, have you got a favourite sport? |
| Candidate A: | Yes, I really enjoy watching football. I often go to see my local team and watch matches if they're on TV. And I like playing tennis and going swimming. |
| Examiner: | Candidate B, do you like to keep fit? |
| [PAUSE FOR YOU TO ANSWER] | |
| Examiner: | Thank you. |

### Part 2

### Track 22

| | |
|---|---|
| Examiner: | Now I'd like each of you to talk on your own about something. I'm going to give each of you a photograph and I'd like you to talk about it. Candidate A, here is your photograph. It shows people out shopping. Please tell us what you can see in the photograph. Candidate B, you just listen. |
| Candidate A: | This photo shows a family out shopping in a supermarket. It's quite a young family. The man and the woman don't look very old, around 30 perhaps and they have a young daughter who looks about four or five years old. She's sitting on her father's shoulders. Either the mother or father has asked her to get a bottle of something from a shelf near the top. Her dad is nearest to the bottles and the girl is reaching out to get one. The mother is holding the shopping trolley, standing next to her husband. All three of them are smiling and look like they're having a good time. |
| Examiner: | Thank you. |
| Examiner: | Candidate B, here is your photograph. It shows some people in a computer room. Please tell us what you can see in the photograph. Candidate A, you just listen. |

[PAUSE FOR YOU TO ANSWER]

Examiner: Thank you.

## Part 3

## Track 23

Examiner: Now, in this part of the test you're going to talk about something together for about two minutes. I'm going to describe a situation to you. A young woman works very hard and wants to get fitter. She has decided to take up an activity to help her get fit. Here are some things she could do. Talk together about the different activities she could try and say which one would be best. All right? Now talk together.

Candidate A: OK, the question has asked us to choose the best activity for a young woman. I don't think playing golf will help her to get fit. What do you think?

[PAUSE FOR YOU TO ANSWER]

Candidate A: That's true. Swimming or cycling are good if you want to take exercise on your own. And what about running as well?

[PAUSE FOR YOU TO ANSWER]

Candidate A: I agree. So, running and cycling are our favourite activities so far. What about dancing? Going dancing is good fun and she can join a dance class on her own, can't she? And she will meet some new people and might make new friends.

[PAUSE FOR YOU TO ANSWER]

Candidate A: Yes, I think that's the best choice.
Examiner: Thank you.

## Part 4

## Track 24

Examiner: Do you do any sports, Candidate A?
Candidate A: Yes, I play tennis and I often go swimming. I'm lucky because there's a sports centre near my house and it's easy for me to get there.
Examiner: And what about you, Candidate B?

[PAUSE FOR YOU TO ANSWER]

Examiner: Candidate B, do you like to watch sport on TV?

[PAUSE FOR YOU TO ANSWER]

Examiner: And how about you, Candidate A?
Candidate A: I don't watch TV very often, but I do like to watch videos of tennis matches on the internet. I prefer playing tennis though.
Examiner: Candidate B, is it important to try to be the best when you do a sport or just to take part?

[PAUSE FOR YOU TO ANSWER]

Examiner: And what about you, Candidate A?
Candidate A: Yes, I agree. The most important thing is you enjoy what you're doing. Most people want to get better but only so they can improve their fitness or skill. I think that's important.
Examiner: Thank you. That is the end of the test.

## TEST 4    LISTENING

## Part 1

## Track 25

*Preliminary English Test, Listening*
*There are four parts to the test. You will hear each part twice.*
*We will now stop for a moment.*
*Please ask any questions now, because you must not speak during the test.*
*Now look at the instructions for Part 1.*
*For each question, choose the correct answer.*
*Look at Question 1.*

**1**   *Which activity wasn't available?*

Woman: Hiya … just back from the business trip … I didn't get to see the museum as there wasn't much time. The hotel where I was staying was OK. It had a really nice restaurant with a good selection of food. There was something to suit everyone's tastes. I was hoping to use the gym over the weekend but it wasn't open, so I spent time at the swimming pool, which was better than nothing.

*Now listen again.*

**2**   *How does the man travel if there's a problem?*

Woman: Could you tell me how you travel to work and why you travel that way?
Man: I usually get the train. I enjoy driving but I only use the car at weekends when it's quieter and more relaxing to drive. I can work on the train, read reports, that kind of thing.
Woman: And do you ever use the bus service?
Man: If the trains are delayed and I'm worried about getting into work on time, then sometimes, yes.

*Now listen again.*

**3**   *What is the building going to be used for?*

Woman: So that's the end of my report on this building's fascinating history. If you get the chance to see it, I'm sure you'll agree it looks wonderful now the repair work has been completed. And it's great to know the community will benefit. There was talk about it being used as flats or even a library, but we hear it's going to be used as a local art gallery.

I think the council have done a very good job bringing this building back to life.

*Now listen again.*

**4**  *Which membership allows a person to attend a presentation?*

Man:  Hello, I'm interested in taking out membership of your book club. Can you explain how it works?

Woman:  OK, well there are three options. You can become a member for three months, six months or one year and each month you'll receive a book in the post. If you sign up for six months we will give you free entrance to listen to an author talk. Sign up for 12 months and you'll be able to join other members online to ask the author questions.

*Now listen again.*

**5**  *When does the woman want to book a library computer?*

Woman:  Hi, I'm just calling about booking the use of a computer. I was planning on coming in on Monday, but I understand there aren't any PCs available that day. I was wondering whether Wednesday was possible. I've been coming in on a Tuesday to work over the past few weeks and there hasn't been a problem getting one then, but I'm busy on that day this week. If you could call me back before you close on Monday, I'd be grateful.

*Now listen again.*

**6**  *What is the man doing on Saturday?*

Woman:  Hi Mark. Have you got anything planned for Saturday?

Man:  Yes, I think so.

Woman:  What are you doing?

Man:  Well, it's Sally's party soon and I need to buy her a present. I was going to do that, but Jim called earlier and wants to go for a coffee. I was thinking of asking him to meet on Sunday instead but a friend's coming over with her elderly mother then, so I'll be seeing Jim as we planned and get the present later in the week.

*Now listen again.*

**7**  *Which item of food has the man's mother tried before?*

Man:  I'm not sure what to take back for mum from our holiday.

Woman:  What does she like?

Man:  I could get her a packet of those biscuits I bought for her last year. She liked them.

Woman:  What about some of that cheese we saw in the shop?

Man:  She'd love that, but I'm not sure it would stay fresh. No, on second thoughts I think I'll get her some chocolate.

*Now listen again.*

*That is the end of Part 1.*

**Part 2**

# Track 26

*Now look at Part 2. For each question, choose the correct answer.*

**8**  *You will hear two friends talking about a trip to the theatre.*

Man:  So, are you ready for the theatre this evening? I can't wait.

Woman:  Yes, I'm really excited too. It's been a while since I went to the theatre. Don't forget your student ID, will you? They always ask to see it before they give you the student discount.

Man:  OK. I'll remind the others in case they forget. I'll text them in a minute.

Woman:  And it's only offered to full-time students, remember. Some of our friends are only part time.

Man:  OK, it's only Tahira who is full time so I'll let her know.

*Now listen again.*

**9**  *You will hear two friends talking about the man's job.*

Man:  I'm going to that employment event in town tomorrow.

Woman:  Really? Are you looking for a new job? I always thought you enjoyed it where you work.

Man:  Well, I'm thinking of having a change of career. I've been working as an accountant for years now and I feel like doing something different. I've got a few friends who are teachers and they think I'd enjoy doing something like that. It would mean a lower salary but that's OK. So, I'm just going to find out about the qualifications I need.

*Now listen again.*

**10**  *You will hear a husband and wife talking about breakfast.*

Man:  OK, my turn to make breakfast, I think. What would you like?

Woman:  I'd love a bowl of cereal, but the last time I looked in the cupboard we'd run out. Did you get any when you went shopping?

Man:  No, I forgot to put that on the list. Sorry. How about some ham and cheese?

Woman:  Yes, that would be nice. We could use some of that nice bread you bought. And can I have coffee for a change instead of tea?

Man:  OK. Oh, I'm feeling quite hungry now!

*Now listen again.*

**11** *You will hear two friends talking about buying a bed.*

Man: I need to get a new bed for my flat. Is there anywhere you can recommend?

Woman: The furniture store in town has some and they're good quality.

Man: Really? I might go there later. I was thinking of looking online but it's difficult to tell how comfortable they'd be if you can't try them out first.

Woman: Well, you might find a bargain that way. You could try one out in the shop and then order the same one online if you find one that costs less than the shop.

Man: Good idea. I might do that.

*Now listen again.*

**12** *You will hear two friends talking about going for a walk.*

Woman: I feel like getting outside in the country today and having a fast walk. Do you fancy joining me?

Man: I'm not sure. We might need to take our umbrellas. The weather forecast says there's going to be heavy rain.

Woman: I know I've just checked. But it's not expected until later this afternoon so I'll just take my jacket. Anyway, a bit of rain won't hurt you. And the fresh air will be good for us.

Man: Yes, I suppose so. And I've got nothing to do today so let's go now, shall we?

*Now listen again.*

**13** *You will hear two friends talking about a passport photograph.*

Woman: I need to get a new passport before we go on holiday. Where can I get my photograph taken?

Man: There's a machine in the pharmacy round the corner but I think it's out of order. I saw someone asking one of the shop assistants for help last week.

Woman: That's a pity. I might have to go into town.

Man: There are a lot of places in town. I know you can get it done in the post office. That one probably works OK, and if you want one that's open in the evening you could try the machine at the train station.

*Now listen again.*

*That is the end of Part 2.*

## Part 3

## Track 27

*Now look at Part 3.*
*For each question, write the correct answer in the gap.*
*Write one or two words or a number or a date or a time.*
*Look at Questions 14 to 19 now. You have 20 seconds.*

*You will hear a man called Russell talking about a new club in the community centre.*

Russell: And finally, news of an interesting club that started recently and meets here every week. The Speakers' Club is aimed at anyone who needs to develop their public speaking skills. Perhaps you have to give talks to colleagues at work or need to practise a presentation you have prepared for a job interview.

The Speakers' Club offers a weekly meeting in the main hall, where members can learn from each other as well as through talks given by highly experienced speakers from the world of business or entertainment. We look at everything from body language and eye contact to storytelling and delivery.

A typical session starts at 7.00 with tea, coffee and biscuits before we listen to the speaker and start looking at a particular topic. Members are then given the chance to change a presentation they've prepared before the session so that it includes the ideas presented by the speaker. We also invite you to enter one of our speech competitions each year.

We understand that clubs like ours might not suit everyone and we like to give you the chance to see for yourself how we operate before you join. So, we invite anyone to attend their first session for free. However, in order for us to manage the numbers of people attending, please make sure you reserve a place first or you may not be able to attend.

If you do decide to join us, annual membership is £170 per year. Arrangements can be made to pay the membership fee once a month. Membership allows you to attend all sessions during the year and gives you access to private areas of the website and the chance to take part in our social events.

*Now listen again.*

*That is the end of Part 3.*

## Part 4

## Track 28

*Now look at Part 4.*
*For each question, choose the correct answer.*
*Look at Questions 20 to 25 now.*
*You have 45 seconds.*

*You will hear an interview with a student called Emily, who walks people's dogs.*

Interviewer: Hi everyone. Today on Student Radio I'm talking to someone who has solved her financial problems at university by starting her own business. Isn't that right, Emily?

Emily: Well, I'm not sure I'd call it a business actually, but it has certainly helped me to buy a few books and a meal or takeaway once a week while I'm studying at university. I offer to walk people's dogs, people who either can't leave their homes easily or are out at work during the day.

Interviewer: What gave you the idea?

Emily: I was talking to my neighbour one day and she told me about a friend of hers who had just come out of hospital and wasn't able to take her dog out for its daily walk. I thought it would be a kind thing to do to offer to help. I didn't even think about charging her, but she insisted on giving me a few pounds.

Interviewer: So how did this develop into you becoming a dog walker?

Emily: After I'd done it for a few weeks I realised what a pleasant way it was to earn a little money. But most importantly I thought I'd be able to fit it in around my studies at university. So, I decided to put an advert in a few of the local shops to see if there was any interest.

Interviewer: And was it successful?

Emily: It took a while before I heard from anyone new but then one day I got a phone call from an old lady asking to meet me. I offered to go to her home but she suggested meeting in the local park so she could see how I was with her dog. We got on really well and the woman booked me to take the dog out every weekend.

Interviewer: And have you taken on any more customers?

Emily: That was about six months ago and now I walk three more dogs. I was expecting to hear from people who had a busy work life and needed help, but all my customers are older people. And their dogs have been trained well and are a pleasure to walk.

Interviewer: What a brilliant idea. And for anyone listening, do you have a set fee?

Emily: At first, I thought about having an hourly fee and that's what my friends recommended. But I enjoy what I'm doing and I know that there are some customers, especially older people, who might not be able to afford to pay much. So, we just agree an amount when we first meet.

*Now listen again.*

*That is the end of Part 4.*

*You now have six minutes to write your answers on the answer sheet.*

*That is the end of the test.*

## TEST 4    SPEAKING

### Part 1

### Track 29

Examiner: Good morning.
Can I have your mark sheets, please? I'm Gareth Reynolds and this is Mary Roberts.
What's your name?

Candidate A: My name's Pierre Rioche.

Examiner: Where do you come from?

Candidate A: I come from Nantes in France.

Examiner: And what's your name, Candidate B?

[PAUSE FOR YOU TO ANSWER]

Examiner: Where do you live, Candidate B?

[PAUSE FOR YOU TO ANSWER]

Examiner: Candidate B, do you work or are you a student?

[PAUSE FOR YOU TO ANSWER]

Examiner: What do you study, Candidate B?

[PAUSE FOR YOU TO ANSWER]

Examiner: And Candidate A, do you work or are you a student?

Candidate A: I work.

Examiner: What do you do?

Candidate A: I'm a librarian.

Examiner: Thank you.

Examiner: Do you live in a house or an apartment, Candidate A?

Candidate A: I live in a small apartment on my own. There's a bedroom, a kitchen, a living room and shower room.

Examiner: Candidate B, what about you?

[PAUSE FOR YOU TO ANSWER]

Examiner: Candidate A, are there any good restaurants where you live?

Candidate A: Yes, there are lots. My favourite is an Italian restaurant just round the corner from my apartment. I go there as often as I can.

Examiner: Candidate B, have you got a favourite meal?

[PAUSE FOR YOU TO ANSWER]

Examiner: Thank you.

### Part 2

### Track 30

Examiner: Now I'd like each of you to talk on your own about something. I'm going to give each of you a photograph and I'd like you to talk about it.

**Candidate A,** here is your photograph. It shows people working.
Please tell us what you can see in the photograph.
Candidate B, you just listen.

**Candidate A:** The people in this photograph are in an office, I think. It might also be in a university or college in the IT room, but I think these people are at work. There are five people, two men are near the front and they're both looking at a computer screen. One man is sitting and the other is standing by his side. It looks like they are discussing something. They're both quite young and wearing casual clothes and they both have beards. There are three women at computers in the background. One woman is standing next to another one who's sitting at her desk and they're talking, and the third woman is looking at them.

**Examiner:** Thank you.
Candidate B, here is your photograph. It shows people in a hairdressers.
Please tell us what you can see in the photograph.
Candidate A, you just listen.

[PAUSE FOR YOU TO ANSWER]

**Examiner:** Thank you.

## Part 3

## Track 31

**Examiner:** Now, in this part of the test you're going to talk about something together for about two minutes. I'm going to describe a situation to you.
A man is at home with a broken leg and wants to find something to do to entertain himself.
Here are some things he could do. Talk together about the different things he could do and say which one would be best.
All right? Now talk together.

**Candidate A:** OK, this person has a broken leg, so do you think any of these things would be good for him?

[PAUSE FOR YOU TO ANSWER]

**Candidate A:** I agree. He might enjoy a game of chess, but he might be on his own. What about the TV?

[PAUSE FOR YOU TO ANSWER]

**Candidate A:** Yes, I think the laptop is better than the TV, actually. But maybe the phone is even better. I use my phone to watch things online. The man can also use it to call his friends. I think this is better than the cards because he might get bored with them.

[PAUSE FOR YOU TO ANSWER]

**Candidate A:** Definitely. Let's say the phone.
**Examiner:** Thank you.

## Part 4

## Track 32

**Examiner:** What do you like to do if you're very tired, Candidate A?
**Candidate A:** If I'm feeling very tired, I like to stay at home and lie on the sofa with a good book or watch the TV.
**Examiner:** And what about you, Candidate B?

[PAUSE FOR YOU TO ANSWER]

**Examiner:** Do you think it's important for people to keep as active as possible, Candidate B?

[PAUSE FOR YOU TO ANSWER]

**Examiner:** And how about you, Candidate A?
**Candidate A:** I agree. A lot of people spend hours on their phones, and this isn't healthy. I also think going for a walk is a good idea, especially for people who don't like exercise.
**Examiner:** Candidate B, do you go to bed very late sometimes?

[PAUSE FOR YOU TO ANSWER]

**Examiner:** And what about you, Candidate A?
**Candidate A:** It's important for me that I get a lot of sleep or I feel tired at work. If there's something I want to watch on TV I sometimes stay up late but that's really the only time.
**Examiner:** Thank you. That is the end of the test.

## TEST 5     LISTENING

## Part 1

## Track 33

*Preliminary English Test, Listening*
*There are four parts to the test. You will hear each part twice.*
*We will now stop for a moment.*
*Please ask any questions now, because you must not speak during the test.*
*Now look at the instructions for Part 1.*
*For each question, choose the correct answer.*

*Look at Question 1.*

**1   Which of the following needs attention?**

**Man:** Barbara, it's me, Charlie. I've just got back from work. I've noticed the window in the garage has been broken. I think one of the branches came down from next door's tree during the storm and hit it. The branch is in front of the garden gate. I'll call someone to have a look at it tomorrow. See you when you get home from work.

*Now listen again.*

**2**  *Which item will be cheaper soon?*

Woman:  Can I help you sir?

Man:  I'm just looking at the moment. I bought my trainers from you a few months ago during the sale and I thought I'd come back to see what else you have in store.

Woman:  Well, we're planning to reduce some of our running shorts next week, so feel free to have a look at them.

Man:  Thanks. I'll buy a pair of running socks while I'm here. I can get them cheaper online, but I like to support local shops.

*Now listen again.*

**3**  *When is the man starting his course?*

Woman:  Have you organised everything for your training course?

Man:  Yes, I think so. I've booked the train tickets. I leave on Friday and return on Sunday.

Woman:  And what about accommodation?

Man:  I've got somewhere for Friday night. The course begins on Saturday and there's a chance they can provide a room for Saturday so I'm going to wait and see.

Woman:  OK, have a great time.

*Now listen again.*

**4**  *What does the woman say they need for the party?*

Man:  I'm just going to the shops. Do we need anything else for the kids' party?

Woman:  We've got plenty of plates. I bought some paper ones yesterday. I'm not sure about paper cups though.

Man:  I think there are some in the cupboard. I'll check before I go out.

Woman:  OK. We've got enough knives and forks. But I wonder if they're suitable. I think small wooden ones might be better for the children as they can be recycled. See if you can find any in the supermarket.

*Now listen again.*

**5**  *What did the man leave at work?*

Man:  Hi, it's John here from the sales department. If someone could get a message to the cleaners, I'd be very grateful. I was in a hurry this evening to get ready to leave and dropped my wallet. All the cards and money fell out. I thought I'd found everything but I've just noticed there's a credit card missing. If one of the cleaners finds it, could they give me a ring on my mobile? My number's on the staff noticeboard.

*Now listen again.*

**6**  *Where is the woman going on holiday?*

Man:  Do you have a holiday planned for this year?

Woman:  I think so. I was hoping we'd go to Italy again. We went there last year, to Rome, and had a wonderful time.

Man:  So, it's Italy then?

Woman:  Well, the children say they want to go somewhere different. Our eldest daughter is studying Spanish, so somewhere in Spain would have been perfect. But eventually we agreed on Greece as none of us have been there before. Spain will have to wait until next year.

*Now listen again.*

**7**  *Which platform is the 9.30 train to London leaving from?*

Woman:  Good morning ladies and gentlemen. Please listen carefully to the following announcement about arrivals and departures. Passengers travelling to London should catch the 9.30 train from Platform 11. This is a change from the timetable and it isn't departing from Platform 10 now. For those of you waiting for the arrival of the 9.15 train from London, we regret to inform you that this has been delayed but it will be arriving at Platform 14 at 9.45.

*Now listen again.*

*That is the end of Part 1.*

## Part 2

## Track 34

*Now look at Part 2. For each question, choose the correct answer.*

**8**  *You will hear two friends discussing what to do in the afternoon.*

Man:  Do you still fancy going out for a walk this afternoon?

Woman:  Yes, but shall we see what the weather's like first? The forecast says we're going to get heavy rain.

Man:  OK, but I really don't want to stay in. We can have a look around the shopping centre in town if it rains. That's all indoors.

Woman:  I want to go out too but not more shopping, please. I've already spent too much money this month.

Man:  Yes, me too. Yes, let's see if the forecast is correct before we decide.

*Now listen again.*

**9**  *You will hear two friends talking about keeping fit.*

Man:  Have you decided to renew your gym membership?

Woman:  I'm not sure really. I don't know if it's doing me any good.

Man:  Why don't you try swimming? You're a good swimmer.

| Woman: | I could do I suppose. It might be more fun than the gym. |
|---|---|
| Man: | I don't think there's a better way to keep fit. Plus, that new swimming pool is huge. I always find swimming pools get crowded and you get in each other's way, but that's not a problem in the new one. |

*Now listen again.*

**10** *You will hear a woman telling a friend about a handbag.*

| Woman: | Can you pass me the laptop? I need to write an email complaining about that handbag. |
|---|---|
| Man: | What's the problem with it? |
| Woman: | Well, I've already sent one back. I ordered one in brown and they sent me a black one. I really don't like black so I returned it and they sent me the correct one. But look, the handle is coming off. |
| Man: | Oh yes. That's not very good is it? |
| Woman: | No, it's not. And what makes me angry is I have to keep going to the post office to post it back. It doesn't cost anything but it's annoying and a waste of time. |

*Now listen again.*

**11** *You will hear two friends talking about a new doctor.*

| Man: | I've got to make an appointment with that new doctor tomorrow. Have you seen him yet? |
|---|---|
| Woman: | Yes, I went to the clinic a couple of weeks ago. Doctor Collins. He's a lot younger than the last doctor, and very caring. |
| Man: | Good, I was hoping he'd be better than the last doctor we had. |
| Woman: | I know. That one never seemed to listen to what you were saying, did he? You should phone early for your appointment though. The new one is the only doctor there at the moment, so he'll get booked up very quickly. |

*Now listen again.*

**12** *You will hear two friends talking about a storm.*

| Woman: | Was there anything interesting on the news tonight? |
|---|---|
| Man: | They're still reporting on the storm that happened last night. They said we had a month's rain in one night. |
| Woman: | It was terrible, wasn't it? There's been so much damage to people's property. |
| Man: | Our area escaped the worst of it. It seemed to affect the northern parts of the country most. They think there's another storm heading our way at the end of the week. It's not going to be quite as bad but we still need to take care. |

*Now listen again.*

**13** *You will hear a woman telling a friend about her noisy neighbours.*

| Woman: | Ever since those people moved into the flat upstairs, I haven't been able to sleep properly. |
|---|---|
| Man: | Why is that? Do they make a noise? |
| Woman: | Yes, they play music quite loudly late at night and they seem to have a party almost every weekend. |
| Man: | Have you spoken to them about it? |
| Woman: | Not yet. My husband thinks we should knock on their door and tell them to be quiet but I'm thinking of asking them round for dinner. It will be a nice thing to do and then if we do need to complain in the future, they might be more likely to agree. |

*Now listen again.*

*That is the end of Part 2.*

# Part 3

# Track 35

*Now look at Part 3.*
*For each question, write the correct answer in the gap.*
*Write one or two words or a number or a date or a time.*
*Look at Questions 14 to 19 now. You have 20 seconds.*

*You will hear a radio presenter called William talking about a photography course he did.*

| William: | I had a great time away on holiday and one of the things I did was go on a two-day photography course about taking photos of people. It was for beginners and I was given quite a few tips, some of which I think are really useful. |
|---|---|
| | For example, getting your position correct is really important. They said a common mistake is to stand too far away from the person. You get a much better result if you get close to them as they take up more of the photo. It's also important to make sure the camera is at the same height as the person, especially if you're taking one of a child. A really useful tip was to pay attention to the background. The person will stand out much more if the background is as plain as possible. This will help you to focus on the subject of your photo. Although most smartphones come with a flash to provide extra light, they suggested try to make as much use as possible of daylight. Doing this will make the colours more accurate and the photo will appear more natural. We're all used to asking someone to 'say cheese' when we're about to take their photo. To get a more interesting picture, they recommended taking a photo of |

the person when they don't know you're about to do it. Perhaps they're reading or looking out of the window.

Finally, they told us to take plenty of photos so we can practise our skills. They said we should aim to take at least three photos of people every day. These can be of friends and family or even strangers, if you ask their permission.

*Now listen again.*

*That is the end of Part 3.*

## Part 4

## Track 36

*Now look at Part 4.*
*For each question, choose the correct answer.*
*Look at Questions 20 to 25 now.*
*You have 45 seconds.*

*You will hear an interview with a woman called Penelope Leigh, giving advice on how to revise.*

| | |
|---|---|
| Interviewer: | I'm really pleased to have Penelope Leigh with us today to talk about the best ways to revise in preparation for an exam. What's your number one piece of advice, Penelope? |
| Penelope: | Well, some students might not like to hear this but there's no easy solution. The best way to learn something is to understand it. This will put the information into your long-term memory and you're less likely to forget it. |
| Interviewer: | So how do we do that? It sounds quite challenging. |
| Penelope: | Some people choose to read things again and again, hoping this will help them remember. But most of the time, this doesn't work. You should underline or make a note of key points, and a great tip is to try explaining these points to a friend or relative. If you can explain it clearly, you probably understand it. |
| Interviewer: | What do you think about trying to revise a few days before an exam? |
| Penelope: | This isn't always a good idea. It's OK if you just want to go over things you've learnt in previous weeks or months but not to rely on this method on its own. Organise your revision over weeks, or even months, going over your notes occasionally to remind yourself of key points. |
| Interviewer: | Are some subjects easier to revise than others? |
| Penelope: | I'm not sure the subject matter is important. I think it's more about being interested in what you are learning. If the subject is boring it's more difficult to understand and |

learn the main points. Unfortunately, some of us have to learn subjects like these, so try to make them interesting by revising with someone who loves the subject. They may be able to help make it more interesting.

| | |
|---|---|
| Interviewer: | What about music? Can that help us concentrate? |
| Penelope: | It's difficult to say. I know some people love listening to their favourite tunes when they revise. I personally find it difficult to concentrate if a song comes on that I love. And actually, research has been carried out that showed listening to music doesn't improve our ability to revise, so it's not something I would do. |
| Interviewer: | OK, so any more tips for students who are listening? |
| Penelope: | OK, let's imagine you've successfully understood key points and just want to remember them for the exam. Try making a word out of the first letters of each key point. Then all you need to do is remember the word. Or make a story using the key points. These are better ways of learning than trying to remember lists on their own. |

*Now listen again.*

*That is the end of Part 4.*

*You now have six minutes to write your answers on the answer sheet.*

*That is the end of the test.*

## TEST 5    SPEAKING

## Part 1

## Track 37

| | |
|---|---|
| Examiner: | Good afternoon.<br>Can I have your mark sheets, please?<br>I'm Louise Reece and this is Patrick Lovell.<br>What's your name? |
| Candidate A: | My name's Ester Boydochenko. |
| Examiner: | Where do you live? |
| Candidate A: | I live near Moscow, in Russia. |
| Examiner: | And what's your name, Candidate B? |
| [PAUSE FOR YOU TO ANSWER] | |
| Examiner: | Where do you come from, Candidate B? |
| [PAUSE FOR YOU TO ANSWER] | |
| Examiner: | Candidate B, do you work or are you a student? |
| [PAUSE FOR YOU TO ANSWER] | |
| Examiner: | What do you do, Candidate B? |
| [PAUSE FOR YOU TO ANSWER] | |

| | |
|---|---|
| Examiner: | And Candidate A, do you work or are you a student? |
| Candidate A: | I'm a student. |
| Examiner: | What do you study? |
| Candidate A: | I'm studying physics at university. I started my course last year. |
| Examiner: | Thank you. |
| Examiner: | Candidate A, what kind of films do you like to watch? |
| Candidate A: | I enjoy lots of different films. Sometimes I like to see a thriller and another time a comedy. I don't really like romantic films though. |
| Examiner: | Candidate B, what about you? |

[PAUSE FOR YOU TO ANSWER]

| | |
|---|---|
| Examiner: | Candidate A, do you prefer watching films at home or at the cinema? |
| Candidate A: | I prefer going to the cinema. It's much better to see films on a big screen and the sound effects are much clearer in a cinema |
| Examiner: | Candidate B, how often do you see your friends? |

[PAUSE FOR YOU TO ANSWER]

| | |
|---|---|
| Examiner: | Thank you. |

## Part 2

## Track 38

| | |
|---|---|
| Examiner: | Now I'd like each of you to talk on your own about something. I'm going to give each of you a photograph and I'd like you to talk about it. Candidate A, here is your photograph. It shows people doing some exercise outside. Please tell us what you can see in the photograph. Candidate B, you just listen. |
| Candidate A: | This photo was taken outside in a park. There are five people all looking at the camera while they do their exercises. They're standing on the grass near a tree. I think this looks like a park in a city. There are two women and three men. They look like they are wearing a kind of uniform. They all have dark tracksuit trousers on and a top. They are all quite old and the exercise they are doing is quite easy. They are lifting their right arms over their heads. It's a nice sunny day and they all seem to be enjoying themselves. |
| Examiner: | Thank you. |
| Examiner: | Candidate B, here is your photograph. It shows three people in a kitchen. |

| | |
|---|---|
| | Please tell us what you can see in the photograph. Candidate A, you just listen. |

[PAUSE FOR YOU TO ANSWER]

| | |
|---|---|
| Examiner: | Thank you. |

## Part 3

## Track 39

| | |
|---|---|
| Examiner: | Now, in this part of the test you're going to talk about something together for about two minutes. I'm going to describe a situation to you. A family are thinking of buying a pet for their young son. They want to get something that the boy can help take care of. Here are some pets they could get. Talk together about the different pets they could get for their son and say which one would be best. All right? Now talk together. |
| Candidate A: | Shall I start? |

[PAUSE FOR YOU TO ANSWER]

| | |
|---|---|
| Candidate A: | Well, we don't know how old the boy is but if he is very young they need something that is OK with little children. Do you think the snake is a good idea? |

[PAUSE FOR YOU TO ANSWER]

| | |
|---|---|
| Candidate A: | I agree. A fish like this one would be easy to keep, wouldn't it? You only need to feed it occasionally and change the water sometimes. The boy could do that, couldn't he? |

[PAUSE FOR YOU TO ANSWER]

| | |
|---|---|
| Candidate A: | I think that would be better than the fish. You can hold the rabbit and it's not as small as the mouse. I don't think the child would hurt it. Do you agree? |

[PAUSE FOR YOU TO ANSWER]

| | |
|---|---|
| Candidate A: | Yes, let's say the rabbit. |
| Examiner: | Thank you. |

## Part 4

## Track 40

| | |
|---|---|
| Examiner: | Do you have a pet, Candidate A? |
| Candidate A: | Yes, we have a cat. She's called Penny. She's quite old now and spends most of the day sleeping. |
| Examiner: | And what about you, Candidate B? |

[PAUSE FOR YOU TO ANSWER]

| | |
|---|---|
| Examiner: | Candidate B, which do you think is the best pet? |

[PAUSE FOR YOU TO ANSWER]

| | |
|---|---|
| Examiner: | And how about you, Candidate A? |

| Candidate A: | Well, apart from our cat I think a rabbit would be good. Some rabbits are really pretty and they're quite easy to take care of, I think. |
| Examiner: | Candidate B, is it important for a child to have a pet? |

[PAUSE FOR YOU TO ANSWER]

| Examiner: | And what about you, Candidate A? |
| Candidate A: | Yes, I agree. I think we have to be responsible when we have a pet. We have to remember to feed it, to make sure it's healthy. A child can learn from this. |
| Examiner: | Thank you. That is the end of the test. |

## TEST 6   LISTENING

### Part 1

# Track 41

*Preliminary English Test, Listening*
*There are four parts to the test. You will hear each part twice.*
*We will now stop for a moment.*
*Please ask any questions now, because you must not speak during the test.*
*Now look at the instructions for Part 1.*
*For each question, choose the correct answer.*

*Look at Question 1.*

**1**   *Where does the man think he last saw his keys?*

| Man: | Hiya. I've just got into work and realised I don't have my house keys in my pocket. Could you have a look to see if you can find them? The last thing I remember is putting them on the kitchen table when I was having breakfast, but I'm sure I picked them up. I sometimes leave them on the bed while I'm getting ready, or maybe they fell out of my pocket and they're on the chair. Call me back if you find them. |

*Now listen again.*

**2**   *What does the man want to eat more of?*

| Man: | I'm going to start being more careful about what I eat. |
| Woman: | That's good to hear. |
| Man: | You know how much I love cheese. It's delicious but not exactly healthy. |
| Woman: | I keep telling you to eat more fruit. We buy it each week and it never gets eaten. |
| Man: | I know. I'll start taking an apple to work every day, I think. And I might try to reduce the amount of bread I eat too. That will be a good start at least. |

*Now listen again.*

**3**   *What is the woman going to do next Wednesday?*

| Man: | I hear you've got a day's holiday next Wednesday. I was wondering whether you fancied a game of tennis. |
| Woman: | I'm not sure. My husband's playing golf that day and I need to collect the kids from school in the afternoon. What time were you thinking of going? |
| Man: | What about lunchtime? |
| Woman: | Well, I was planning to meet a friend to go cycling in the morning but she can't come, so I think I'm free then. |
| Man: | OK, let's put it in the diary. |

*Now listen again.*

**4**   *What is the woman interested in buying?*

| Man: | Hello, madam. Can I help you? |
| Woman: | Yes, hello. I was in here the other week. You were showing me some of the rugs you have. |
| Man: | Yes, I remember. Have you chosen one you like? |
| Woman: | I've changed my mind about that now. But I was looking at the sofa over there. I'm wondering whether it would fit in my room. I have quite a large cupboard and I'm not sure there's enough space. Could you tell me how long it is? |
| Man: | No problem, I'll measure it for you. |

*Now listen again.*

**5**   *Why has the walk been cancelled?*

| Woman: | Hello, I'm phoning to tell you some disappointing news about the walk that we'd planned for this weekend. We've decided to cancel it because of the latest weather forecast. They say the snow that had been forecast isn't likely to arrive, but they're forecasting heavy rain and we think it would make walking unpleasant. Never mind. At least there's going to be less wind than we've had, so we can use our umbrellas when we go out. |

*Now listen again.*

**6**   *What did the woman enjoy most about her holiday?*

| Man: | Welcome home. Did you have a nice holiday? |
| Woman: | We had a lovely time thanks. The hotel was OK for the price. |
| Man: | Great. So what did you do? |
| Woman: | Well, the kids spent most of the time in the hotel swimming pool. It was lovely to see them having so much fun, even though I can't swim and had to sit and watch them. On one afternoon I had the best time of all taking some photographs of the local area, which was absolutely beautiful. |

*Now listen again.*

**7**   *Which day does the man want to meet?*

Man: Hiya. I hope you're OK. I'm just calling about our night out next week. I know we'd arranged to go out on Thursday, but it looks like I've got visitors coming then, so I'll need to stay at home. Wednesday is usually a problem for me but I finish work early that day so I could meet then. Let's avoid Friday though, shall we? I know you love going out on Fridays, but it gets so busy in town, doesn't it? Let me know what you think.

*Now listen again.*

*That is the end of Part 1.*

## Part 2

## Track 42

*Now look at Part 2. For each question, choose the correct answer.*

**8** *You will hear a wife and her husband talking about housework.*

Woman: Have you seen how untidy the living room is? The children have left it in a mess again.

Man: I know. To be fair, they've done a lot more around the house since we spoke to them last week.

Woman: They started well, but I think we need to have another talk with them. We're both so busy trying to organise work and home. And I'd love to get some outside help but I'm not sure about your idea of getting a cleaner.

Man: OK, I'll have another talk with them later.

*Now listen again.*

**9** *You will hear two friends talking about a university.*

Man: So I hear you've decided on Melchester University. Is that right?

Woman: Yes. I've looked at a few now and I think that's the best for me.

Man: You were saying there are better ones for your subject area but I've been told it's still good.

Woman: I know, I'm happy with the course. I've now got to organise my accommodation.

Man: I've heard rent isn't too expensive there so you may be able to find somewhere nice. Once you've made some friends at university, you'll be able to share a place.

*Now listen again.*

**10** *You will hear two friends talking about the weather.*

Man: I'm really enjoying this sunny weather we've had lately, aren't you?

Woman: I know. It's lovely to wake up to a blue sky every morning, isn't it? It makes a change from all the rain we had last month.

Man: So, what are your plans for today?

Woman: I want to do some exercise if I can. I might go the gym as it's a bit cooler there. It's too warm to go running. I can't remember it being this warm before. I'm certainly not complaining though!

*Now listen again.*

**11** *You will hear two friends talking about a journey to work.*

Man: Getting to work in the morning seems to take longer each day. I was half an hour late this morning.

Woman: Are you still driving in?

Man: Yes, but I might stop using the car. The traffic is so bad early in the morning. It's a shame as I like using the car but it's just one traffic jam after another. There's no way I'm cycling in – it's too dangerous.

Woman: What about getting the train?

Man: I might do that. I know there were always delays in the past, but I've heard the service has improved.

*Now listen again.*

**12** *You will hear two friends talking about the local swimming pool.*

Woman: I haven't seen you at the swimming pool for a while. Have you stopped going?

Man: Yes, I haven't been recently, although last time I went there weren't too many people. We've been quite busy at work lately and I get home feeling really tired. That's no excuse though. I could always go at the weekend I suppose.

Woman: You should. It sounds like a swim is just what you need.

Man: I thought the changing rooms were clean and tidy, but I think they need better security. I didn't feel confident leaving my things in the locker, and after that I stopped going.

*Now listen again.*

**13** *You will hear two friends talking about visiting someone in hospital.*

Man: I'm going to visit Simon in hospital on Saturday if you want to join me.

Woman: Sorry but I can't make it at the weekend. Too much to do. I was planning to see him next week. If I give you some grapes could you give them to him?

Man: Of course.

Woman: How are you getting there? I was planning to go on the bus as it stops right outside.

Man: I'm driving there. You can park on the street outside quite easily.

Woman: OK, I'll see how I feel next week.

*Now listen again.*

*That is the end of Part 2.*

## Part 3

## Track 43

*Now look at Part 3.*
*For each question, write the correct answer in the gap.*
*Write one or two words or a number or a date or a time.*
*Look at Questions 14 to 19 now. You have 20 seconds.*

*You will hear a radio presenter called Ellen talking about local activities taking place over the summer.*

Ellen: If you're looking for things to do over the summer, there's lots going on in the area. I'll give you an idea of what you can do now, but for a full programme of events text 1576 and we'll send you a link to all the information you need.
To give you a taste of what's on offer, the Activity Centre is running a wide range of activities for all the family. There's climbing for beginners. This is indoors and will be led by experienced teachers. The centre has also organised a walk along the coast path for a look at some of the creatures you can find there. The centre is open seven days a week, with a special open day on the thirteenth of June to give you an idea of what else is on offer.
As you know, our town has a very long history, and those with an interest in the past can sign up for one of the guided walks the History Group has organised. Find out where a very well-known celebrity was born and learn about local industry in the past. You can find out more at the History Centre, which is located in the central library.
For film lovers, the Arts Centre has a full programme of films running throughout the summer months. And the Book Festival, which starts on the fourteenth of August, has several speakers on its programme and book readings by some well-known authors. This year they'll be organising a question and answer session for anyone interested in writing poetry. The Arts Centre expects this to be quite popular, so you should call them first to book a place.

*Now listen again.*

*That is the end of Part 3.*

## Part 4

## Track 44

*Now look at Part 4.*
*For each question, choose the correct answer.*
*Look at Questions 20 to 25 now.*
*You have 45 seconds.*

*You will hear an interview with a man called Matt Jennings, who helps people with online security.*

Interviewer: Today I'm speaking to Matt Jennings about using email safely.
Matt: Hi. Thanks for inviting me on. People are generally taking more care to protect themselves and noticing things that aren't correct, but at the same time criminals are getting better at inventing new ways to get what they want.
Interviewer: So give us some of your tips for email safety.
Matt: Let's start with the emails you might receive. Every day I get at least one telling me I need to change my password on a company website. Sometimes I don't even have an account with the company, so I know immediately that this email needs deleting. But if you do recognise the company and think you may have an account with them, do not click any links in the email.
Interviewer: So what should we do?
Matt: Go to the company website and log in with your personal details. If you're concerned about security, simply change your password on the website itself. The link in the email might take you to a website that looks like the company's but could be a copy. Any information you add will be seen by the criminals.
Interviewer: OK, so what's your next tip?
Matt: OK, there are emails that arrive telling you that someone is in trouble and needs your help urgently. I had one the other day from an email address of someone I know. It said they had lost their purse and needed money to get home. It started 'Dear Matt' and ended with the name of the person. To a lot of people, it would look OK.
Interviewer: So what did you do?
Matt: I certainly didn't send any money. Not long after, I received another email from the same address, this time from my friend. She explained that someone had got into her email account and had sent the earlier message. But even if she hadn't contacted me, I would have tried to phone her to check that everything was OK.
Interviewer: We need a strong password on our email account then?
Matt: Yes, on all your accounts really. And don't use passwords that people can easily guess. If you use words, and people do because they can remember them, change some letters for numbers, so use

1 instead of *i*, or zero instead of *o*. And start the password with an unusual character like a question mark or full stop. And make sure one of the letters is a capital.

*Now listen again.*

*That is the end of Part 4.*

*You now have six minutes to write your answers on the answer sheet.*

*That is the end of the test.*

## TEST 6    SPEAKING

### Part 1

## Track 45

| | |
|---|---|
| Examiner: | Good evening.<br>Can I have your mark sheets, please?<br>I'm Donald Edmondson and this is Sarah Hunt.<br>What's your name? |
| Candidate A: | My name's Martin Mostermans. |
| Examiner: | Where do you come from? |
| Candidate A: | I come from Amsterdam in the Netherlands. |
| Examiner: | And what's your name, Candidate B? |

[PAUSE FOR YOU TO ANSWER]

| | |
|---|---|
| Examiner: | Where do you live, Candidate B? |

[PAUSE FOR YOU TO ANSWER]

| | |
|---|---|
| Examiner: | Candidate B, do you work or are you a student? |

[PAUSE FOR YOU TO ANSWER]

| | |
|---|---|
| Examiner: | What do you study, Candidate B? |

[PAUSE FOR YOU TO ANSWER]

| | |
|---|---|
| Examiner: | And Candidate A, do you work or are you a student? |
| Candidate A: | I work. |
| Examiner: | What do you do? |
| Candidate A: | I'm an architect. Our office is in the centre of Amsterdam. |
| Examiner: | Thank you. |
| Examiner: | Candidate A, do you come from a big family? |
| Candidate A: | No, not really. I have a brother and a sister, but I don't have any uncles or aunts so it's quite a small family. |
| Examiner: | Candidate B, what about you? |

[PAUSE FOR YOU TO ANSWER]

| | |
|---|---|
| Examiner: | Candidate A, do you prefer to relax at the weekend or find a job to do? |
| Candidate A: | I like to find something to do. We have a garden so I often spend time working out there or doing jobs in the house. |
| Examiner: | Candidate B, how about you? |

[PAUSE FOR YOU TO ANSWER]

| | |
|---|---|
| Examiner: | Thank you. |

### Part 2

## Track 46

| | |
|---|---|
| Examiner: | Now I'd like each of you to talk on your own about something. I'm going to give each of you a photograph and I'd like you to talk about it.<br>Candidate A, here is your photograph. It shows people waiting for a train. Please tell us what you can see in the photograph.<br>Candidate B, you just listen. |
| Candidate A: | This photo shows four people waiting for a train on the platform at an underground train station. They're all dressed in smart clothes and it looks like they are going to work or going home at the end of the day. It could also be late at night because these are the only people on the platform. The woman nearest the camera is looking at her watch so the train might be late. Behind her in the photo are three men. Two of them are using their phones. One man is talking to someone and laughing about something and the other is looking at the screen and reading. |
| Examiner: | Thank you.<br>Candidate B, here is your photograph. It shows children at a party. Please tell us what you can see in the photograph.<br>Candidate A, you just listen. |

[PAUSE FOR YOU TO ANSWER]

| | |
|---|---|
| Examiner: | Thank you. |

### Part 3

## Track 47

| | |
|---|---|
| Examiner: | Now, in this part of the test you're going to talk about something together for about two minutes. I'm going to describe a situation to you.<br>A woman is going on a business trip for a few days. She is deciding what she needs to take with her.<br>Here are some things she could take. Talk together about the different things she could take and say which one would be most important.<br>All right? Now talk together. |
| Candidate A: | So, we have to decide how important these things are for the woman to take. What do you think? |

[PAUSE FOR YOU TO ANSWER]

| | |
|---|---|
| Candidate A: | That's true. And the camera isn't important either. She probably has a camera on her phone. What about the headphones and the radio? |

[PAUSE FOR YOU TO ANSWER]

Candidate A: I think they're all important. She probably needs the laptop for files or documents for meetings.

[PAUSE FOR YOU TO ANSWER]

Candidate A: I think the mobile phone is the most important. She can email any documents or files she needs before she leaves so she might not have to take her laptop. But it will be difficult if she doesn't have her phone.

[PAUSE FOR YOU TO ANSWER]

Candidate A: OK, let's say the mobile phone.
Examiner: Thank you.

## Part 4

## Track 48

Examiner: Candidate A, do you travel much?
Candidate A: I don't have to travel very much for work but I like travelling when I'm on holiday.
Examiner: And what about you, Candidate B?

[PAUSE FOR YOU TO ANSWER]

Examiner: Candidate B, do you find it easy to decide what to take when you travel?

[PAUSE FOR YOU TO ANSWER]

Examiner: And how about you, Candidate A?
Candidate A: I'm different. I always take lots of luggage, especially clothes. Last time I went on a trip I took too many clothes. I had a really big suitcase which was very heavy to carry. And then I didn't wear a lot of the clothes because it was very hot.
Examiner: Candidate B, is it important to be organised before we make a long journey?

[PAUSE FOR YOU TO ANSWER]

Examiner: And what about you, Candidate A?
Candidate A: Yes, I agree. Sometimes, getting ready for a trip can be quite stressful. I remember when I was younger, and we were going on holiday, my parents got stressed trying to organise everything for me and my brother.
Examiner: Thank you. That is the end of the test.

## TEST 7    LISTENING

## Part 1

## Track 49

*Preliminary English Test, Listening*
*There are four parts to the test. You will hear each part twice.*
*We will now stop for a moment.*
*Please ask any questions now, because you must not speak during the test.*
*Now look at the instructions for Part 1.*
*For each question, choose the correct answer.*

*Look at Question 1.*

**1**  *What time is the man's appointment?*
Man: Hello, I was wondering if I could get my hair cut sometime today.
Woman: Certainly, sir. Let me have a look. I'm afraid we're quite busy today. We don't have anything this morning, our hairdressers are all booked until 12.30. What about this afternoon? We have an empty hour at 1.30 and another at 3.30.
Man: 3.30 then. 1.30 would be great but I don't think I can get into town by then.
Woman: OK, we'll see you later today then.

*Now listen again.*

**2**  *Why is the woman going to be late for work?*
Woman: Hiya, I'm just calling to say I might be a little late this morning. I collected the car from the garage earlier and was hoping to get in on time, but I've just had a message to say my son's motorbike has been stolen. I've got to drive back and wait for the police to come round. Could someone meet my visitor at the station for me? He's arriving on the 9 o'clock train and I don't want him to think we've forgotten about him.

*Now listen again.*

**3**  *Which sport was the man unable watch on TV?*
Woman: Did you enjoy the match on Saturday?
Man: Yes, it was a great game and we won, which made it worth standing out in the rain all afternoon. I could have watched it on TV but I fancied going to the game.
Woman: And what about the basketball?
Man: I know, I was hoping to see that on TV when I got home but the kids were watching a film. I did get to see the swimming later in the evening though, after the children had gone to bed.

*Now listen again.*

**4**  *Where are floods expected to cause problems?*
Woman: If you're thinking of travelling over the next 24 hours you may need to pay attention to the weather. The heavy rain we've had over the past two days has meant there are likely to be floods, which will cause problems for travellers. Police have informed us they aren't expecting problems on the motorways at the moment but trains may be affected if water levels continue to rise. We've had no reports of flights being cancelled at the airports but please keep listening in case we have any updates.

*Now listen again.*

**5**  *How many people are going to the party so far?*
Woman: So we need to decide on food for the party. Any ideas?

**Man:** Yes, I know. I was going to order something this afternoon. I've got the numbers of about seven different companies. I'll call them all and try to get the best price. But I need to know how many people are coming.

**Woman:** I've invited about 30 people but I've only heard back from about 18 of them. I'm not sure about the others. Maybe we should wait a few more days before organising the food.

*Now listen again.*

**6** *What does the woman finally buy to drink?*

**Man:** Good afternoon, can I help you?

**Woman:** Yes, I just ordered this coffee but I'm afraid it's almost cold.

**Man:** Oh, I'm sorry about that. Let me get you another one.

**Woman:** Thanks, but the coffee looks a bit too strong for me. Is there any chance of having tea instead?

**Man:** No problem. Anything else, madam? Would you like a glass of water to go with the hot drink?

**Woman:** That's OK thanks. I had one with the coffee.

*Now listen again.*

**7** *When does the caller want to move into the flat?*

**Man:** Hello, I'm just phoning about the flat I went to look at yesterday. I really like it and I'm planning to come in today to ask a few questions before I sign the contract. Your colleague told me it was possible to move into the flat from the eleventh of August. However, I'm away on business until the eighteenth of August so wouldn't be able to move in that early. Is it possible to wait until the first of September and start paying rent from then?

*Now listen again.*

*That is the end of Part 1.*

## Part 2

## Track 50

*Now look at Part 2. For each question, choose the correct answer.*

**8** *You will hear a man talking to his wife about a podcast.*

**Man:** I downloaded a really interesting podcast yesterday about history.

**Woman:** Really? Do you think Jennifer would find it useful for her exams?

**Man:** I'm not sure it covers the subjects she's studying but the presenter is that guy on TV she loves, so that might interest her.

**Woman:** Does it cost anything?

**Man:** You can download the podcast for nothing. There's a course he offers that you need to pay for. But she might not want that if the topic is different. Let's see what she thinks of the podcast first.

*Now listen again.*

**9** *You will hear two friends talking about a new mobile phone.*

**Man:** So, are you enjoying your new phone? It certainly looks fantastic.

**Woman:** It's OK. It certainly cost enough! I'm not sure it's a big improvement on the previous one, to be honest.

**Man:** Why did you get a new one then?

**Woman:** Well, I was getting these emails encouraging me to get the latest model. The other one had a little bit of damage to the screen, which didn't look very nice. But it worked and I could do all the things I needed to do with it. Oh well, never mind!

*Now listen again.*

**10** *You will hear a woman talking to her husband about washing clothes.*

**Woman:** There's something wrong with the washing machine. It seems to go on forever!

**Man:** Not again! We've had problems with it ever since we bought it.

**Woman:** So, what should we do? We need to do the washing. Shall we get someone to have a look at it?

**Man:** I don't think it's worth it. We've had people out before and they're never cheap. I know we only bought it a couple of years ago but maybe it's time to think about getting a new one. Shall we have a look online?

*Now listen again.*

**11** *You will hear two friends talking about living in the countryside.*

**Man:** I've been watching that programme on TV about moving to the countryside.

**Woman:** That one about people who don't want to live in the city anymore? I like having lots of people around me. Being on my own somewhere in the countryside wouldn't suit me.

**Man:** True, but if you have a car it doesn't take long to get what you need. That wouldn't bother me. I know people think it's good for your health but not if you're unhappy living there.

*Now listen again.*

**12** *You will hear two friends talking about travelling by plane.*

Man: I've been thinking about the number of flights I take a year. It's not good for the environment.

Woman: I know. It's a worry, isn't it?

Man: It's more expensive to travel by train than to fly on some short journeys. No wonder people choose to go by plane.

Woman: I don't think putting the price up would be very popular, do you?

Man: I certainly wouldn't like it. I think we should avoid travelling abroad for our holidays. That would probably make a difference.

*Now listen again.*

**13** *You will hear two friends talking about a local businesswoman.*

Woman: I was reading about Emily Wainwright, the local businesswoman of the year.

Man: Mmm, she sounds like an interesting person, doesn't she? That new shop she has in town is doing really well. It's always busy when I go past.

Woman: She seems to be popular with other businesspeople too.

Man: I know. Her new business partner was on the radio the other day. He was explaining that she always recommends other local companies to customers and helps other women who are thinking of starting their own business.

*Now listen again.*

*That is the end of Part 2.*

## Part 3

## Track 51

*Now look at Part 3.*
*For each question, write the correct answer in the gap.*
*Write one or two words or a number or a date or a time.*
*Look at Questions 14 to 19 now. You have 20 seconds.*

*You will hear an announcement in a supermarket.*

Woman: Welcome to Milburn's. If you're looking for a sale or for something unusual, don't forget our Thursday 'Special Buy' day where you'll find some great offers. These change every week and are removed from the shelves at the end of the day. This Thursday you'll be able to buy a special gift for your pet with lots of items at low, low prices. Come early and don't miss our offers.

Are you interested in a career with Milburn's? We're looking for new staff in various areas of the business. There are now opportunities to join our trainee manager programme and several jobs for cleaners. We are proud of our staff and like to think they're proud to be part of the Milburn family. Why not speak to our manager today if you're interested in joining us? Or pick up our magazine at the exit for details about how to apply.

As the New Year approaches we know you'll need to get your shopping done ready for all the celebrations. We'll be opening until 10.30 on Friday evening to give you time to get ready for the big day. Don't forget we'll be closed on the first but open again on the second, when we return to normal opening hours.

We value our local community and are always looking for the chance to help out where we can. This month we're supporting the local Arts Project and the Children's Theatre Group. When you pay for your shopping you'll be given a ticket. To show your support, choose which of the organisations you would like to give this to by putting it in the box by the exit. We'll turn these into cash when they are counted up at the end of the month.

*Now listen again.*

*That is the end of Part 3.*

## Part 4

## Track 52

*Now look at Part 4.*
*For each question, choose the correct answer.*
*Look at Questions 20 to 25 now.*
*You have 45 seconds.*

*You will hear an interview with a woman called Florence Adams, who helps people with job interviews.*

Interviewer: Today I'm speaking to Florence Adams about how to prepare for job interviews. Florence, how should we prepare for an interview?

Florence: Start by researching the company. This will help you understand how you might 'fit' with them. Do they have strong links with the local area? Do they have offices abroad, are they serious about environmental issues? If these things matter to you you'll have lots in common.

Interviewer: I suppose we need to show we really want the job.

Florence: Yes, it's important that you're clear why you want to work for the company. Going back to what I said earlier, perhaps your values are similar, or maybe having researched the company you can see they offer great career opportunities. What is it about the job that appeals to you?

Interviewer: And what about those difficult questions we get asked?

| Florence: | Think about your weak areas and how you might answer any challenging questions. Few of us are perfect and you may not have much experience in a particular area. Ask if there are any training opportunities the company can offer. Is there anything you can do before the interview? If you tell them you're already intending to improve these things, it will look great. |
|---|---|
| Interviewer: | And we need to ask the company questions as well, don't we? |
| Florence: | Certainly. Don't feel you need to wait to be asked. As well as helping you understand what you'll be responsible for in the job, some questions you ask can show employers more about what you're like. For example, questions about career opportunities will show you're serious about working for the company. Questions about training will show you want to develop your skills. |
| Interviewer: | And I suppose it's useful to practise before the interview. |
| Florence: | Definitely. There are lots of sites on the internet where you can download example interview questions. Ask a friend or relative to download some questions and interview you. Don't ask to see the list first. This will give you the chance to try to answer questions without preparing for them. |
| Interviewer: | Anything else we should do? |
| Florence: | The first few minutes or even seconds of the interview are extremely important. Smile at the interviewer when you enter the room. Look confident when you walk in – stand tall with your shoulders back. Wait until you're invited to sit down and then try to relax. Don't look at the floor or ceiling when you're answering a question but at the person or people in front of you. |

*Now listen again.*

*That is the end of Part 4.*

*You now have six minutes to write your answers on the answer sheet.*

*That is the end of the test.*

### TEST 7    SPEAKING

### Part 1

### Track 53

| Examiner: | Good morning. Can I have your mark sheets, please? I'm Hannah King and this is Richard Brown. What's your name? |
|---|---|
| Candidate A: | My name's Anne-Marie Dubois. |

| Examiner: | Where do you live? |
|---|---|
| Candidate A: | I live in Lyon, in France. |
| Examiner: | And what's your name, Candidate B? |

[PAUSE FOR YOU TO ANSWER]

| Examiner: | Where do you come from, Candidate B? |
|---|---|

[PAUSE FOR YOU TO ANSWER]

| Examiner: | Candidate B, do you work or are you a student? |
|---|---|

[PAUSE FOR YOU TO ANSWER]

| Examiner: | What do you do, Candidate B? |
|---|---|

[PAUSE FOR YOU TO ANSWER]

| Examiner: | And Candidate A, do you work or are you a student? |
|---|---|
| Candidate A: | I'm a student. |
| Examiner: | What do you study? |
| Candidate A: | I'm studying history but I don't know what job I want to do when I finish my course. |
| Examiner: | Thank you. |
| Examiner: | Candidate A, what's your favourite way of travelling? |
| Candidate A: | I like travelling by train. It's usually quite fast and you can also relax and do some work or read during the journey. |
| Examiner: | Candidate B, what about you? |

[PAUSE FOR YOU TO ANSWER]

| Examiner: | Candidate A, how often do you eat in a restaurant? |
|---|---|
| Candidate A: | Not very often. I go if it's a special occasion like a birthday party, but I'm a student and I haven't got much money, so I usually eat at home. |
| Examiner: | Candidate B, and what about you? |

[PAUSE FOR YOU TO ANSWER]

| Examiner: | Thank you. |
|---|---|

### Part 2

### Track 54

| Examiner: | Now I'd like each of you to talk on your own about something. I'm going to give each of you a photograph and I'd like you to talk about it. Candidate A, here is your photograph. It shows a group of people. Please tell us what you can see in the photograph. Candidate B, you just listen. |
|---|---|
| Candidate A: | In this photo I can see four people sitting together in the living room of someone's house. I think they're watching TV and it's probably a football match because one of the men in the group is holding a football. There's another man sitting on the floor. He has a beard. He looks worried. He's waiting to see what will happen in the match. There's a woman and she's holding a bowl. I |

think there is food in the bowl. She looks very happy so I think the team she supports has scored a goal. No one is eating the food in the bowl because everyone is waiting to see what happens.

| Examiner: | Thank you. |
| | Candidate B, here is your photograph. It shows two people. |
| | Please tell us what you can see in the photograph. |
| | Candidate A, you just listen. |

[PAUSE FOR YOU TO ANSWER]

| Examiner: | Thank you. |

## Part 3

## Track 55

| Examiner: | Now, in this part of the test you're going to talk about something together for about two minutes. I'm going to describe a situation to you. A couple want to buy their six-year-old daughter a present for her birthday. |
| | Here are some things they could get. Talk together about the different things they could buy and say which one would be best. |
| | All right? Now talk together. |
| Candidate A: | So, we have to decide on a birthday present and the girl is six years old. |

[PAUSE FOR YOU TO ANSWER]

| Candidate A: | I agree. We should choose something that she will get excited about. I don't think a birthday cake is a good present. The parents should get her one of those anyway, don't you think? |

[PAUSE FOR YOU TO ANSWER]

| Candidate A: | Yes, children love it when their parents read them stories. That's one idea. I don't think they should buy her sweets. That's like the cake. Not really a good present. |

[PAUSE FOR YOU TO ANSWER]

| Candidate A: | Well, children love drawing so I definitely think the pencils are the best present. What about you? |

[PAUSE FOR YOU TO ANSWER]

| Candidate A: | Yes, so we say the colouring pencils. |
| Examiner: | Thank you. |

## Part 4

## Track 56

| Examiner: | Candidate A, do you remember birthdays when you were young? |
| Candidate A: | Yes, my mum and dad used to invite my relations to our house. We played |

party games and had lots of food. We had a big family and I really enjoyed these parties.

| Examiner: | Candidate B, and what about you? |

[PAUSE FOR YOU TO ANSWER]

| Examiner: | Candidate B, can you remember any presents you were given when you were young? |

[PAUSE FOR YOU TO ANSWER]

| Examiner: | And how about you, Candidate A? |
| Candidate A: | I can't remember one present but I did spend a lot of time drawing and painting when I was little so I'm sure I got pens and paints for my birthday. |
| Examiner: | Candidate B, is it important for children to have a birthday party? |

[PAUSE FOR YOU TO ANSWER]

| Examiner: | Candidate A, and what about you? |
| Candidate A: | I think a party is a nice idea because it's something you remember when you're older. But some children don't want a party. My brother was shy when he was little and never wanted to have a party. |
| Examiner: | Thank you. That is the end of the test. |

## TEST 8    LISTENING

## Part 1

## Track 57

*Preliminary English Test, Listening*
*There are four parts to the test. You will hear each part twice.*
*We will now stop for a moment.*
*Please ask any questions now, because you must not speak during the test.*
*Now look at the instructions for Part 1.*
*For each question, choose the correct answer.*

*Look at Question 1.*

**1**  *What time does reception open?*

| Woman: | Hello. You are through to Doctor Andrews. I'm afraid we are now closed for the weekend and we open again on Monday. If you have medicine or a note to collect, you can speak to a receptionist who will be able to assist you from 8.30. I will be available to see patients from 9.00. If you can't come in, another doctor may be able to help you on the phone. She can be contacted from 9.30, though may not be available if she's out visiting someone at home. |

*Now listen again.*

**2**  *When is the best month to plant the seeds?*

| Man: | I was thinking of planting some of these flowers out next year, but I've never grown them before. |

| Woman: | Oh, they'll be lovely if you can time everything just right. I made the mistake of planting them out in January, but the ground was too wet. |
|---|---|
| Man: | So a little later then? |
| Woman: | Definitely. It says you can start them in February on the packet. Personally, I don't think it's a bad idea to wait until March. The ground will be much drier then. |

*Now listen again.*

**3** *Where did the man buy his shirt?*

| Woman: | You're looking very smart. I love your shirt. |
|---|---|
| Man: | Thanks. Yes, I got it the other week. I'd seen one in that new shop in town and loved it. I tried it on and it was a perfect fit. But it was really expensive! |
| Woman: | I know. Things in that shop aren't cheap. |
| Man: | Anyway, I saw a similar one in the market at the weekend. It wasn't anywhere as nice quality, so I looked online and got this one. I'm really pleased with it. |

*Now listen again.*

**4** *How much is one adult ticket to the football match?*

| Woman: | Turning now to football, and Mark phoned to ask about the cost of tickets for him and his 13-year-old son. Well Mark, now would be a good time to book your ticket. The club are organising a family day and are offering tickets for four people at £60. If there are just the two of you, a single ticket is £25 and children under 14 can get in for £15. So, the question is, are there any other family members you can persuade to join you, Mark? |
|---|---|

*Now listen again.*

**5** *What is it that needs replacing?*

| Woman: | I'm going into town later. Did you say the iron wasn't working? I might get a new one. |
|---|---|
| Man: | I thought there was something wrong with it but it's OK. We did say we would get another microwave. Have you noticed the door doesn't shut properly? |
| Woman: | I know but I can't carry one of them back home on my own. Let's look for one at the weekend. |
| Man: | OK. Hopefully the kettle still works. Do you want a cup of tea? |

*Now listen again.*

**6** *Where does the man want his wife to come?*

| Man: | Hiya. Just phoning to let you know we're having a lovely time. We spent the morning walking around the city centre. |
|---|---|

Jamie wanted to have a tour of the football stadium but they only do those on Wednesdays so I said we'd come back and do that another week. He wants you to come and meet us later, so I thought we could go and see a film together. I suggested the museum, but he didn't like that idea. Call me and let me know if you can come.

*Now listen again.*

**7** *When is Janine's birthday?*

| Man: | Have you bought Janine's birthday present yet? |
|---|---|
| Woman: | No, not yet. We're seeing her on the fifteenth, aren't we? I'll give her the present then. |
| Man: | Yes, we still have plenty of time. Are you going to her party? |
| Woman: | I've told her I can't go. It's on the sixteenth and I'm away at a conference that weekend. Still, I'll give her a call on her birthday. |
| Man: | Yes, that's the thirteenth. I've arranged to see her, so I'll send her your love. |

*Now listen again.*

*That is the end of Part 1.*

## Part 2

## Track 58

*Now look at Part 2. For each question, choose the correct answer.*

**8** *You will hear two friends talking about a sales assistant.*

| Man: | Have you just been shopping? |
|---|---|
| Woman: | Yes, I went to that computer shop to have a look at their laptops. |
| Man: | Did you buy one? |
| Woman: | No, not yet, but I had an interesting chat with one of the sales assistants who worked there. I thought he was new but he's worked there for quite a while. He was so helpful. He took the time to explain the difference between the laptops and if he wasn't able to answer a question, he went and found the manager to ask for his opinion. |

*Now listen again.*

**9** *You will hear two friends talking about saving for when they retire.*

| Woman: | My bank sent me a letter about opening a savings account for when I retire. |
|---|---|
| Man: | Did they? It's a really good idea. Even when you're young like us, the sooner you start to save something each month the more you'll have when you finish work. If you leave it too long, you end up having to save more each month. |

Woman: Not everyone can afford it though, can they?

Man: Some people would definitely find it hard, I agree. But I think young people realise how important it is and are willing to make an effort.

*Now listen again.*

**10** *You will hear a husband and wife talking about a holiday.*

Woman: What about this year's holiday? Where do you fancy going? Anywhere nice?

Man: Somewhere warm and sunny, hopefully. Claire and Adam were talking about going with them again.

Woman: Were they? I think the kids would prefer to have a family holiday this year. Just the four of us. What do you think?

Man: OK. Shall we have a look on the internet?

Woman: Let's go into the travel agents instead. It might be more expensive, but I'd like to go somewhere we haven't been to before and they might be able to suggest somewhere.

*Now listen again.*

**11** *You will hear two friends talking about the local library.*

Woman: Have you heard? They're thinking of closing our library.

Man: I know. They've been recording the number of visitors that libraries in the city get, and our one is supposed to be very quiet.

Woman: But I'll really miss it if we lose it.

Man: Me too. And it's so important to have a local library for the children. Some families don't have a house full of books and a library is somewhere children can discover the pleasure in reading. And once they close it I don't suppose there will ever be another one.

*Now listen again.*

**12** *You will hear two friends talking about doing a presentation.*

Man: It's your interview tomorrow, isn't it?

Woman: Yes, 9.30 in the morning. I finally finished my presentation last night. I just hope nothing goes wrong with the laptop. You know what it's like relying on things like that.

Man: How about speaking in front of people? Have you done a presentation before?

Woman: Yes, a few times. I'll be nervous for sure, but once I get started, I'll be OK. And I've spent ages researching the subject, so I'll have plenty to talk about. Wish me luck!

Man: Yes, good luck. I'm sure you'll do well.

*Now listen again.*

**13** *You will hear two friends talking about working from home.*

Woman: How's your business going?

Man: It's good. It's strange working for myself and not having any meetings to go to, but I'm enjoying it.

Woman: Do you like working from home?

Man: I get jobs done more quickly. When I was working in the office I was always talking to other people and didn't concentrate on the job I was doing. I thought I'd feel a bit lonely working for myself, but I make sure I get out of the house every day and have a chat with people, so that's not a problem.

*Now listen again.*

*That is the end of Part 2.*

## Part 3

## Track 59

*Now look at Part 3.*
*For each question, write the correct answer in the gap. Write one or two words or a number or a date or a time. Look at Questions 14 to 19 now. You have 20 seconds.*

*You will hear a radio presenter telling new students about the first week at university.*

Woman: This will be a very exciting time for you. You've got the grades you needed and you're off to university. For many of you this will be the first time away from home. Write a list of things you should take with you, for example, your passport if you're planning to go travelling. You'll certainly need all the documentation the university has sent you about your course or accommodation. Don't bring too many household items with you. You'll be able to buy a lot of things at university. When you arrive and go to your room, check that everything is as it should be and in good condition. Report anything that looks damaged. You don't want to be blamed for this and be asked to pay any costs involved. This is also the time to get to meet new people. Don't lock yourself away in your room, but go to the kitchen as this is always the first place to introduce yourself to other students. During your first week you can enjoy Freshers' Week. This is the time to find out about all the clubs and societies you can join at university. These are great ways to get to know students doing different subjects. These people will help you forget about your studies when you need to relax and not talk about work. It's sensible to limit yourself to signing up to a maximum of five groups or you'll be receiving emails for weeks to come.

Don't forget the important things like registering with the local doctor as soon as you can. And think about your weekly shopping list. Don't spend too much but at the same time make sure you don't go hungry. And remember to put your name on your food. A shared fridge sometimes leads to arguments!

*Now listen again.*

*That is the end of Part 3.*

## Part 4

## Track 60

*Now look at Part 4.*
*For each question, choose the correct answer.*
*Look at Questions 20 to 25 now.*
*You have 45 seconds.*

*You will hear an interview with a woman called Carrie Lewis, who is talking about her reasons for travelling.*

| | |
|---|---|
| Interviewer: | We have Carrie Lewis on the show today, who has just returned from a four-month holiday in Europe. Have you always spent so long travelling? |
| Carrie: | During the past few years I have tried to do as much travelling as possible. I'm 22 and I know eventually I have to start a career, but at the moment I want to see as much of the world as possible before I have responsibilities like children. |
| Interviewer: | But where do you find the money to go on such long holidays? |
| Carrie: | Well, I certainly don't stay in expensive hotels. I wish I could. I often go camping or stay with people I have met on an earlier holiday. Most places have youth hostels that can be fairly cheap, though I haven't stayed in one for a while. Then of course you can always find work while you're travelling. |
| Interviewer: | Is that easy to do? |
| Carrie: | It depends where you are. It's usually easy to find work as a waiter or waitress, but it's a good idea to arrive early in the year as the jobs get taken quickly. In some countries you can work on farms picking fruit. A friend of mine found work in a hotel and I might try that myself next year. |
| Interviewer: | So where did you go this year? |
| Carrie: | I started in France and spent time travelling around some of the big cities. But I wanted to get to Greece to work in a restaurant. I had written to a few places before I left home and one of them had offered me work so I wanted to get there as soon as possible. I went by train and found a place to stay in Athens. |

| | |
|---|---|
| Interviewer: | And did you get the job? |
| Carrie: | I did. It was a lovely family restaurant in Athens, and they were looking for someone who could speak English to help with the customers. They've got children who can speak it but they weren't around over the summer, so they employed me. |
| Interviewer: | So that paid for your holiday then? |
| Carrie: | Most of it, yes. It was perfect for me as they only wanted me to work there during the week. That meant I could visit the islands at the weekend. I used to catch the boat on Friday evening, have two nights on an island somewhere and then get back on Sunday night ready for work. |

*Now listen again.*

*That is the end of Part 4.*

*You now have six minutes to write your answers on the answer sheet.*

*That is the end of the test.*

## TEST 8    SPEAKING

## Part 1

## Track 61

| | |
|---|---|
| Examiner: | Good afternoon. Can I have your mark sheets please? I'm Greg Miller and this is Gill Matthews. What's your name? |
| Candidate A: | My name's Suzanne Vojtek. |
| Examiner: | Where do you come from? |
| Candidate A: | I come from a small village in the Czech Republic. |
| Examiner: | And what's your name, Candidate B? |

[PAUSE FOR YOU TO ANSWER]

| | |
|---|---|
| Examiner: | Where do you live, Candidate B? |

[PAUSE FOR YOU TO ANSWER]

| | |
|---|---|
| Examiner: | Candidate B, do you work or are you a student? |

[PAUSE FOR YOU TO ANSWER]

| | |
|---|---|
| Examiner: | What do you do, Candidate B? |

[PAUSE FOR YOU TO ANSWER]

| | |
|---|---|
| Examiner: | And Candidate A, do you work or are you a student? |
| Candidate A: | I'm a student. |
| Examiner: | What do you study? |
| Candidate A: | I'm studying sports science. I started my course last year. |
| Examiner: | Thank you. |
| Examiner: | Candidate A, what kind of books do you like to read? |

| Candidate A: | I don't really read many books. I read a newspaper every day though and I get a magazine on photography once a month. |
| Examiner: | Candidate B, what about you? |

[PAUSE FOR YOU TO ANSWER]

| Examiner: | Candidate A, do you prefer books or e-books? |
| Candidate A: | I prefer books. I don't really like reading books on a screen. Reading a book is more enjoyable and I think it's often easier than looking at a small screen. |
| Examiner: | Candidate B, how often do you go to the cinema? |

[PAUSE FOR YOU TO ANSWER]

| Examiner: | Thank you. |

## Part 2

## Track 62

| Examiner: | Now I'd like each of you to talk on your own about something. I'm going to give each of you a photograph and I'd like you to talk about it. Candidate A, here is your photograph. It shows two young women enjoying themselves. Please tell us what you can see in the photograph. Candidate B, you just listen. |
| Candidate A: | This photo shows two young women enjoying themselves. I think they're on a bus on the top floor. It's the kind of bus that tourists use to go sightseeing around a city. It looks like summer as the women are wearing sunglasses and summer clothes. One of the women has a camera around her neck. One of the women who is furthest away from the camera is pointing at something and her friend is looking at what it is. It looks like you can see the sea in the background. I think they're on holiday or they've gone on a trip for the day. |
| Examiner: | Thank you. Candidate B, here is your photograph. It shows three people outside. Please tell us what you can see in the photograph. Candidate A, you just listen. |

[PAUSE FOR YOU TO ANSWER]

| Examiner: | Thank you. |

## Part 3

## Track 63

| Examiner: | Now, in this part of the test you're going to talk about something together for about two minutes. I'm going to describe a situation to you. |

A teenager is on his way home before dinner and wants to eat something on the way.
Here are some things he could eat on the way home.
Talk together about the different things he could eat and say which one would be best.
All right? Now talk together.

| Candidate A: | Would you like to start? |

[PAUSE FOR YOU TO ANSWER]

| Candidate A: | I agree. And really, he shouldn't eat anything that is too sweet. So I don't think the cake or the ice cream is a good idea, do you? And what about the chocolate? |

[PAUSE FOR YOU TO ANSWER]

| Candidate A: | He could try, but I think he'll probably eat it all. So, we don't think the ice cream, the cake or the chocolate are sensible. What about the pizza? |

[PAUSE FOR YOU TO ANSWER]

| Candidate A: | That's true. And the sandwich is the same. I don't think he should eat that. Isn't the best thing really the apple? |

[PAUSE FOR YOU TO ANSWER]

| Candidate A: | OK, I agree. He should have the apple on his way home. |
| Examiner: | Thank you. |

## Part 4

## Track 64

| Examiner: | Candidate A, do you like to eat snacks? |
| Candidate A: | Yes, sometimes, but I try to eat healthy food. I used to eat a lot of sweets and chocolate when I was younger, but I try to avoid that now. |
| Examiner: | Candidate B, and what about you? |

[PAUSE FOR YOU TO ANSWER]

| Examiner: | Candidate B, what do you think are the best things to eat for snacks? |

[PAUSE FOR YOU TO ANSWER]

| Examiner: | And how about you, Candidate A? |
| Candidate A: | I agree. Fruit is nice but eating chocolate makes you feel great. I try not to eat too much now though. |
| Examiner: | Candidate B, is it important to eat three meals a day? |

[PAUSE FOR YOU TO ANSWER]

| Examiner: | And what about you, Candidate A? |
| Candidate A: | I like to eat thee meals. We always go to a café for lunch at university and I have a meal when I go home. And I have breakfast of course. |
| Examiner: | Thank you. That is the end of the test. |

# Sample answer sheets

## Cambridge Assessment
English

| Candidate Name | | Candidate Number | |
|---|---|---|---|
| Centre Name | | Centre Number | |
| Examination Title | | Examination Details | |
| Candidate Signature | | Assessment Date | |

Supervisor: If the candidate is ABSENT or has WITHDRAWN shade here ○

## Preliminary Reading Candidate Answer Sheet

**Instructions**
Use a PENCIL (B or HB)
Rub out any answer you want to change with an eraser.

**For Parts 1, 2, 3, 4 and 5:**
Mark ONE letter for each answer.
For example: If you think A is the right answer to
the question, mark your answer sheet like this:

0  A● B○ C○

**Part 1**

| | A | B | C |
|---|---|---|---|
| 1 | ○ | ○ | ○ |
| 2 | ○ | ○ | ○ |
| 3 | ○ | ○ | ○ |
| 4 | ○ | ○ | ○ |
| 5 | ○ | ○ | ○ |

**Part 2**

| | A | B | C | D | E | F | G | H |
|---|---|---|---|---|---|---|---|---|
| 6 | ○ | ○ | ○ | ○ | ○ | ○ | ○ | ○ |
| 7 | ○ | ○ | ○ | ○ | ○ | ○ | ○ | ○ |
| 8 | ○ | ○ | ○ | ○ | ○ | ○ | ○ | ○ |
| 9 | ○ | ○ | ○ | ○ | ○ | ○ | ○ | ○ |
| 10 | ○ | ○ | ○ | ○ | ○ | ○ | ○ | ○ |

**Part 3**

| | A | B | C | D |
|---|---|---|---|---|
| 11 | ○ | ○ | ○ | ○ |
| 12 | ○ | ○ | ○ | ○ |
| 13 | ○ | ○ | ○ | ○ |
| 14 | ○ | ○ | ○ | ○ |
| 15 | ○ | ○ | ○ | ○ |

**Part 4**

| | A | B | C | D | E | F | G | H |
|---|---|---|---|---|---|---|---|---|
| 16 | ○ | ○ | ○ | ○ | ○ | ○ | ○ | ○ |
| 17 | ○ | ○ | ○ | ○ | ○ | ○ | ○ | ○ |
| 18 | ○ | ○ | ○ | ○ | ○ | ○ | ○ | ○ |
| 19 | ○ | ○ | ○ | ○ | ○ | ○ | ○ | ○ |
| 20 | ○ | ○ | ○ | ○ | ○ | ○ | ○ | ○ |

**Part 5**

| | A | B | C | D |
|---|---|---|---|---|
| 21 | ○ | ○ | ○ | ○ |
| 22 | ○ | ○ | ○ | ○ |
| 23 | ○ | ○ | ○ | ○ |
| 24 | ○ | ○ | ○ | ○ |
| 25 | ○ | ○ | ○ | ○ |
| 26 | ○ | ○ | ○ | ○ |

**Continues over ➡**

2150

**For Part 6:**

Write your answers clearly in the spaces next to the numbers (27 to 32) like this:

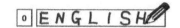

Write your answers in CAPITAL LETTERS.

| Part 6 | | Do not write below here |
|--------|--|-------------------------|
| 27 | | 27 1   0    O   O |
| 28 | | 28 1   0    O   O |
| 29 | | 29 1   0    O   O |
| 30 | | 30 1   0    O   O |
| 31 | | 31 1   0    O   O |
| 32 | | 32 1   0    O   O |

2150

## Cambridge Assessment
English

| Candidate Name | | Candidate Number | |
| --- | --- | --- | --- |
| Centre Name | | Centre Number | |
| Examination Title | | Examination Details | |
| Candidate Signature | | Assessment Date | |

Supervisor: If the candidate is ABSENT or has WITHDRAWN shade here ○

### Preliminary Listening Candidate Answer Sheet

**Instructions**
**Use a PENCIL (B or HB).** Rub out any answer you want to change with an eraser.

**For Parts 1, 2 and 4:**
Mark one letter for each answer. For example: If you think **A** is the right answer to the question, mark your answer sheet like this:

**For Part 3:**
Write your answers clearly in the spaces next to the numbers (14 to 19) like this:

Write your answers in CAPITAL LETTERS.

**Part 1**

| | A | B | C |
| --- | --- | --- | --- |
| 1 | ○ | ○ | ○ |
| 2 | ○ | ○ | ○ |
| 3 | ○ | ○ | ○ |
| 4 | ○ | ○ | ○ |
| 5 | ○ | ○ | ○ |
| 6 | ○ | ○ | ○ |
| 7 | ○ | ○ | ○ |

**Part 2**

| | A | B | C |
| --- | --- | --- | --- |
| 8 | ○ | ○ | ○ |
| 9 | ○ | ○ | ○ |
| 10 | ○ | ○ | ○ |
| 11 | ○ | ○ | ○ |
| 12 | ○ | ○ | ○ |
| 13 | ○ | ○ | ○ |

**Part 3**

| No. | Answer | Do not write below here |
| --- | --- | --- |
| 14 | | 14 1 ○  0 ○ |
| 15 | | 15 1 ○  0 ○ |
| 16 | | 16 1 ○  0 ○ |
| 17 | | 17 1 ○  0 ○ |
| 18 | | 18 1 ○  0 ○ |
| 19 | | 19 1 ○  0 ○ |

**Part 4**

| | A | B | C |
| --- | --- | --- | --- |
| 20 | ○ | ○ | ○ |
| 21 | ○ | ○ | ○ |
| 22 | ○ | ○ | ○ |
| 23 | ○ | ○ | ○ |
| 24 | ○ | ○ | ○ |
| 25 | ○ | ○ | ○ |

220

You must write within the grey lines.

Write your answer for Part 1 below. Do not write on the barcodes.

| Question 1 |
|---|
| |
| |
| |
| |
| |
| |
| |
| |
| |
| |
| |
| |
| |
| |
| |
| |
| |
| |
| |
| |

This section for use by Examiner only:

| C | CA | O | L |
|---|---|---|---|
| | | | |

* 0010437500302 *

You must write within the grey lines.

Answer only one of the two questions for Part 2.
Tick the box to show which question you have answered.
Write your answer below. Do not write on the barcodes.

| Part 2 | Question 2 | | Question 3 | |
|--------|------------|--|------------|--|
| | | | | |

This section for use by Examiner only:

| C | CA | O | L |
|---|----|---|---|
| | | | |

# Answer key for the Reading and Listening papers

This is the Answer key for the Reading and Listening papers of Tests 1-8.

## TEST 1

### Reading

**Part 1**
1  C
2  B
3  A
4  C
5  B

**Part 2**
6  H
7  A
8  F
9  C
10 D

**Part 3**
11 B
12 A
13 A
14 C
15 C

**Part 4**
16 C
17 H
18 G
19 F
20 B

**Part 5**
21 B
22 C
23 D
24 A
25 B
26 A

**Part 6**
27 of
28 they
29 per/every/each
30 enough/plenty
31 are
32 the

### Listening

**Part 1**
1  B
2  C
3  B
4  C
5  A
6  B
7  A

**Part 2**
8  B
9  A
10 B
11 B
12 A
13 A

**Part 3**
14 shopping
15 plastic bags
16 charity shops
17 environmental
18 rivers
19 neighbour

**Part 4**
20 C
21 C
22 B
23 B
24 A
25 C

## TEST 2

### Reading

**Part 1**
1  B
2  C
3  B
4  B
5  A

**Part 2**
6  C
7  B
8  H
9  D
10 G

**Part 3**
11 B
12 C
13 D
14 B
15 C

**Part 4**
16 G
17 A
18 C
19 H
20 E

**Part 5**
21 A
22 C
23 D
24 D
25 B
26 A

**Part 6**
27 have
28 the
29 and
30 by
31 to
32 are/get

### Listening

**Part 1**
1  B
2  C
3  C
4  A
5  B
6  B
7  A

**Part 2**
8  C
9  B
10 C
11 B
12 A
13 B

**Part 3**
14 changes
15 wild flowers
16 published
17 cancelled
18 10.00/10 am
19 library

**Part 4**
20 B
21 C
22 B
23 B
24 A
25 C

# TEST 3

## Reading

### Part 1
1 B
2 C
3 A
4 A
5 C

### Part 2
6 F
7 B
8 H
9 D
10 A

### Part 3
11 C
12 A
13 C
14 B
15 C

### Part 4
16 G
17 B
18 E
19 D
20 A

### Part 5
21 C
22 A
23 B
24 D
25 C
26 D

### Part 6
27 of
28 was
29 have
30 as
31 the
32 Whatever

## Listening

### Part 1
1 C
2 C
3 A
4 B
5 B
6 C
7 A

### Part 2
8 B
9 A
10 A
11 C
12 C
13 B

### Part 3
14 different building
15 13 September
16 exercises
17 training manager
18 (company) restaurant
19 134

### Part 4
20 A
21 B
22 B
23 C
24 A
25 B

---

# TEST 4

## Reading

### Part 1
1 A
2 B
3 A
4 B
5 C

### Part 2
6 G
7 F
8 H
9 E
10 B

### Part 3
11 C
12 A
13 C
14 D
15 C

### Part 4
16 G
17 C
18 E
19 A
20 F

### Part 5
21 B
22 A
23 B
24 D
25 B
26 C

### Part 6
27 do
28 This
29 as
30 are
31 which
32 the

## Listening

### Part 1
1 B
2 C
3 C
4 B
5 C
6 A
7 A

### Part 2
8 A
9 B
10 A
11 B
12 B
13 C

### Part 3
14 interview
15 entertainment
16 7.00 / 7 pm / 7 o'clock
17 speech competitions
18 free
19 £170

### Part 4
20 B
21 C
22 A
23 A
24 C
25 B

# TEST 5

## Reading

### Part 1
1 C
2 A
3 A
4 A
5 B

### Part 2
6 E
7 B
8 A
9 G
10 H

### Part 3
11 C
12 B
13 A
14 D
15 C

### Part 4
16 F
17 C
18 H
19 A
20 D

### Part 5
21 C
22 A
23 D
24 B
25 A
26 C

### Part 6
27 been
28 who
29 the
30 was
31 his
32 it

## Listening

### Part 1
1 B
2 A
3 B
4 C
5 C
6 A
7 B

### Part 2
8 B
9 B
10 A
11 B
12 A
13 B

### Part 3
14 two days
15 height
16 plain
17 accurate
18 reading
19 three photos

### Part 4
20 C
21 A
22 B
23 B
24 A
25 C

# TEST 6

## Reading

### Part 1
1 A
2 B
3 A
4 B
5 C

### Part 2
6 E
7 G
8 A
9 B
10 C

### Part 3
11 C
12 B
13 B
14 C
15 C

### Part 4
16 D
17 E
18 G
19 B
20 C

### Part 5
21 B
22 C
23 A
24 C
25 B
26 D

### Part 6
27 have
28 that/which
29 the/a
30 If
31 There
32 to

## Listening

### Part 1
1 A
2 C
3 A
4 A
5 B
6 C
7 A

### Part 2
8 B
9 C
10 B
11 B
12 C
13 A

### Part 3
14 1576
15 climbing
16 coast path
17 13/13th
18 celebrity
19 poetry

### Part 4
20 A
21 B
22 C
23 A
24 C
25 C

## TEST 7

### Reading

**Part 1**
1 C
2 B
3 C
4 A
5 A

**Part 2**
6 H
7 E
8 C
9 F
10 B

**Part 3**
11 C
12 B
13 D
14 B
15 A

**Part 4**
16 D
17 G
18 A
19 F
20 B

**Part 5**
21 A
22 B
23 D
24 B
25 A
26 C

**Part 6**
27 been
28 at
29 has
30 as
31 more
32 until

### Listening

**Part 1**
1 C
2 B
3 B
4 A
5 B
6 B
7 C

**Part 2**
8 C
9 A
10 B
11 C
12 A
13 B

**Part 3**
14 pet
15 cleaners
16 magazine
17 10.30 / 10.30 pm / 22:00
18 Children's Theatre / children's theatre
19 ticket

**Part 4**
20 A
21 B
22 A
23 C
24 B
25 C

## TEST 8

### Reading

**Part 1**
1 C
2 C
3 B
4 A
5 C

**Part 2**
6 H
7 C
8 A
9 D
10 G

**Part 3**
11 B
12 A
13 C
14 D
15 C

**Part 4**
16 D
17 A
18 F
19 B
20 G

**Part 5**
21 C
22 D
23 A
24 C
25 A
26 C

**Part 6**
27 of
28 There
29 at
30 who
31 to
32 until

### Listening

**Part 1**
1 A
2 C
3 B
4 A
5 C
6 B
7 A

**Part 2**
8 A
9 C
10 B
11 C
12 A
13 B

**Part 3**
14 accommodation
15 damaged
16 kitchen
17 different subjects
18 five/5
19 local doctor

**Part 4**
20 B
21 C
22 A
23 A
24 C
25 B

# Model answers for the Writing papers

These are the model answers for the Writing papers of Tests 1–8.

## Test 1

## Writing Part 1

### Question 1

Hi Tania,
I'm really looking forward to the party too. I haven't seen you for such a long time and we have a lot to talk about.
It's very kind of you to offer to buy a present. Clothes are difficult to choose, aren't they? What about a CD? You know the music I like.
The party starts at 7.00 but it would be great to see you before that. You could come at lunchtime and we can go for a coffee and something to eat. Email me when you know the time.
Please don't worry about bringing food. There will be plenty here!
See you soon!

## Writing Part 2

### Question 2

I go on holiday every year and I like to visit different places every time. But I always like to go somewhere that is by the sea.
A busy seaside town is my favourite place because I think it's good to have a shopping centre. If the weather is bad there is somewhere you can go and not get wet.
I usually go with my family and we book a hotel that has a view of the ocean. I like getting up early in the morning, walking along the beach on my own and having an ice-cream. When I get back my family are awake and are ready to go somewhere.

### Question 3

When I opened the door, I couldn't believe my eyes. My friend Sue was standing there with some flowers and a present.
'Congratulations,' said Sue. 'I heard you've got a new job.'
Sue was an old friend from school and she always did nice things like this. I invited her in and we sat at the table while I opened the present. It was a photo of Sue and me together on our holiday. We had lots of happy memories from this trip and we talked for a long time about all the things we'd done. It was a lovely afternoon.

## TEST 2

## Writing Part 1

### Question 1

Hi Martin,
I'm very well thanks! Yes, it was lovely to speak with you. I enjoyed hearing about your news, especially your holiday plans!
It's difficult to say what the weather will be like in November. Some years we have a late summer with warm sunny days. Other years the weather can be terrible – rain and wind and sometimes even snow! Bring a warm jumper and something to keep you dry, just in case it rains.
I'd love to meet you when you come! Let's meet as soon as we can after you arrive.
And you don't have to bring anything from England, but some chocolate would be nice.
See you soon!

## Writing Part 2

### Question 2

I don't think I have one meal that I like the best, but I'm keen on Italian food.

I don't cook often but pasta is quite easy. I also know how to make a tomato sauce, which tastes nice with some good Italian cheese.

Of course, pasta is better when I eat it in a restaurant. Luckily, we have an excellent one near where I live. We often go there to celebrate a special occasion and I've tried a few different dishes. Actually, the one I order most often is risotto, so maybe that's my favourite meal.

### Question 3

As the bus turned the corner, I saw my hotel at the end of the road.

It had been a very long journey and I was looking forward to having a walk along the beach.

I checked in and took the lift to my room. It was bigger than I had imagined, and the sun was shining through the window.

I went out on to the balcony and looked down at the scene below. There were lots of interesting shops and restaurants on one side of the road and a long golden beach on the other side. I knew this was going to be a wonderful holiday.

## TEST 3

## Writing Part 1

### Question 1

Hi Mark,

We're all OK thanks. My family send you their love.

We have our meals at similar times to you although the evening meal is a bit later. I have breakfast before I go to work at 8.00 and I eat lunch at about 12.00 or 12.30. Our main meal is usually around 7.00 and we always sit at the table together to eat.

Yes, Chinese and Indian food are very popular in my country. We have a takeaway once a week and it's usually one of these.

I don't know if I'm a good cook but I enjoy making a curry and my family seem to like it!

Best wishes,

## Writing Part 2

### Question 2

My main interest is reading, especially novels. Ever since I was a young child at school, I have loved books. I think this is because my parents used to read me lots of stories from colourful children's books and as I got older my interest continued.

There are lots of reasons why I enjoy reading. To begin with, it's a way to relax and forget about work or studying. Then, if it's a good book you become very interested in the events and the characters. Finally, I think some novels can help you learn about life and help you to understand people better.

### Question 3

The house was much bigger than I had expected. It was a Saturday morning and we were on our family holiday. I had only seen photographs of the place we were staying in and so I was feeling very excited as we all got out of the car. There was a lovely front garden with colourful flowers and a path going up to the front door.

My wife put the key in the lock and my children pushed past her to be the first ones inside. It was lovely inside and we were all looking forward to our two-week holiday.

## TEST 4

## Writing Part 1

### Question 1

> Hi Lisa,
> I'm OK thanks! I'm working very hard at college at the moment as we have exams coming soon but I'm feeling confident!
> A film night is a great idea! Thanks for inviting me. Actually, I can't think of a film I'd like to see but I know we have the same taste, so I'll let you choose one. And I'll buy some crisps and biscuits to bring as well.
> The only problem is I'm working until 6.00 so I can't come until 7.00. Will that be OK? I hope so.
> Looking forward to seeing you on Saturday!

## Writing Part 2

### Question 2

I have been studying English ever since I went to high school and it has always been my favourite subject.

I'm at university now, doing a degree in business and I need English for my studies. I hope to get a job in advertising when I finish and it will be very useful to have a second language.

However, another reason I'm still enjoying learning the language is because I love finding out more about different cultures. I like reading novels and when my English is good enough, I'm looking forward to reading books written by famous English authors.

### Question 3

I left my car in the car park and went through the front door to the reception desk. It was my first day in the new job and I was feeling a little nervous but very excited. It was a lovely bright building and everyone seemed happy and friendly. The receptionist was talking to someone on the phone and while I was waiting I thought about my future with this company. I was looking forward to learning new skills and meeting new people and I knew it was going to be much more enjoyable than the job I had just left.

## TEST 5

## Writing Part 1

### Question 1

> Hi Maura,
> Good to hear from you! Congratulations on finishing your exams. I'm sure you'll do really well!
> That new restaurant was fantastic! We went there the day after it opened and had a lovely time. The food was delicious and the staff were very friendly. It wasn't too expensive either so I know you'll like it.
> Yes, they do have a children's menu. Your nephew and niece can have things like chips or pizza, but they would like the adult meals too.
> It was very busy when we went and that was the week it opened. I expect it will be very popular now, so I think you should definitely book a table.
> Write after you've been and tell me what it was like!

# Writing Part 2

### Question 2

I work very hard and always look forward to the weekend. I always get up early on both days to make sure I don't spend too long in bed. I don't really like to waste my time doing nothing, even if I'm feeling tired.

I usually go to the shops on Saturday with my friends. We often meet in a café and sit around the table talking for ages. On Sunday I enjoy going for a long walk if the weather is nice. We live near the countryside and it's always a great way to spend a few hours. I always feel better afterwards.

### Question 3

When I saw who it was, I ran across the road to meet her. I hadn't seen Sophie for at least three years. We worked for the same company and quickly became best friends. But Sophie had moved away to start a new job and we hadn't seen each other since then.

We gave each other a huge hug, found ourselves a nice place to have lunch and spent the afternoon telling each other about our news. As we were talking, I thought how much I had missed our friendship. So you can imagine how pleased I was when she told me she was returning to her old job and moving back to our town.

# TEST 6

# Writing Part 1

### Question 1

> Hi Kelly,
> Thanks for your email! I think it's a great idea to study together. I'm looking forward to it.
> I'd like to eat first too. Shall we get a takeaway? That's better than you cooking as we'll be able to concentrate on work. We can decide what to order when I arrive!
> Thanks for offering me your computer to work on. But most of my study notes are on my laptop so I'll bring that.
> If it's OK I'd like to come on Wednesday evening. But if that's not possible let me know.
> Write back soon!

# Writing Part 2

### Question 2

TV is still very popular with older people in my country but younger people don't watch TV very often and I'm the same. If there's a programme on that all my friends at university are interested in or my family are watching, I'll try to see it so we can talk about it. But that's really the only time I watch television.

I prefer to choose what I'm interested in and watch it on my laptop. There are lots of films and documentaries online that aren't on TV and you can watch them whenever you want, so I find that much more convenient.

### Question 3

I was so pleased that the food tasted as nice as before. It was my friend's birthday and I had suggested we all go to the Italian restaurant in town. It was a lovely place to eat with friends and the food was always very nice. I was a little nervous when we arrived because I really wanted my friend to enjoy the meal and have a positive experience.

But I didn't need to worry. The waiters were really kind and as we all began to eat, I was so pleased to see everyone laughing and joking and enjoying the dishes they had ordered.

## TEST 7

## Writing Part 1

### Question 1

Hi Karen,

Thanks for your email. I'm really happy you can be there to take care of my apartment although it's a pity we won't see each other this time.

There's lots to do on Saturday. We have a local cinema that shows the latest films and a busy shopping centre you can visit if that interests you. Actually, it's not at all quiet in my area on Sunday – it's almost as busy as on Saturday. The shops are always open but when the weather is nice and I want some fresh air I go to the park near the apartment. It's beautiful in the summer. Once again, thanks for looking after the apartment while I'm away.

Have a good time!

## Writing Part 2

### Question 2

I live in a small apartment and we have quite a big family. We also have lots of visitors, which means the house is always full of people. This is nice but it makes it difficult to relax.

For this reason, I love to spend time on our balcony. I'm very lucky as we live on the coast, our apartment is on the fifth floor and we have a wonderful view of the sea. I love to sit in a chair with my feet up and enjoy the feeling of the sun on my face. It's the perfect place to relax!

### Question 3

As my friend waved goodbye I wondered when we would see each other again. I watched her as she went through passport control and thought about all the good times we had spent together. She was flying to Australia and was planning to stay there for a year, and I knew it would be a while before we could get together again.

But it was also a lovely moment, as I realised what a good friend she was. Even though I would miss her, I also knew that our friendship was strong and would last until we saw each other the following summer.

## Test 8

## Writing Part 1

### Question 1

Hi Marcela,

Good to hear from you. Yes, it was lovely chatting to you last month. I'm very glad you're coming here next week. I think the library would be a good place to meet. It's on the corner of St John's Square. It's not far from my office and it will only take us a few minutes to walk to the restaurant. Let's meet there at 6.30 pm. Is that OK?

I know your dad likes watching films and there's a good cinema opposite the library. I can see him to say hello first, I hope!

Yes, I'd love to see your photos so please bring them – mine weren't very good and I think yours are probably better. Wasn't it a lovely holiday?

See you soon.

# Writing Part 2

### Question 2

I have a friend called Rob who I met a few years ago while I was studying at university. We were both doing the same course and sat next to each other in the first lecture, where we introduced ourselves. We became very close friends, and after university finished we promised to keep in contact. Rob lives quite a long way from me so we don't see each other very often. But we both love football and we sometimes arrange to meet at a match. When we do, we spend the time finding out about each other's lives and remembering the great times we had at university.

### Question 3

The van drove past and a box fell from the back of it. I saw it just as I was walking to work. As I turned to look, I noticed the back door of the van was open. It was clearly a delivery vehicle as there were many more boxes of different shapes and sizes inside. The driver didn't realise the door was open and continued driving down the road and two more boxes fell from the back.

Luckily for the people who were waiting for a delivery, two kind people collected the boxes and took them to the local post office, which was just across the road. As I continued on my journey to work, I hoped the driver wouldn't get into too much trouble.

# Model answers for the Speaking papers

The model answers for the Speaking papers of Tests 1-8 are highlighted in grey here. You can listen to these model answers online at: **www.collins.co.uk/eltresources**

## Test 1

### Speaking Part 1

05a

| | |
|---|---|
| Examiner | Good morning.<br>Can I have your mark sheets, please?<br>I'm Fiona Evans and this is Michael Hale.<br>What's your name, Candidate A? |
| Candidate A | My name's Marta Gonzalez. |
| Examiner | Where do you live? |
| Candidate A | I live in Madrid. |
| Examiner | And what's your name, Candidate B? |
| Candidate B | My name's Daniel Garofoli. |
| Examiner | Where do you come from, Candidate B? |
| Candidate B | I come from Rome. |
| Examiner | Candidate B, do you work or are you a student? |
| Candidate B | I work. |
| Examiner | What do you do, Candidate B? |
| Candidate B | I'm a dentist's assistant. I help the dentist with the patients. |
| Examiner | And Candidate A, do you work or are you a student? |
| Candidate A | I'm a student. |
| Examiner | What do you study? |
| Candidate A | I'm studying biological sciences. I'm going to finish my course next year. |
| Examiner | Thank you. |
| | |
| Examiner | Candidate A, do you enjoy studying English? |
| Candidate A | Yes, I do. I like being able to speak to other people in English and reading English books. |
| Examiner | Candidate B, what did you do last weekend? |
| Candidate B | I went to the cinema with my friends. We usually meet in the afternoon and decide what we want to do. |
| Examiner | Candidate A, what are you going to do next weekend? |
| Candidate A | I'm going to visit my grandparents. They live quite close to us and we're going there for dinner. |
| Examiner | Candidate B, what do you enjoy doing in your free time? |
| Candidate B | I like to keep fit. I go to the gym a few times every week. I also enjoy reading and going to the theatre. |
| Examiner | Thank you. |

### Speaking Part 2

06a

| | |
|---|---|
| Examiner | Now I'd like each of you to talk on your own about something. I'm going to give each of you a photograph and I'd like you to talk about it.<br>Candidate A, here is your photograph. It shows two people on bicycles.<br>Please tell us what you can see in the photograph.<br>Candidate B, you just listen. |
| Candidate A: | OK, in this photograph I can see two people and they are riding bicycles. There's a young girl, she's on the left. She looks about ten years old. She's wearing a nice dress. Next to her, on the right is an older lady. I think it could be her grandmother. |

|             |                                                                      |
| ----------- | -------------------------------------------------------------------- |
|             | This lady is wearing jeans and a white shirt. They're in a park and there are trees in the background. Maybe it's summer because they're both wearing sunglasses. They're both smiling and they look very happy. It's a nice family photograph. |
| Examiner    | Thank you.                                                           |

| | |
| --- | --- |
| Examiner | Candidate B, here is your photograph. It shows a group of children. Please tell us what you can see in the photograph. Candidate A, you just listen. |
| Candidate B: | My photograph has five children in it. I think they're in a school gym or dance room. Somewhere children can do exercise. There are three girls in the front and two boys are at the back. They're all wearing shorts and T-shirts, which are different colours. Most of them are looking at the camera and are smiling. I don't know if they're dancing. They're standing on one leg, doing something that looks a bit difficult. Maybe they're exercising, but they're enjoying it. |
| Examiner | Thank you. |

## Speaking Part 3

07a

| | |
| --- | --- |
| Examiner | Now, in this part of the test you're going to talk about something together for about two minutes. I'm going to describe a situation to you. A woman has been invited to her friend's wedding. She is trying to decide what she could buy her friend for a wedding gift. Here are some things she could buy. Talk together about the different things she could buy and say which one would be best. All right? Now talk together. |
| Candidate A: | OK, I think they're interesting presents but some are more expensive. Do you agree? |
| Candidate B: | Yes ... the washing machine costs a lot of money and I don't think it's a good present really. |
| Candidate A: | Yes, I agree. I think if you need a washing machine you choose one yourself. The money would be a good idea. Her friend could buy something she needed. |
| Candidate B: | Yes, money is a good thing to give her but do you think she would prefer a present more than money? What about the clock? It looks like one you can put on the kitchen wall. It could be useful. |
| Candidate A: | That's a good idea. I think the microwave and the television are too expensive. Shall we forget about them? There are also the towels and the cushions. What do you think about them? |
| Candidate B: | The towels are a good idea but the person might not like the cushions. They might be the wrong colour or pattern. So, I think the towels or the clock. I would prefer the clock. Shall we decide to buy that? |
| Candidate A: | Yes, I agree with you. |
| Examiner: | Thank you. |

## Speaking Part 4

08a

| | |
| --- | --- |
| Examiner: | Candidate A, do you enjoy going to parties? |
| Candidate A: | Yes, I do. I enjoy talking and being with my friends. We always have a good time. |
| Examiner: | And what about you, Candidate B? |
| Candidate B: | Yes, I do too. I have lots of parties with my friends. We sometimes have one at the weekend when we finish our studies. |
| Examiner: | Do you prefer to dance at parties or talk with people? |
| Candidate B: | I like to do both things. We usually talk a lot at the beginning of the party but then we like to dance when we feel relaxed. |
| Examiner: | And how about you, Candidate A? |

| Candidate A: | I'm not very good at dancing so I usually sit with my friends and talk. When we know a song that's playing, we all sing as well. |
|---|---|
| Examiner: | What makes a good party, Candidate B? |
| Candidate B: | I think the people are important. It's a good idea to invite people who are friends or who like each other. When you do this the guests are happy. |
| Examiner: | And what about you, Candidate A? |
| Candidate A: | Yes, I agree. The people are important. I also think it's good to have lots of food because people are always hungry. |
| Examiner: | Thank you. That is the end of the test. |

## Test 2

## Speaking Part 1

🎧
13a

| Examiner | Good afternoon. |
|---|---|
| | Can I have your mark sheets please? |
| | I'm Steve Malpas and this is Sue Hudson. |
| | What's your name? |
| Candidate A | My name's Stephan Eglin. |
| Examiner | Where do you come from? |
| Candidate A | I come from a small village in Switzerland. |
| Examiner | And what's your name, Candidate B? |
| Candidate B | My name's Ana Sousa. |
| Examiner | Where do you live, Candidate B? |
| Candidate B | I live in Brazil, but my town is a long way from Rio de Janeiro. |
| Examiner | Candidate B, do you work or are you a student? |
| Candidate B | I'm a student. |
| Examiner | What do you study, Candidate B? |
| Candidate B | I'm doing a degree in computer science at university. |
| Examiner | And Candidate A, do you work or are you a student? |
| Candidate A | I work. |
| Examiner | What do you do? |
| Candidate A | I'm a designer. I work in a design studio. |
| Examiner | Thank you. |
| | |
| Examiner | Do you like it where you live? |
| Candidate A | Yes, I do. I enjoy living in a busy city. I live near the shopping centre and I like leaving my flat and being in crowds of people. |
| Examiner | Candidate B, what about you? |
| Candidate B | Yes, I like it where I live too. We have a lovely park near my house and I often go there to relax. |
| Examiner | Candidate A, have you got any hobbies or interests? |
| Candidate A | I play the guitar. I spend a lot of time practising on my own but I also play in a group with some friends. |
| Examiner | Candidate B, what do you do to relax? |
| Candidate B | I enjoy reading and I go to the cinema quite often. I also like to spend time drawing or painting. |
| Examiner | Thank you. |

## Speaking Part 2

🎧
14a

| Examiner | Now I'd like each of you to talk on your own about something. I'm going to give each of you a photograph and I'd like you to talk about it. |
|---|---|
| | Candidate A. Here is your photograph. It shows two people in a kitchen. |

|  |  |
|---|---|
| | Please tell us what you can see in the photograph. |
| | Candidate B, you just listen. |
| Candidate A: | This photo shows two people in a kitchen. It looks like a kitchen in someone's house, not one you see in a restaurant. There's a man and a woman preparing food. They look middle-aged and they might be a husband and wife. They are both wearing something to protect their clothes. I don't know the word for this, but everyone has one hanging in the kitchen and you put it on when you prepare food. It looks like the woman is getting the vegetables ready and the man is cutting something up, it looks like meat. I think they are making the evening meal and they both look very happy. |
| Examiner | Thank you. |
| Examiner | Candidate B. Here is your photograph. It shows people in a shopping centre. Please tell us what you can see in the photograph. Candidate A, you just listen. |
| Candidate B: | There are more than three people in this photo but there are three together at the front. They look like three friends who are out shopping. There is another person in the background, but I don't know if he is with them or not. The girl on the left is wearing a long top and dark trousers, the man in the middle is wearing a jacket and a jumper and the girl on the right is wearing a scarf round her neck, a dark top, jeans and a long dark cardigan. They're all carrying shopping bags. One of the girls is pointing to something, it might be something in a shop window, and the other two are looking in the same direction. |
| Examiner: | Thank you. |

## Speaking Part 3

🎧 **15a**

| | |
|---|---|
| Examiner: | Now, in this part of the test you're going to talk about something together for about two minutes. I'm going to describe a situation to you. A man's daughter is going on a camping holiday. He wants to buy her something she can take with her. Here are some things he could get. Talk together about the different things he could get her and say which one would be best. All right? Now talk together. |
| Candidate A: | So, we need to choose something that's good for a camping holiday. I don't think the shoes are useful, do you? |
| Candidate B: | No, I agree, but the walking boots might be a good present if the person is doing a lot of walking in the countryside. What about the bags? |
| Candidate A: | I think the backpack is better than the suitcase. It's the kind of bag someone uses for camping, isn't it? |
| Candidate B: | That's true. I don't think the alarm clock is a good idea. When you go on holiday you don't need to get up early. Do you? But the map could be useful if she's walking and she doesn't know the area very well. |
| Candidate A: | I agree, but the map is very cheap. I think her father would like to spend a bit more money on her present. I think your idea for him to buy walking boots is the best so far. What about the camera? |
| Candidate B: | That's another special present. But she probably has a phone with a camera so it might not be very useful. Shall we agree he should buy her the walking boots then? |
| Candidate A: | Yes, let's say that. |
| Examiner: | Thank you. |

## Speaking Part 4

16a

| | |
|---|---|
| Examiner: | Candidate A, have you ever been camping? |
| Candidate A: | Yes, but a long time ago. When I was younger I went with my family. I enjoyed cooking our food outside in a field. |
| Examiner: | And what about you, Candidate B? |
| Candidate B: | No, I've never been camping. I always stay in a hotel when I go on holiday. My friends go and they always enjoy it. |
| Examiner: | Candidate B, do you prefer a holiday in a town or the countryside? |
| Candidate B: | I prefer going to a town or a city. I like walking around the shops and going sightseeing to visit old buildings. But it's really good if it's near the sea as well. |
| Examiner: | And how about you, Candidate A? |
| Candidate A: | I agree. That's the kind of place I prefer. When I go on holiday with my friends, we always look for places that have good shops but also a nice beach. |
| Examiner: | Candidate B, is it better to go on holiday on your own or with other people? |
| Candidate B: | I like going with my friends or my family. If you see something interesting or do something exciting, it's nice to do it with another person. |
| Examiner: | And what about you, Candidate A? |
| Candidate A: | Yes, I agree. I think I would be lonely on my own. I like to have people to talk to on the journey and to have fun with on the holiday. |
| Examiner: | Thank you. That is the end of the test. |

## Test 3

## Speaking Part 1

21a

| | |
|---|---|
| Examiner: | Good evening. |
| | Can I have your mark sheets, please? |
| | I'm Lorna MacDonald and this is Mark Farrington. |
| | What's your name? |
| Candidate A: | My name's Aleksandra Kaminski. |
| Examiner: | Where do you live? |
| Candidate A: | I live in Krakow in Poland. |
| Examiner: | And what's your name, Candidate B? |
| Candidate B: | My name's Li Jing. |
| Examiner: | Where do you come from, Candidate B? |
| Candidate B: | I come from China. |
| Examiner: | Candidate B, do you work or are you a student? |
| Candidate B: | I work. |
| Examiner: | What do you do, Candidate B? |
| Candidate B: | I'm an architect. |
| Examiner: | And Candidate A, do you work or are you a student? |
| Candidate A: | I'm a student. |
| Examiner: | What do you study? |
| Candidate A: | I'm studying Polish literature. |
| Examiner: | Thank you. |
| | |
| Examiner: | Candidate A, who do you live with? |
| Candidate A: | I live with my family. There's my mum, my dad and my two sisters. They're both younger than me. |
| Examiner: | And what about you, Candidate B? |
| Candidate B: | I live with two colleagues. We have a small flat a long way from the office where we work. |
| Examiner: | Candidate A, have you got a favourite sport? |

| | |
|---|---|
| Candidate A: | Yes, I really enjoy watching football. I often go to see my local team and watch matches if they're on TV. And I like playing tennis and going swimming. |
| Examiner: | Candidate B, do you like to keep fit? |
| Candidate B: | Yes, I play football every week. I walk quite a lot but I'm not keen on going to the gym or things like that. |
| Examiner: | Thank you. |

## Speaking Part 2

22a

| | |
|---|---|
| Examiner: | Now I'd like each of you to talk on your own about something. I'm going to give each of you a photograph and I'd like you to talk about it.<br>Candidate A, here is your photograph. It shows people out shopping.<br>Please tell us what you can see in the photograph.<br>Candidate B, you just listen. |
| Candidate A: | This photo shows a family out shopping in a supermarket. It's quite a young family. The man and the woman don't look very old, around 30 perhaps and they have a young daughter who looks about four or five years old. She's sitting on her father's shoulders. Either the mother or father has asked her to get a bottle of something from a shelf near the top. Her dad is nearest to the bottles and the girl is reaching out to get one. The mother is holding the shopping trolley, standing next to her husband. All three of them are smiling and look like they're having a good time. |
| Examiner: | Thank you. |
| | |
| Examiner: | Candidate B, here is your photograph. It shows some people in a computer room. Please tell us what you can see in the photograph.<br>Candidate A, you just listen. |
| Candidate B: | This photo is of a group of people in a training session, I think. It might be taking place at work or at university. They're sitting at computers so it could be an IT lesson, or they could be learning new software for the company they work for. I can see five people sitting at the desks, two men, two women and I think another woman in the background. It looks like there are two trainers. The one nearest to the camera is a man in a white shirt. Behind him there's a female trainer. She's helping the person who I can't see very clearly. |
| Examiner: | Thank you. |

## Speaking Part 3

23a

| | |
|---|---|
| Examiner: | Now, in this part of the test you're going to talk about something together for about two minutes. I'm going to describe a situation to you.<br>A young woman works very hard and wants to get fitter. She has decided to take up an activity to help her get fit.<br>Here are some things she could do.<br>Talk together about the different activities she could try and say which one would be best.<br>All right? Now talk together. |
| Candidate A: | OK, the question has asked us to choose the best activity for a young woman. I don't think playing golf will help her to get fit. What do you think? |
| Candidate B: | I agree. People just walk around when they play golf. She needs a friend to play golf with as well and we don't know if she wants something she can do by herself. |
| Candidate A: | That's true. Swimming or cycling are good if you want to take exercise on your own. And what about running as well? |

| | |
|---|---|
| Candidate B: | Running and swimming are really good exercise and they don't cost much money. You have to buy a bike to go cycling and they can cost a lot. And skiing is very expensive. |
| Candidate A: | I agree. So, running and cycling are our favourite activities so far. What about dancing? Going dancing is good fun and she can join a dance class on her own, can't she? And she will meet some new people and might make new friends. |
| Candidate B: | That's a good point. So, let's say dancing is the best if she wants to try an activity on her own. Is that OK? |
| Candidate A: | Yes, I think that's the best choice. |
| Examiner: | Thank you. |

## Speaking Part 4

24a

| | |
|---|---|
| Examiner: | Do you do any sports, Candidate A? |
| Candidate A: | Yes, I play tennis and I often go swimming. I'm lucky because there's a sports centre near my house and it's easy for me to get there. |
| Examiner: | And what about you, Candidate B? |
| Candidate B: | I play football every week. I also walk a lot and I sometimes do some exercise at home too. I try to make sure I keep fit. |
| Examiner: | Candidate B, do you like to watch sport on TV? |
| Candidate B: | Yes. I love watching football, especially the big games. And I enjoy athletics when it's on. |
| Examiner: | And how about you, Candidate A? |
| Candidate A: | I don't watch TV very often, but I do like to watch videos of tennis matches on the internet. I prefer playing tennis though. |
| Examiner: | Candidate B, is it important to try to be the best when you do a sport or just to take part? |
| Candidate B: | It depends. If you go in for competitions, you need to try your hardest to win. But if you're doing the sport to keep fit, I think it's best just to take part. |
| Examiner: | And what about you, Candidate A? |
| Candidate A: | Yes, I agree. The most important thing is you enjoy what you're doing. Most people want to get better but only so they can improve their fitness or skill. I think that's important. |
| Examiner: | Thank you. That is the end of the test. |

## Test 4

## Speaking Part 1

29a

| | |
|---|---|
| Examiner: | Good morning.<br>Can I have your mark sheets, please?<br>I'm Gareth Reynolds and this is Mary Roberts.<br>What's your name? |
| Candidate A: | My name's Pierre Rioche. |
| Examiner: | Where do you come from? |
| Candidate A: | I come from Nantes in France. |
| Examiner: | And what's your name, Candidate B? |
| Candidate B: | My name's Marta Filipek. |
| Examiner: | Where do you live, Candidate B? |
| Candidate B: | I live near Prague, in the Czech Republic. |
| Examiner: | Candidate B, do you work or are you a student? |
| Candidate B: | I'm a student. |
| Examiner: | What do you study, Candidate B? |
| Candidate B: | I'm doing my training to be a maths teacher. |

| | |
|---|---|
| Examiner: | And Candidate A, do you work or are you a student? |
| Candidate A: | I work. |
| Examiner: | What do you do? |
| Candidate A: | I'm a librarian. |
| Examiner: | Thank you. |

| | |
|---|---|
| Examiner: | Do you live in a house or an apartment, Candidate A? |
| Candidate A: | I live in a small apartment on my own. There's a bedroom, a kitchen, a living room and shower room. |
| Examiner: | Candidate B, what about you? |
| Candidate B: | I live in a house with my family. I've lived there all my life. |
| Examiner: | Candidate A, are there any good restaurants where you live? |
| Candidate A: | Yes, there are lots. My favourite is an Italian restaurant just round the corner from my apartment. I go there as often as I can. |
| Examiner: | Candidate B, have you got a favourite meal? |
| Candidate B: | I can't think of just one meal. I love Chinese or Indian food and especially meals that are spicy. |
| Examiner: | Thank you. |

## Speaking Part 2

🎧 30a

| | |
|---|---|
| Examiner: | Now I'd like each of you to talk on your own about something. I'm going to give each of you a photograph and I'd like you to talk about it.<br>Candidate A, here is your photograph. It shows people working.<br>Please tell us what you can see in the photograph.<br>Candidate B, you just listen. |
| Candidate A: | The people in this photograph are in an office, I think. It might also be in a university or college in the IT room, but I think these people are at work. There are five people, two men are near the front and they're both looking at a computer screen. One man is sitting and the other is standing by his side. It looks like they are discussing something. They're both quite young and wearing casual clothes and they both have beards. There are three women at computers in the background. One woman is standing next to another one who's sitting at her desk and they're talking, and the third woman is looking at them. |
| Examiner: | Thank you.<br>Candidate B, here is your photograph. It shows people in a hairdressers.<br>Please tell us what you can see in the photograph.<br>Candidate A, you just listen. |
| Candidate B: | This photograph shows people having their hair done. There are seven people altogether and they're all women except one man. He's sitting nearest to the camera and two women are standing behind him. One of them might be a hairdressing student and the other is teaching her. It looks like the man's haircut is nearly finished. There are two more women sitting in chairs and each one has a hairdresser who is doing their hair. I don't know what it's called but all the customers are wearing something black to protect their clothes. |
| Examiner: | Thank you. |

## Speaking Part 3

🎧 31a

| | |
|---|---|
| Examiner: | Now, in this part of the test you're going to talk about something together for about two minutes. I'm going to describe a situation to you.<br>A man is at home with a broken leg and wants to find something to do to entertain himself. |

Here are some things he could do.

Talk together about the different things he could do and say which one would be best.

All right? Now talk together.

Candidate A: OK, this person has a broken leg, so do you think any of these things would be good for him?

Candidate B: Well, he can still do all these things with a broken leg, can't he? So where can we start? He might not be able to play the guitar so shall we say not that?

Candidate A: I agree. He might enjoy a game of chess, but he might be on his own. What about the TV?

Candidate B: That's one idea, yes. But the laptop is like the TV, isn't it? He can use it to watch videos for example. He can also do some work if he feels like it.

Candidate A: Yes, I think the laptop is better than the TV, actually. But maybe the phone is even better. I use my phone to watch things online. The man can also use it to call his friends. I think this is better than the cards because he might get bored with them.

Candidate B: Yes, I agree. The book is a good idea too, but you can also use the phone to read, can't you? The phone does everything, so I think that's the best idea. What about you?

Candidate A: Definitely. Let's say the phone.

Examiner: Thank you.

## Speaking Part 4

*32a*

Examiner: What do you like to do if you're very tired, Candidate A?

Candidate A: If I'm feeling very tired, I like to stay at home and lie on the sofa with a good book or watch the TV.

Examiner: And what about you, Candidate B?

Candidate B: I'm the same. When I'm tired and don't have to go to college I relax at home. I still get up quite early though because I don't like staying in bed too long.

Examiner: Do you think it's important for people to keep as active as possible, Candidate B?

Candidate B: I think it's better to be active if you can. If you spend the day doing nothing it's a waste of time and you might get bored. I think going out for a nice walk is better for you than staying at home and doing nothing.

Examiner: And how about you, Candidate A?

Candidate A: I agree. A lot of people spend hours on their phones, and this isn't healthy. I also think going for a walk is a good idea, especially for people who don't like exercise.

Examiner: Candidate B, do you go to bed very late sometimes?

Candidate B: Sometimes, yes. If I go out with my friends, I normally get home quite late. But when I'm at home I try to go to bed early.

Examiner: And what about you, Candidate A?

Candidate A: It's important for me that I get a lot of sleep or I feel tired at work. If there's something I want to watch on TV I sometimes stay up late but that's really the only time.

Examiner: Thank you. That is the end of the test.

## Test 5   SPEAKING TEST

## Speaking Part 1

*37a*

Examiner: Good afternoon.

Can I have your mark sheets, please?

I'm Louise Reece and this is Patrick Lovell.

What's your name?

Candidate A: My name's Ester Boydochenko.

Examiner: Where do you live?

| | |
|---|---|
| Candidate A: | I live near Moscow, in Russia. |
| Examiner: | And what's your name, Candidate B? |
| Candidate B: | My name's Mattias Busing. |
| Examiner: | Where do you come from, Candidate B? |
| Candidate B: | I come from Munich, in Germany. |
| Examiner: | Candidate B, do you work or are you a student? |
| Candidate B: | I work. |
| Examiner: | What do you do, Candidate B? |
| Candidate B: | I'm a journalist. I work on a news website. |
| Examiner: | And Candidate A, do you work or are you a student? |
| Candidate A: | I'm a student. |
| Examiner: | What do you study? |
| Candidate A: | I'm studying physics at university. I started my course last year. |
| Examiner: | Thank you. |

| | |
|---|---|
| Examiner: | Candidate A, what kind of films do you like to watch? |
| Candidate A: | I enjoy lots of different films. Sometimes I like to see a thriller and another time a comedy. I don't really like romantic films though. |
| Examiner: | Candidate B, what about you? |
| Candidate B: | I like action films and thrillers, that kind of thing. I also enjoy any films that are about historical events. |
| Examiner: | Candidate A, do you prefer watching films at home or at the cinema? |
| Candidate A: | I prefer going to the cinema. It's much better to see films on a big screen and the sound effects are much clearer in a cinema |
| Examiner: | Candidate B, how often do you see your friends? |
| Candidate B: | I don't see my friends every day because I don't have time. But I sometimes meet up with some of my old friends from university at the weekend. |
| Examiner: | Thank you. |

## Speaking Part 2

38a

| | |
|---|---|
| Examiner: | Now I'd like each of you to talk on your own about something. I'm going to give each of you a photograph and I'd like you to talk about it.<br>Candidate A, here is your photograph. It shows people doing some exercise outside. Please tell us what you can see in the photograph.<br>Candidate B, you just listen. |
| Candidate A: | This photo was taken outside in a park. There are five people all looking at the camera while they do their exercises. They're standing on the grass near a tree. I think this looks like a park in a city. There are two women and three men. They look like they are wearing a kind of uniform. They all have dark tracksuit trousers on and a top. They are all quite old and the exercise they are doing is quite easy. They are lifting their right arms over their heads. It's a nice sunny day and they all seem to be enjoying themselves. |
| Examiner: | Thank you. |
| Examiner: | Candidate B, here is your photograph. It shows three people in a kitchen.<br>Please tell us what you can see in the photograph.<br>Candidate A, you just listen. |
| Candidate B: | There are three girls in this photo. They're about 20 years old. They're sitting at a table having something to eat. Perhaps it's the kitchen where one of them lives. I can't see what everything is on the table but there is a large pizza box with some pizza in it. There's a bowl of salad as well and it looks like some fried chicken. The girls are wearing tops which are different colours. Two of them are wearing a shirt |

with a T-shirt underneath it. They're all laughing and they are having a great time. Perhaps one of them is telling the others a funny story.

Examiner: Thank you.

## Speaking Part 3

39a

Examiner: Now, in this part of the test you're going to talk about something together for about two minutes. I'm going to describe a situation to you.
A family are thinking of buying a pet for their young son. They want to get something that the boy can help take care of.
Here are some pets they could get.
Talk together about the different pets they could get for their son and say which one would be best.
All right? Now talk together.

Candidate A: Shall I start?
Candidate B: Yes, OK.
Candidate A: Well, we don't know how old the boy is but if he is very young they need something that is OK with little children. Do you think the snake is a good idea?
Candidate B: No, I wouldn't buy him a snake. And I'm not sure the mouse is a good idea. A mouse is very small and a young child might hurt it by mistake. What do you think?
Candidate A: I agree. A fish like this one would be easy to keep, wouldn't it? You only need to feed it occasionally and change the water sometimes. The boy could do that, couldn't he?
Candidate B: That's true. He might like a dog or a cat but they need a lot of attention. You need to be in the house with them as much as possible. What about the rabbit?
Candidate A: I think that would be better than the fish. You can hold the rabbit and it's not as small as the mouse. I don't think the child would hurt it. Do you agree?
Candidate B: Yes, I think the rabbit would be a good pet. I like that idea better than a bird. Shall we choose the rabbit then?
Candidate A: Yes, let's say the rabbit.
Examiner: Thank you.

## Speaking Part 4

40a

Examiner: Do you have a pet, Candidate A?
Candidate A: Yes, we have a cat. She's called Penny. She's quite old now and spends most of the day sleeping.
Examiner: And what about you, Candidate B?
Candidate B: No, I don't. There is a cat that comes to our house every day for food. I think it belongs to someone along the road.
Examiner: Candidate B, which do you think is the best pet?
Candidate B: I think I'd like a cat. My friend's cat always waits at the window for the family to come home and it always goes to the door to say hello.
Examiner: And how about you, Candidate A?
Candidate A: Well, apart from our cat I think a rabbit would be good. Some rabbits are really pretty and they're quite easy to take care of, I think.
Examiner: Candidate B, is it important for a child to have a pet?
Candidate B: I don't know if it's important but I think a pet can be fun to have when you're young. It's also good for children to have contact with animals and learn how to be responsible for them.
Examiner: And what about you, Candidate A?
Candidate A: Yes, I agree. I think we have to be responsible when we have a pet. We have to remember to feed it, to make sure it's healthy. A child can learn from this.
Examiner: Thank you. That is the end of the test.

## Test 6   SPEAKING TEST

### Speaking Part 1

🎧 45a

| | |
|---|---|
| Examiner: | Good evening. |
| | Can I have your mark sheets, please? |
| | I'm Donald Edmondson and this is Sarah Hunt. |
| | What's your name? |
| Candidate A: | My name's Martin Mostermans. |
| Examiner: | Where do you come from? |
| Candidate A: | I come from Amsterdam in the Netherlands. |
| Examiner: | And what's your name, Candidate B? |
| Candidate B: | My name's Alena Simic. |
| Examiner: | Where do you live, Candidate B? |
| Candidate B: | I live in Zagreb in Croatia. |
| Examiner: | Candidate B, do you work or are you a student? |
| Candidate B: | I'm a student. |
| Examiner: | What do you study, Candidate B? |
| Candidate B: | I'm a medical student – it's a very long course! |
| Examiner: | And Candidate A, do you work or are you a student? |
| Candidate A: | I work. |
| Examiner: | What do you do? |
| Candidate A: | I'm an architect. Our office is in the centre of Amsterdam. |
| Examiner: | Thank you. |
| | |
| Examiner: | Candidate A, do you come from a big family? |
| Candidate A: | No, not really. I have a brother and a sister, but I don't have any uncles or aunts so it's quite a small family. |
| Examiner: | Candidate B, what about you? |
| Candidate B: | My family is quite big, yes. My father has four brothers and sisters and we see them quite often when we have family parties. If my cousins come as well, there are a lot of us. |
| Examiner: | Candidate A, do you prefer to relax at the weekend or find a job to do? |
| Candidate A: | I like to find something to do. We have a garden so I often spend time working out there or doing jobs in the house. |
| Examiner: | Candidate B, how about you? |
| Candidate B: | Yes, I'm the same. I try to relax because I work hard during the week. But I don't like sitting on the sofa doing nothing. |
| Examiner: | Thank you. |

### Speaking Part 2

🎧 46a

| | |
|---|---|
| Examiner: | Now I'd like each of you to talk on your own about something. I'm going to give each of you a photograph and I'd like you to talk about it. |
| | Candidate A, here is your photograph. It shows people waiting for a train. |
| | Please tell us what you can see in the photograph. |
| | Candidate B, you just listen. |
| Candidate A: | This photo shows four people waiting for a train on the platform at an underground train station. They're all dressed in smart clothes and it looks like they are going to work or going home at the end of the day. It could also be late at night because these are the only people on the platform. The woman nearest the camera is looking at her watch so the train might be late. Behind her in the photo are three men. Two of them are using their phones. One man is talking to someone and laughing about something and the other is looking at the screen and reading. |

Examiner:    Thank you.
             Candidate B, here is your photograph. It shows children at a party.
             Please tell us what you can see in the photograph.
             Candidate A, you just listen.
Candidate B: This is a happy photograph of children enjoying themselves at a party. There are seven children altogether, three boys and four girls. They're different ages but they're all young – two or three of them are about five years old but some of them are bigger. I imagine it's a birthday party. Most of them are wearing party hats and they're standing or sitting at a table that's got lots of cakes, biscuits and drinks on it. They're all holding their hands out and I think they are playing with balloons. They're trying to catch something. They all look like they are having a great time.
Examiner:    Thank you.

## Speaking Part 3

47a

Examiner:    Now, in this part of the test you're going to talk about something together for about two minutes. I'm going to describe a situation to you.
             A woman is going on a business trip for a few days. She is deciding what she needs to take with her.
             Here are some things she could take.
             Talk together about the different things she could take and say which one would be most important.
             All right? Now talk together.

Candidate A: So, we have to decide how important these things are for the woman to take. What do you think?
Candidate B: They're all useful but shall we start by saying things she doesn't need? For example, I think she can buy a magazine when she gets there, so she doesn't really have to take that.
Candidate A: That's true. And the camera isn't important either. She probably has a camera on her phone. What about the headphones and the radio?
Candidate B: I don't think she needs them, do you? That leaves the laptop, the mobile phone and the suit.
Candidate A: I think they're all important. She probably needs the laptop for files or documents for meetings.
Candidate B: Yes, I agree. She also definitely needs her mobile phone and I suppose the suit is important when she has meetings with businesspeople.
Candidate A:  I think the mobile phone is the most important. She can email any documents or files she needs before she leaves so she might not have to take her laptop. But it will be difficult if she doesn't have her phone.
Candidate B: Yes, I think you're right. There are two or three things she needs to take but the mobile phone is probably the most important.
Candidate A: OK, let's say the mobile phone.
Examiner:    Thank you.

## Speaking Part 4

48a

Examiner:    Candidate A, do you travel much?
Candidate A: I don't have to travel very much for work but I like travelling when I'm on holiday.
Examiner:    And what about you, Candidate B?
Candidate B: I'm a student now so I don't have much money for holidays. But three years ago I went to stay with a cousin in Australia and I had a great time there.
Examiner:    Candidate B, do you find it easy to decide what to take when you travel?

Candidate B:   Well, I try to take as little as possible. I don't take many clothes because I don't like carrying lots of luggage. If I can put everything I need in a backpack I'm very happy.

Examiner:   And how about you, Candidate A?

Candidate A:   I'm different. I always take lots of luggage, especially clothes. Last time I went on a trip I took too many clothes. I had a really big suitcase which was very heavy to carry. And then I didn't wear a lot of the clothes because it was very hot.

Examiner:   Candidate B, is it important to be organised before we make a long journey?

Candidate B:   Yes, I think it is. If you are travelling to another country for example, there are important things you need to remember. Your passport for example, and your tickets. If you aren't organised you could have serious problems.

Examiner:   And what about you, Candidate A?

Candidate A:   Yes, I agree. Sometimes, getting ready for a trip can be quite stressful. I remember when I was younger, and we were going on holiday, my parents got stressed trying to organise everything for me and my brother.

Examiner:   Thank you. That is the end of the test.

# Test 7

## Speaking Part 1

🎧
53a

Examiner:   Good morning.
Can I have your mark sheets, please?
I'm Hannah King and this is Richard Brown.
What's your name?

Candidate A:   My name's Anne-Marie Dubois.

Examiner:   Where do you live?

Candidate A:   I live in Lyon, in France.

Examiner:   And what's your name, Candidate B?

Candidate B:   My name's Victor Trubinov.

Examiner:   Where do you come from, Candidate B?

Candidate B:   I come from Kiev, in Ukraine.

Examiner:   Candidate B, do you work or are you a student?

Candidate B:   I work.

Examiner:   What do you do, Candidate B?

Candidate B:   I work in a bank. I started there last year.

Examiner:   And Candidate A, do you work or are you a student?

Candidate A:   I'm a student.

Examiner:   What do you study?

Candidate A:   I'm studying history but I don't know what job I want to do when I finish my course.

Examiner:   Thank you.

Examiner:   Candidate A, what's your favourite way of travelling?

Candidate A:   I like travelling by train. It's usually quite fast and you can also relax and do some work or read during the journey.

Examiner:   Candidate B, what about you?

Candidate B:   I enjoy driving my car. I drive to work every day. I have to leave early in the morning, but there isn't too much traffic.

Examiner:   Candidate A, how often do you eat in a restaurant?

Candidate A:   Not very often. I go if it's a special occasion like a birthday party, but I'm a student and I haven't got much money, so I usually eat at home.

Examiner:   Candidate B, and what about you?

Candidate B:   I love going to restaurants. We have some good restaurants and cafes where I live. I like Georgian and Italian restaurants, and Ukrainian of course. I probably eat out once or twice every month.

Examiner:   Thank you.

## Speaking Part 2

54a

| Examiner: | Now I'd like each of you to talk on your own about something. I'm going to give each of you a photograph and I'd like you to talk about it. |
|---|---|
| | Candidate A, here is your photograph. It shows a group of people. |
| | Please tell us what you can see in the photograph. |
| | Candidate B, you just listen. |
| Candidate A: | In this photo I can see four people sitting together in the living room of someone's house. I think they're watching TV and it's probably a football match because one of the men in the group is holding a football. There's another man sitting on the floor. He has a beard. He looks worried. He's waiting to see what will happen in the match. There's a woman and she's holding a bowl. I think there is food in the bowl. She looks very happy so I think the team she supports has scored a goal. No one is eating the food in the bowl because everyone is waiting to see what happens. |
| Examiner: | Thank you. |
| | Candidate B, here is your photograph. It shows two people. |
| | Please tell us what you can see in the photograph. |
| | Candidate A, you just listen. |
| Candidate B: | This photo shows two people standing outside a building. The man is on the right and is wearing a light T-shirt. The woman has long hair and has a long-sleeved top on. The man and the woman are holding a map and the woman is pointing at something on the right. They are both smiling and they look like they are enjoying themselves. I think they're probably boyfriend and girlfriend and are on holiday together. |
| Examiner: | Thank you. |

## Speaking Part 3

55a

| Examiner: | Now, in this part of the test you're going to talk about something together for about two minutes. I'm going to describe a situation to you. |
|---|---|
| | A couple want to buy their six-year old daughter a present for her birthday. |
| | Here are some things they could get. |
| | Talk together about the different things they could buy and say which one would be best. |
| | All right? Now talk together. |
| | |
| Candidate A: | So, we have to decide on a birthday present and the girl is six years old. |
| Candidate B: | I think as she's six years old she doesn't really want money. What do you think? |
| Candidate A: | I agree. We should choose something that she will get excited about. I don't think a birthday cake is a good present. The parents should get her one of those anyway, don't you think? |
| Candidate B: | Yes, they should. I think I would be disappointed if that was my present. I like the colouring pencils, they look like good ones. All children love drawing at that age. What about some books? |
| Candidate A: | Yes, children love it when their parents read them stories. That's one idea. I don't think they should buy her sweets. That's like the cake. Not really a good present. |
| Candidate B: | That's true. And the toy car might not be very interesting. She could get bored with it quickly. So, we have the camera, the pencils and the books. Which one do you think is the best? |
| Candidate A: | Well, children love drawing so I definitely think the pencils are the best present. What about you? |
| Candidate B: | I agree. The girl will enjoy using those, won't she? |
| Candidate A: | Yes, so we say the colouring pencils. |
| Examiner: | Thank you. |

## Speaking Part 4

56a

| | |
|---|---|
| Examiner: | Candidate A, do you remember birthdays when you were young? |
| Candidate A: | Yes, my mum and dad used to invite my relations to our house. We played party games and had lots of food. We had a big family and I really enjoyed these parties. |
| Examiner: | Candidate B, and what about you? |
| Candidate B: | Yes, I had some nice parties too. I remember my friends coming to my house when I was about six or seven. We played games too and I remember eating lots of ice cream. |
| Examiner: | Candidate B, can you remember any presents you were given when you were young? |
| Candidate B: | Yes, my best present when I was about six was a James Bond car. It was only small but when you pressed it down hard the top came off and the driver came out of the roof. I think they're worth a lot of money now. |
| Examiner: | And how about you, Candidate A? |
| Candidate A: | I can't remember one present but I did spend a lot of time drawing and painting when I was little so I'm sure I got pens and paints for my birthday. |
| Examiner: | Candidate B, is it important for children to have a birthday party? |
| Candidate B: | I don't think it's very important. The important thing is that the child feels loved by their parents, so if that happens on their birthday they will be happy. |
| Examiner: | Candidate A, and what about you? |
| Candidate A: | I think a party is a nice idea because it's something you remember when you're older. But some children don't want a party. My brother was shy when he was little and never wanted to have a party. |
| Examiner: | Thank you. That is the end of the test. |

## Test 8

## Speaking Part 1

61a

| | |
|---|---|
| Examiner: | Good afternoon. |
| | Can I have your mark sheets please? |
| | I'm Greg Miller and this is Gill Matthews. |
| | What's your name? |
| Candidate A: | My name's Suzanne Vojtek. |
| Examiner: | Where do you come from? |
| Candidate A: | I come from a small village in the Czech Republic. |
| Examiner: | And what's your name, Candidate B? |
| Candidate B: | My name's Oliver Correa. |
| Examiner: | Where do you live, Candidate B? |
| Candidate B: | I live in São Paulo, in Brazil. |
| Examiner: | Candidate B, do you work or are you a student? |
| Candidate B: | I work. |
| Examiner: | What do you do, Candidate B? |
| Candidate B: | I'm a nurse. I work in a big hospital. |
| Examiner: | And Candidate A, do you work or are you a student? |
| Candidate A: | I'm a student. |
| Examiner: | What do you study? |
| Candidate A: | I'm studying sports science. I started my course last year. |
| Examiner: | Thank you. |
| | |
| Examiner: | Candidate A, what kind of books do you like to read? |
| Candidate A: | I don't really read many books. I read a newspaper every day though and I get a magazine on photography once a month. |
| Examiner: | Candidate B, what about you? |

Candidate B:    I like to read novels and short stories and since I've been studying English, I try to read things in English.

Examiner:    Candidate A, do you prefer books or e-books?

Candidate A:    I prefer books. I don't really like reading books on a screen. Reading a book is more enjoyable and I think it's often easier than looking at a small screen.

Examiner:    Candidate B, how often do you go to the cinema?

Candidate B:    Not very often. There isn't a cinema near my house but if there's a film I want to see I go to a cinema in the city centre.

Examiner:    Thank you.

## Speaking Part 2

62a

Examiner:    Now I'd like each of you to talk on your own about something. I'm going to give each of you a photograph and I'd like you to talk about it.
Candidate A, here is your photograph. It shows two young women enjoying themselves.
Please tell us what you can see in the photograph.
Candidate B, you just listen.

Candidate A:    This photo shows two young women enjoying themselves. I think they're on a bus on the top floor. It's the kind of bus that tourists use to go sightseeing around a city. It looks like summer as the women are wearing sunglasses and summer clothes. One of the women has a camera around her neck. One of the women who is furthest away from the camera is pointing at something and her friend is looking at what it is. It looks like you can see the sea in the background. I think they're on holiday or they've gone on a trip for the day.

Examiner:    Thank you.
Candidate B, here is your photograph. It shows three people outside.
Please tell us what you can see in the photograph.
Candidate A, you just listen.

Candidate B:    In this photo there are three people sitting outside on the grass. It looks like a park, and there are some big trees. There are two men and a woman sitting in the middle. They don't look very old, I think about 30 years old perhaps. I imagine they are having a break from working in the office. It might be lunchtime. They each have a cup of coffee and the men are both wearing shirts and ties. All three are wearing quite smart clothes. The man on the right is typing on a laptop and the other two are looking at the screen. It's a nice sunny day and they all look very happy.

Examiner:    Thank you.

## Speaking Part 3

63a

Examiner:    Now, in this part of the test you're going to talk about something together for about two minutes. I'm going to describe a situation to you.
A teenager is on his way home before dinner and wants to eat something on the way.
Here are some things he could eat on the way home.
Talk together about the different things he could eat and say which one would be best.
All right? Now talk together.

Candidate A:    Would you like to start?

Candidate B:    OK, I think the important information is that he is on his way home before dinner. That means he shouldn't eat too much.

Candidate A:    I agree. And really, he shouldn't eat anything that is too sweet. So I don't think the cake or the ice cream is a good idea, do you? And what about the chocolate?

Candidate B:    No, he shouldn't have the chocolate either. Although he could eat just a little bit and save the rest for after his dinner.

Candidate A:    He could try, but I think he'll probably eat it all. So, we don't think the ice cream, the cake or the chocolate are sensible. What about the pizza?

Candidate B:    One slice of pizza is OK. That's better than eating a bag of crisps. He won't be hungry when he gets home if he eats them.

Candidate A:    That's true. And the sandwich is the same. I don't think he should eat that. Isn't the best thing really the apple?

Candidate B:    Probably, yes. It's healthy and he'll still be hungry when he gets home, which will make his parents happy.

Candidate A:    OK, I agree. He should have the apple on his way home.

Examiner:    Thank you.

## Speaking Part 4

64a

Examiner:    Candidate A, do you like to eat snacks?

Candidate A:    Yes, sometimes, but I try to eat healthy food. I used to eat a lot of sweets and chocolate when I was younger, but I try to avoid that now.

Examiner:    Candidate B, and what about you?

Candidate B:    No, I don't really have many snacks. Not in the week when I'm working. At the weekend I do. But that's often because I feel bored and so I just eat for something to do.

Examiner:    Candidate B, what do you think are the best things to eat for snacks?

Candidate B:    Everyone says fruit is the best and I agree that it's good for you. But sometimes I want something sweet, like a bar of chocolate.

Examiner:    And how about you, Candidate A?

Candidate A:    I agree. Fruit is nice but eating chocolate makes you feel great. I try not to eat too much now though.

Examiner:    Candidate B, is it important to eat three meals a day?

Candidate B:    I don't know if it should be three meals. Dinner in the evening is important, and having something for breakfast is always a good thing to do. But maybe a healthy snack at lunchtime is all we need.

Examiner:    And what about you, Candidate A?

Candidate A:    I like to eat thee meals. We always go to a café for lunch at university and I have a meal when I go home. And I have breakfast of course.

Examiner:    Thank you. That is the end of the test.

# Speaking paper: Additional practice by topic

This section will give you extra practice in the sorts of questions the examiner may ask you in Part 1 of the Speaking test. Listen to the audio and practise answering the questions. Some of the questions mean quite similar things but the words used in the question are different; this gives you more speaking practice and shows you how different questions are formed. Remember that the examiner will choose what questions to ask you and won't ask you lots of questions about the same topic. When you are practising try to give a longer answer, even if you want to just say *No*. For example, you may not like doing sport, but if the question is *Do you like playing tennis?* and your real answer is *No*, you can say something like *No, I don't like playing tennis because I didn't learn how to play it when I was at school.* Once you are feeling confident it would be a good idea not to look at the book – just listen to the audio and answer the questions. And keep practising!

The questions are grouped under different topic headings: family and friends, food, work, studying, travel, accommodation, hobbies and interests, clothes, shopping, sport, music, books and films, celebrations, technology, future plans, the past.

## Family and friends

65

Now let's talk about family and friends.
Tell us about your family.
Are you like anyone in your family?
Is there anyone in your family who is very important to you?
What's your favourite family memory?
Is there anything you and your family like to do together?
Tell us about your friends.
How often do you see your friends?
What do you like doing with your friends?
Where do you like going with your friends?   Why?
What do you do with your friends when you go out?
Do your friends have the same hobbies as you?
Where did you meet your best friends?
Do your friends live near you?
Did you see any of your friends yesterday?
How do you keep in touch with friends when you can't be together?

## Food

66

Now let's talk about food.
Tell us about the food you like.
What time do you have dinner?
Have you got a favourite meal?
How often do you go to a restaurant?
Do you like to eat healthy food?
Do you think it's important to eat three meals a day?
Which meal of the day do you enjoy most?
Are you a good cook?
Do you enjoy cooking?
Do you like to try cooking different meals?
What did you have for breakfast this morning?
Is there any food you dislike?
What did you eat for dinner yesterday?
Do you prefer to eat at home or in a restaurant?
How often do you eat fruit?

## Work
Now let's talk about work.
Tell us about your work.
What job do you do or what do you study?
What job would you like to do?
What kind of job do you think you would be good at?
Is it easy to find work where you live?
Is it more important to enjoy your job or to earn a lot of money?
Would you like to have your own business?
Do you like working alone or with other people?
Is there another country you would like to work in?
Would you like a job where you have to travel?
How important is money to you?
Are there any jobs you would not like to do?
What's your ideal job in the future?

## Studying
Tell us about studying.
Do you enjoy studying English?
Have you got a favourite room to study in at home?
What time of day is your best time for studying?
Do you like to study online?
What are the advantages and disadvantages of studying online?
What do you find most difficult about studying?
How often do you study English every week?
Have you studied English in a class?
Have you tried studying with other people?
Do you prefer studying alone or with other people?
Which area of English do you find most difficult?
Is the internet always useful for studying?
Is there a subject you would like to study?

## Travel
Now let's talk about travel.
Do you like to travel?
Have you ever lived in another country?
What do you like to do on holiday?
Do you prefer lying on the beach or sightseeing?
Which country would you most like to visit?
Do you have many tourists where you live?
What's the most interesting place you've ever visited?
Do you like to buy souvenirs?
Are you going on holiday this year?
Do you like to travel on your own?
What's your favourite way of travelling?

## Accommodation
Now let's talk about accommodation.
Tell us about where you live.
Do you live in a house or an apartment?
How long have you lived in your house or apartment?
Who do you live with?
What's your favourite room where you live?
Is there anything you don't like about where you live?

What kind of place do you think you will live in in the future?
Would you prefer to live in the city or the countryside?
Do you have a garden?
Do you live on your own?
Is it better to live on your own or with other people?
Which room do you spend most time in when you're at home?
Have you ever moved house?

### Hobbies and interests

Now let's talk about hobbies and interests.
Tell us about your hobbies and interests.
Have you got any hobbies?
Are there any hobbies you used to have that you don't do anymore?
Is there a hobby you would like to start?
What do you like to do at the weekend?
What do you like to do to relax?
Do you like doing activities alone or with other people?
How often do you do exercise?
What are the most popular hobbies in your country?
Do any of your friends have an interesting hobby?
What do you do when you get home from your studies or work?
Are there any hobbies you wouldn't like to do?

### Clothes

Now let's talk about clothes.
Tell us about the clothes you like.
What kind of clothes do you usually wear?
How often do you buy new clothes?
Where do you like to shop for clothes?
What are your favourite clothes?
Do you have to wear anything special for work?
Do you like to wear the same clothes as your friends?
Do you wear any jewellery?
Are you interested in the jewellery other people wear?
Do you like to wear clothes that are in fashion?
Did you wear a uniform to school?
What do you like to wear in summer?
Do you like to shop in department stores?
What did you wear last weekend?

### Shopping

Now let's talk about shopping.
Tell us about shopping.
Do you enjoy shopping?
Are there many shops near where you live?
Which shops do you go to most often?
Do you like to shop online?
What was the last thing you bought?
Do you ever go shopping with your friends?
How often do you buy clothes?
How often do you go to a supermarket?
Do you prefer buying food in big superstores or small markets? Why?
Do you prefer to shop online or in a real shop? Why?
What was the last present you bought for someone?
What would you most like to buy if you had enough money?

## Sport

74

Now let's talk about sport.
Tell us about the sports you like.
What sports do you like?
How often do you do sport?
What kind of sports do you play?
Where do you play sports?
Do you play any sports?
Is sport important in your life? Why?
Do you play sport with your family?
Do you play sport at the weekend?
Do you ever watch sport on TV?
Did you play much sport when you were at school?
Who's your favourite sports team or player?
When did you start playing your sport?
Have you ever played sport in a competition?

## Music

75

Now let's talk about music.
Tell us about the type of music you like to listen to.
How often do you listen to music?
What kind of music do you like?
Do you listen to music while you're working?
Have you ever been to a music festival?
Can you play any musical instruments?
Do you like to sing?
Who is your favourite singer?
Do you download songs?
What was the last song you downloaded?
Is there a musical instrument you would like to learn?
Do you listen to music when you do exercise?
Is there a band or singer you would like to see?

## Books and films

76

Now let's talk about books and films.
Tell us about books and films.
Are books and films important to you? Why?
Do you read many books?
What sort of books or magazines do you read most?
Do you like reading?
What sort of things do you like reading most?
What's the best book you've ever read?
Is there a cinema near where you live?
Do you enjoy going to the cinema?
What's your favourite type of film?
How often do you watch films, TV or documentaries?
Are there any films or TV programmes you dislike?
How often do you go to the cinema?
What was the last film you saw?
Do you prefer to see a movie at home or at the cinema?
Have you seen a good documentary recently? What was it about?
Is there a film you want to see?
Who's your favourite actor?
Are you interested in celebrities?

## Celebrations

Now let's talk about celebrations.
Tell us about celebrations in your life.
Do you like going to parties?
When was the last party you went to?
What kind of things do people celebrate in your country?
Have you been to a wedding?
What do you like to do at parties?
What was your favourite party game as a child?
How often do you go to a party?
Do you like to dance when you're at a party?
What's the best food to serve at a celebration?
Have you had a party in your house?
Which famous person would you most like to invite to a party?

## Technology

Now let's talk about technology.
Tell us why it's important to know about technology.
Tell us about the technology you use in different places.
Are you interested in new technology?
Do you know much about new technology?
Could you live without a smartphone? How long for?
Do you think children should be allowed to have mobile phones?
Do you use the internet to practise English?
What are some of the problems with the internet?
Do you like to have the latest mobile phone?
Does technology make our lives easier?
What are your favourite websites?
Do you play computer games?
Do you listen to the radio online?
Do you watch videos online? What kind of videos do you watch online?
Do you watch movies online?

## Future plans

Now let's talk about future plans.
Tell us about your future plans.
What are you going to do at the weekend?
Are you going to have a holiday soon?
Where do you want to live in the future?
Which country would you like to visit in the future? Why?
How much do you think you will use English in the future?
What are you doing for your next holiday?
Do you think you will work or study in a foreign country?
Where do you think you will work in the future?
Have you got a five-year plan?
Is there anywhere you want to visit next year?

80

**The past**
Now let's talk about the past.
Tell us about the past.
Where were you born?
Have you always lived in the same place?
Did you enjoy school?
What was your favourite subject?
What do you remember about the games you played as a child?
Which of your friends have you known the longest?
What do you like to do now that you didn't like in the past?
How has your town or city changed in the past few years?
What was your favourite TV programme when you were younger?
Can you remember a time you were really excited?
Can you remember a birthday present you were given when you were young?